FLASH PROFESSIONAL CS6

Training Guide

by

Satish Jain

B.Sc., B.E. (II Sc), M.E. (II Sc), M.Tech. (IIT Kanpur),
Ex Professor of Information Technology,
Institute of Information Technology & Management,
GGS Indraprastha University, Delhi.

Kratika

B.Com., Advanced Diploma (IT)

BPB PUBLICATIONS

B-14, CONNAUGHT PLACE, NEW DELHI-1

FIRST EDITION 2015

ISBN : 978-81-8333-576-8

Distributors:

COMPUTER BOOK CENTRE
12, Shrungar Shopping Centre, M.G.Road
BENGALURU-560001
Ph: 25587923, 25584641

MICRO BOOKS
Shanti Niketan Building, 8,Camac Street,
KOLKATA-700017 Ph: 22826518,
22826519

MICRO MEDIA
Shop No. 5, Mahendra Chambers,150 DN Rd. Next to Capital Cinema, V.T. (C.S.T.) Station, MUMBAI-400 001, Ph: 22078296, 22078297

DECCAN AGENCIES
4-3-329, Bank Street,
HYDERABAD-500195
Ph: 24756967, 24756400

BPB PUBLICATIONS
B-14,Connaught Place,
NEW DELHI-110001
23325760, 43526249

BPB BOOK CENTRE
376 Old Lajpat Rai Market,
DELHI-110 006, Ph: 23861747

INFOTECH
G-2, Sidhartha Building,
96 Nehru Place,
NEW DELHI-110 019
Ph: 26438245

BPB PUBLICATIONS
20, Ansari Road, NEW DELHI-110002
Ph: 23254990/91

Published by Manish Jain for BPB Publications, B-14, Connaught Place, New Delhi – 110001 and Printed by him at Akash Press, New Delhi.

Dedicated to

Lord Ganesh, Maa Durga and Mata Raj Rajeshwari

whose blessings overcome all hurdles in life

BOOKS *by Prof. Satish Jain*

According to CBSE New Syllabus of year 2010–11 (for Class IX to Class XII)

- **Foundation of Information Technology for Class IX (code 165)**
- **Foundation of Information Technology for Class X (code 165)**
- **Computer Science with C++ Language *made comprehensive* for Class XI (code 083)**
- **Computer Science with C++ Language** *made comprehensive* **for Class XII (code 083)**
- **Informatics Practices *made comprehensive* for Class XI (code 065)**
- **Informatics Practices *made comprehensive* for Class XII (code 065)**

'O' Level made simple Books (According to NIELIT (DOEACC) Syllabus effective from July, 2010 Examination)

- **IT Tools and Business Systems** *(covering M1-R4, A1-R4 and B1.1-R4 papers)* ***(Also available in Hindi)***
- **Internet Technology and Web Design** *(covering M2-R4, A2-R4 and B1.2-R4 papers)* ***(Also available in Hindi)***
- **Programming and Problem Solving through `C' language** *(covering M3-R4, A3-R4 and B1.3-R4 papers)* ***(Also available in Hindi)***
- **Application of .Net Technology** *(covering M4.1-R4 paper)*
- **Introduction to Multimedia** *(covering M4.2-R4 paper)*
- **Introduction to ICT Resources** *(covering M4.3-R4 paper)*
- **BPB 'O' Level** *Course (Covering: IT Tools and Business Systems, Internet Technology & Web Design and Programming and Problem Solving through 'C' Language) (Also covering A1-R4, A2-R4, A3-R4 as well as B1.1-R4, B1.2-R4 and B1.3-R4 papers)*

'A' Level made simple Books (According to NIELIT (DOEACC) Syllabus effective from July, 2010 Examination)

- **Computer System Architecture** *(covering A4-R4 and B1.4-R4 papers)*
- **Structured System Analysis & Design** *(covering A5-R4 and B1.5-R4 papers)* ***(Also available in Hindi)***
- **Data Structure Through C++** *(covering A6-R4 and B2.1-R4 papers)* ***(Also available in Hindi)***
- **Introduction to Database Management Systems** *(covering A7-R4 and B2.2-R4 papers)*
- **Basics of OS, Unix and Shell Programming** *(covering A8-R4 and B2.3-R4 papers)*
- **Data Communication and Network Technologies** *(covering A9-R4 and B2.4-R4 papers)*
- **Introduction to Object Oriented Programming through Java** *(covering A10.1-R4 and B2.5.1-R4 papers)*
- **Software Testing and Quality Management** *(covering A10.2-R4 and B2.5.2-R4 papers)*

PREFACE

The objective of this Training Guide is to meet the growing need of the users to build advance animations using Flash Professional CS6. This latest application package from Adobe® is highly versatile for making animations and publishing. This training guide explains text matter in simple English language, how to design static as well as dynamic animation. It is observed that most of the books available in the market do not explain this package in step-by-step manner from the first time user's point of view.

This book covers basic Interface of Flash Professional CS6. It discusses new features and let you know how to create and manipulate graphics using Drawing and Selection tools. Concepts of Symbols and Instances in Flash Professional CS6 save your time and reduce your file size. With all the animation information, you can create different types of animations. To add interactive power in projects, you can use button symbols with sound effects. You can also attach media files using Flash Professional CS6 to make Projects more interactive. You can also test and publish Flash content for distribution to the Web, mobile devices and even as full-featured desktop applications using Adobe AIR. Last but not least, you can also familiarize with the Flash CC, the latest version of the software package Flash.

Most of the capabilities of this package are explained with many illustrations. A very useful feature of this book is that different types of tools in Flash Professional CS6 are explained with practical examples and screens, so as to enable a reader to understand them without any outside help.

We shall feel obliged to the readers if they send us their critical opinion of the presentation, readability and coverage in this book and send us suggestions in improving the subject matter.

4st August, 2015 — Authors

BOOKS by Prof. Satish Jain *(Contd...)*

'O' & 'A' Level BPB's Golden Solutions for NIELIT (DOEACC) Examination Question Papers

- `O' Level—**IT Tools and Business Systems** (*Also covering A1-R4 and B1.1-R4 papers*)
- `O' Level—**Internet Technology & Web Design** (*Also covering A2-R4 and B1.2-R4 Papers*)
- 'O' Level—**Programming & Problem Solving through `C' language** (*Also covering A3-R4 and B1.3-R4 Papers*)
- `O' Level—**ICT Resources** (*covering M4.3-R4 paper*)
- `O' Level—**Introduction to Multimedia** (*covering M4.2-R4 paper*)
- `A' Level—**Data Communication and Network Technologies** (*Also covering A9-R4 and B2.4-R4 papers*)

'O' Level CHM (Computer Hardware Maintenance) Made Simple (According to NIELIT (DOEACC) Syllabus)

- **Electronics Components and PC Hardware** (*covering CHM–O1 paper*)
- **PC Architecture** (*covering CHM–O2 paper*)
- **Computer Peripherals and Networking** *(covering CHM O3 paper)*
- **System Software, Dignostics and Debugging Tools** (covering CHM O4 paper)
- **Course on Computer Concepts (CCC)** *made simple* (According to NIELIT (DOEACC) Revised Syllabus of year 2011 Examination) (***Also available in Hindi***)
- **Basic Computer Course (BCC)** *made simple* (According to NIELIT (DOEACC) Syllabus of year 2011 Examination)

Training Guides for Application Packages

- **CorelDRAW Graphics Suit X3** (Version 13) ***Training Guide***
- **Photoshop CS3/CS5/CS6** ***Training Guide***
- **PageMaker-6.5 and 7.0** ***Training Guide***
- **MS Office 2007 and 2010** ***Training Guide***
- **MS Word 2007 and 2010 Training Guide**
- **MS Excel 2007 and 2010** ***Training Guide***
- **MS PowerPoint 2007 and 2010** ***Training Guide***
- **Internet** ***Training Guide***
- **Windows 7/8** ***Training Guide***
- **Dreamweaver CS5** ***Training Guide***
- **Flash Professional CS5** ***Training Guide***
- **Illustrator CS5/CS6** ***Training Guide***

CONTENTS

CHAPTER 1

Getting Started with Flash® Professional CS6

Introduction

Adobe® Flash® Professional CS6 provides a complete interactive authoring environment for creating digital animation and interactive Web sites. It is basically used to create rich interactive applications using video, sound, graphics and animation.

With Adobe® Flash® Professional CS6, you can:

- Design expressive contents, write code precisely and efficiently, and deliver superior-quality video to audiences practically everywhere.
- Import images from other Adobe® applications, such as Photoshop or Illustrator.
- Quickly design simple animations.
- Use Adobe ActionScript 3.0 to develop interactive projects.
- Design Web-based training courses and publish them as standalone projector files or AIR (Adobe Integrated Runtime) applications and deliver them students via CDs (Compact Disks), DVDs (Digital Video/Versatile Disks), or mobile apps.
- Create self-running presentations that are more creative and have a higher degree of interactivity.
- Create Customer service kiosks to help customers find what they need. For example, kiosks in banks let customers withdraw funds, check interest rates, and make deposits.
- Create visual effects for TV (Television) shows and even small feature films.
- Create entertaining, professional-looking games using runtime scripting, back-end data transfers, and interactive controls like buttons and text boxes.
- Develop apps for mobile devices, from iPads to Androids.

A Flash SWF file runs in the Flash Player on your browser, in AIR (Adobe Integrated Runtime) on your desktop outside of your browser, or on your mobile phone.

New Features of Flash® Professional CS6

New and improved features of Flash® Professional CS6 are the following:

New Simulator Tool

New tool introduced for mobile device interactions allows testing gestures, such as pinches and swipes while using Flash.

Pin IK Bones

Pinning locks IK (Inverse Kinematics) bone to a specific position on the stage to allow finer control for armatures to create poses.

Symbol Rasterization

The cache as bitmap feature converts Vector to Bitmap and Export as Bitmap, which provide greater control over graphics handling, increasing mobile device performance, CPU (Central Processing Unit) efficiency, and improving battery life.

Auto-save and File Recovery

Like your favorite word processor, Flash now has a new feature that automatically saves your documents and eases your mind over potential lost work due to crashes.

Integrated Ruler on TLF Text Boxes

The integrated ruler that now appears above all active TLF (Text Layout Framework) text boxes on the Stage helps you set margins and other measurements quickly, without having to move to the Properties Inspector.

Scale Content with Stage

Stage resizing that scales all your content proportionally

Templates and Code Snippets for Mobile Services

Adobe has now introduced new Code Snippets, making it easier to develop apps for iPhones, iPads, and Android mobile devices. Flash CS6 add new Code Snippets that show how to interact with touchscreen gestures, such as swipes and pinches. Templates show how to use built-in accelerometers and geo-location features.

PNG Sequence Export

To share graphics or animation sequences (even individual frames) with other applications, you can select any graphic, button, or movie clip symbol and export its contents as a PNG (Portable Network Graphics) Sequence. This results in one or more PNG files that you can easily import into other applications or development environments.

Bitmap Editing with Adobe Photoshop CS6

It is now possible to do on-the-spot editing with Photoshop CS6 for any bitmap in your movie. Right-click any bitmap image in the Library panel or on the Stage for direct editing in Adobe Photoshop CS6; changes to the image are automatically reflected in the Flash CS6 application.

Expanded Publishing and Support for iOS and Android Devices

If you are publishing apps, you will find new device templates in the New Document and Start Page dialog boxes for AIR 3.2 for iOS and AIR 3.2 for Android. Now, you can include the AIR runtime with your apps, saving your audience's time for downloading the runtime.

App Development for Multiple Services

It is now easier to develop an application that works on desktops and mobile devices like smartphones and tablets. Flash enhancements make it easier to share files and scale projects for a variety of screen sizes.

Built-in iPhone, iPad and Android App Packager

Using Flash CS6, you can build apps for all Apple's iDevices and Android smartphones and tablets. Test your apps immediately on devices connected by USB (Universal Serial Bus) cables.

Conversion to HTML and JavaScript

It is now possible to export part or all of an animation made in Flash CS 6 for use in HTML (HyperText Markup Language) or JavaScript projects.

Other Miscellaneous Features

- An updated Document panel for quick access to document settings
- Powerful controls for managing layers
- Better workflow for sharing resources across multiple FLA (Flash) files
- Many more incremental feature improvements and overall better performance.

Starting Flash Professional CS6

To start Flash Professional CS6, do this:

1. Click Start menu, highlight All Programs, again highlight Adobe and then choose Adobe Flash Professional CS6 (See Figure 1.1).
2. When the first time you start Flash Professional CS6 you will see a Welcome screen with links for creating and opening files, including handy, built-in sample templates for common project types, such as Flash movies, advertising banners, and mobile phone application templates, quick access to tutorials, and other help features (See Figure 1.2). You can also see Welcome screen when no documents are open in the application. After opening or creating a new file, the Start page automatically closes to make room on your desktop.

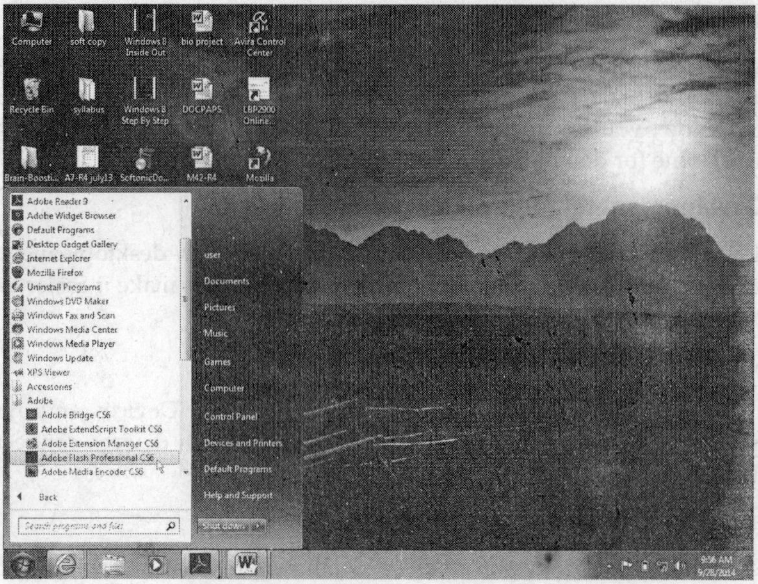

Figure 1.1 Getting started with Adobe Flash Professional CS6

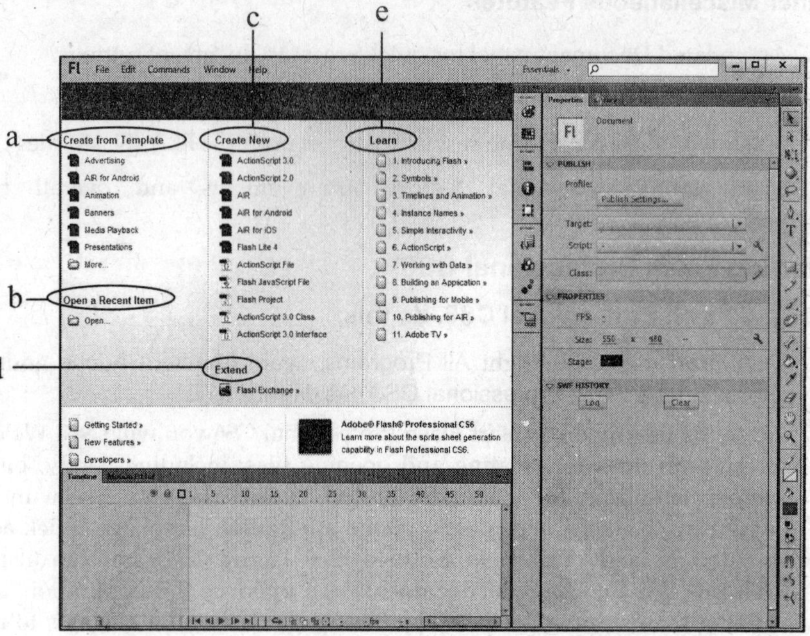

Figure 1.2 Welcome Screen of Flash Professional CS6

3. The **Welcome screen** appears as shown in Figure 1.2 which includes the following areas:
   a. **Create from Template**: Displays the list of templates which are used to create Flash files.
   b. **Open a Recent Item**: Displays a list of recently opened Flash files.
   c. **Create New**: Displays a list of different types of Flash files, such as ActionScript 3.0, ActionScript 2.0, AIR for Android and iOS, and so on.
   d. **Extend**: It contains Flash Exchange option that gives a link to the Flash Exchange Website to download helper applications and information related to Flash Professional CS6.
   e. **Learn**: It provides tutorials related to Flash Professional CS6.

Creating New Flash File

To create a simple animation, we have to add the photos and a title. For that firstly, we have to create new Flash file or more specifically, a **.fla** file where all your work takes place. The extension of the Flash file or movie file is .fla.

To create new flash file, do this:

1. Click the **File** menu and choose **New...** . A New Document dialog box appears as shown in Figure 1.3.

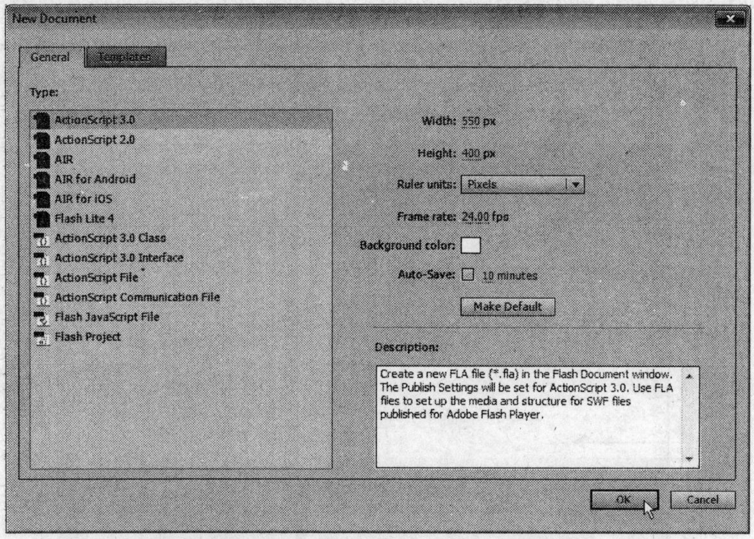

Figure 1.3 New Document Dialog box

2. Select the **Flash file (ActionScript 3.0)** option in **Type**: section, under the **General** tab (ActionScript 3.0 is the latest version of Flash's scripting language, which you use to add interactivity).

3. On the right-hand side of the dialog box, you can choose the dimensions of the Stage by entering new pixel values for the **Width:** and **Height:**. Enter 800 for Width and 600 for Height. Keep the **Ruler units:** as Pixels. Leave the **Frame rate:** and **Background color:** for the Stage at their default settings.
4. Click **Auto-Save:** check box, if you want to save your file automatically.
5. Then click **OK** button.
6. Flash creates a new ActionScript 3.0 file with all the specified settings

---

✍ *To create a new Flash file using the Welcome Screen, select ActionScript 3.0 from the **Create New column** in the middle of the Welcome Screen, select ActionScript 3.0. Your workspace, including the Stage, Timeline, and Tools panel, appears.*

Exploring the Flash Professional CS6 Workspace

Workspace of Adobe Flash Professional CS6 includes the command menus at the top of the screen and a variety of tools and panels for editing. By default, it displays the menu bar, Timeline, Stage, Tools panel, Properties Inspector, and a few other panels. As you work in Flash, you can open, close, dock, undock, and move panels around the screen to fit your work style or your screen resolution.

✍ *You create and manipulate your documents and files using various elements, such as panels, bars, and windows. Any arrangement of these elements is called a **workspace**.*

Let us explore the various components of Flash Professional CS6 workspace. (See Figure 1.4)

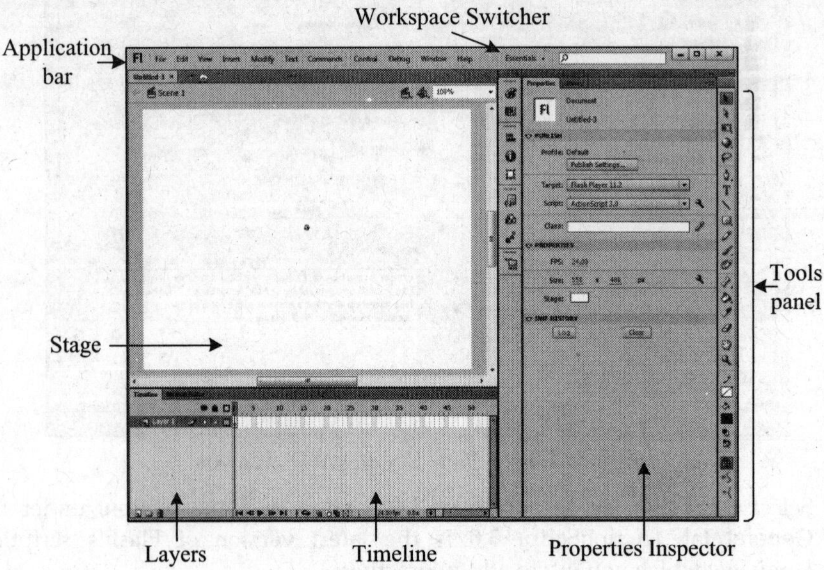

Figure 1.4 Elements of Flash Professional CS6 Workspace

The Application Bar

The Application bar is located at the top of the workspace. This bar contains Application Icon, Menu bar, Search Text box, and the Workspace Switcher (See Figure 1.4).

The elements that are present on the Application bar are as follows:

Application Icon: It displays Minimizes, Maximizes/Restore or Close buttons in Flash Professional CS6 and has its own menu called system icon.

Menu bar: It contains various options to perform specific actions (See Figure 1.5).

Figure 1.5 Menu bar

- File menu: The File menu contains commands for opening, closing, saving, importing, exporting, printing and publishing and quitting from Flash Professional CS6.
- Edit menu: The Edit menu contains the Cut, Copy and Paste command, along with the Find and Replace command, and the Preferences command. In addition to this, it also contains commands related to Timeline, symbols Tools panel and much more.
- View menu: It changes the view settings, such as the Zoom level and ruler, grids and guides. It also specifies snapping preferences for objects.
- Insert menu: It enables you to insert Symbols, Frames, Keyframe, Layers and Scenes.
- Modify menu: It enables you to modify symbols, bitmaps, shapes, frame, timeline features. It also provides tools to change the properties of the currently selected object, such as transforming, aligning, grouping and ungrouping, etc.
- Text menu: It provides various options to format the text.
- Commands menu: This menu is useful to automate tasks and reuse previously performed commands in Flash Professional CS6.
- Control menu: It provides various control options for movies, scenes, sound and buttons.
- Debug menu: It provides tools for debugging ActionScript code.
- Window menu: It enables you to open duplicate windows, panels and workspaces.
- Help menu: This menu contains the command to launch the Extension Manager. There are numerous links to Adobe resources, including the Flash Support Center on the Adobe's Website.

Workspace Switcher: It toggles between the different workspace layout options.

Search Text Box: It allows user to search topics in Flash Professional CS6 application.

Stage

The Stage is a big white rectangular area in the middle of your computer screen (See Figure 1.4). Like a theatre Stage, the Stage in a Flash is the area where viewers can see a movie during playback. It contains the text, images, and video that appears on the screen.

✍ ***Pasteboard** is the grey area off the Stage where you can place elements that will not be visible to your audience.*

To just see the Stage, do this:

1. Click the View menu and click on Pasteboard to deselect the option (See Figure 1.6).

To scale the Stage, do this:

1. Click the View menu and then click Magnification.
2. Then choose Fit in Window option (See Figure 1.6).

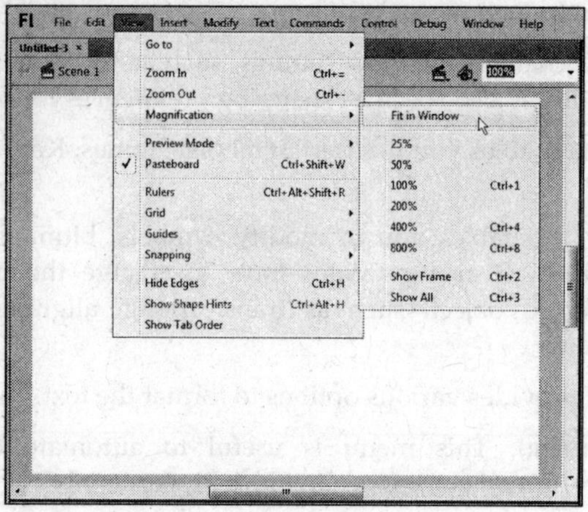

Figure 1.6 Scale the Stage

3. You can also choose different magnification view options from the pop-up menu just above the Stage (See Figure 1.7).

To change the Stage properties, do this:

1. At the bottom of the Properties inspector, click the Edit document properties button. A Document Settings dialog box appears as shown in Figure 1.8.
2. In the Dimensions: group, in width and height boxes, enter new pixel dimensions.

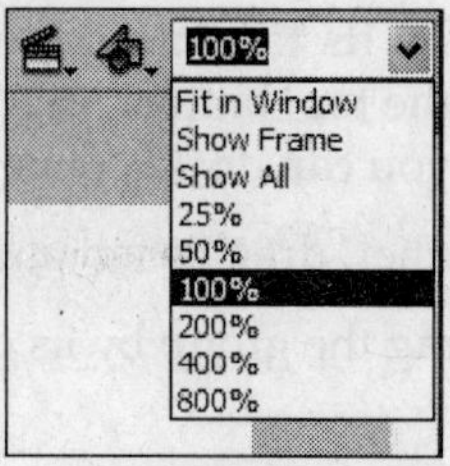

Figure 1.7 Change magnification options

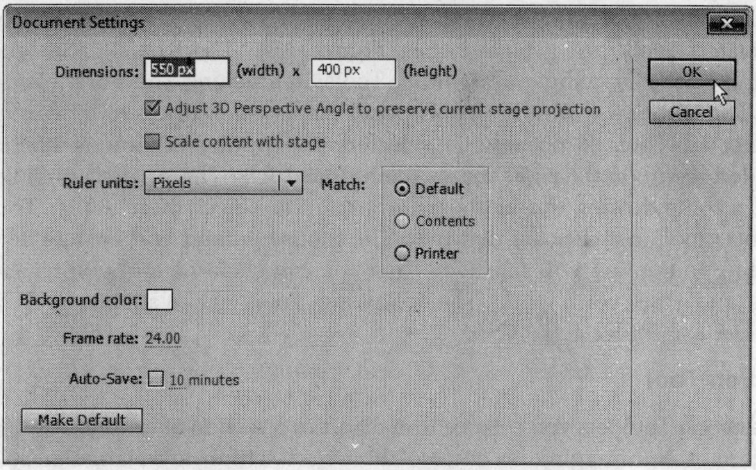

Figure 1.8 Document Setting dialog box

3. Click the Background color: button and choose a new color for the Stage.
4. Then click OK button.

You can also change the Stage color by clicking on the Stage button directly in the Properties Inspector. You can change the Stage properties at any time.

Panels

Panels are small floating windows that let you see and change attributes or properties of objects. It provides an easy access to controls that helps to work with the contents in your document. These can be moved around the screen or closed as and when needed. Each Panel has tabs that let you add actions or add the effects. By default, the Properties Inspector, Library panel, and Tools panel appear together at the right of the screen; the Timeline and Motion Editor are at the bottom; and the Stage is on the top (See Figure 1.4). However, you can move a panel to any position that is convenient for you. For example,

- To undock a panel from the right side of the screen, drag it by its tab to a new location.

- To dock a panel, drag it by its tab into the dock at a new position on the screen. You can drag it to the top, bottom, or in between other panels. A blue highlight indicates where you can dock a panel.
- To group a panel with another, drag its tab onto the other panel's tab.
- To move a panel group, drag the group by its dark gray top bar.

Using Tools Panel

The Tools panel is a long, narrow panel on the far right side of the work area. It contains tools for creating and editing images, artwork, page elements, and so on. Related tools are grouped (See Figure 1.9). The Tools panel contains Selection Tools, Drawing and Painting Tools, Retouching Tools and Navigation Tools. The Options area in the Tools panel displays modifiers to let you modify the Selected Tool. If nothing is selected, the option section is blank. The expanded menu on the right shows the hidden tools. The single capital letter in parentheses indicates the keyboard shortcut to select those tools. To use a particular tool, just click on that tool. The mouse pointer will change its shape according to the tool you selected. Then you can click the tool pointer on your canvas and start your work. The following Tools are available in the Tools panel of Flash Professional CS6.

Selection Tool

The Selection Tool lets you select entire object or a section of an object by clicking an object or by dragging to enclose the object within a rectangular selection called *marquee*.

Subselection Tool

The Subselection Tool lets you select a specific point or line in an object. Subselection Tools select objects by dragging a rectangular selection called *marquee* around the object.

Free Transform Tool

Free Transform Tool is used to change an object's scale, rotation, or skew or distort an object by dragging control points around a bounding box.

Gradient Transform Tool

The Gradient Transform Tool allows you to scale, rotate, or skew an image and its bitmap fill. It can also be used to squeeze the gradient in the front surface and reverse the gradient in the back surface.

3D Rotation Tool

3D Rotation Tool rotate movie clip instances in 3D space. A 3D rotation control appears on the top of selected objects on the Stage. The X control is red, the Y control is green, and the Z control is blue.

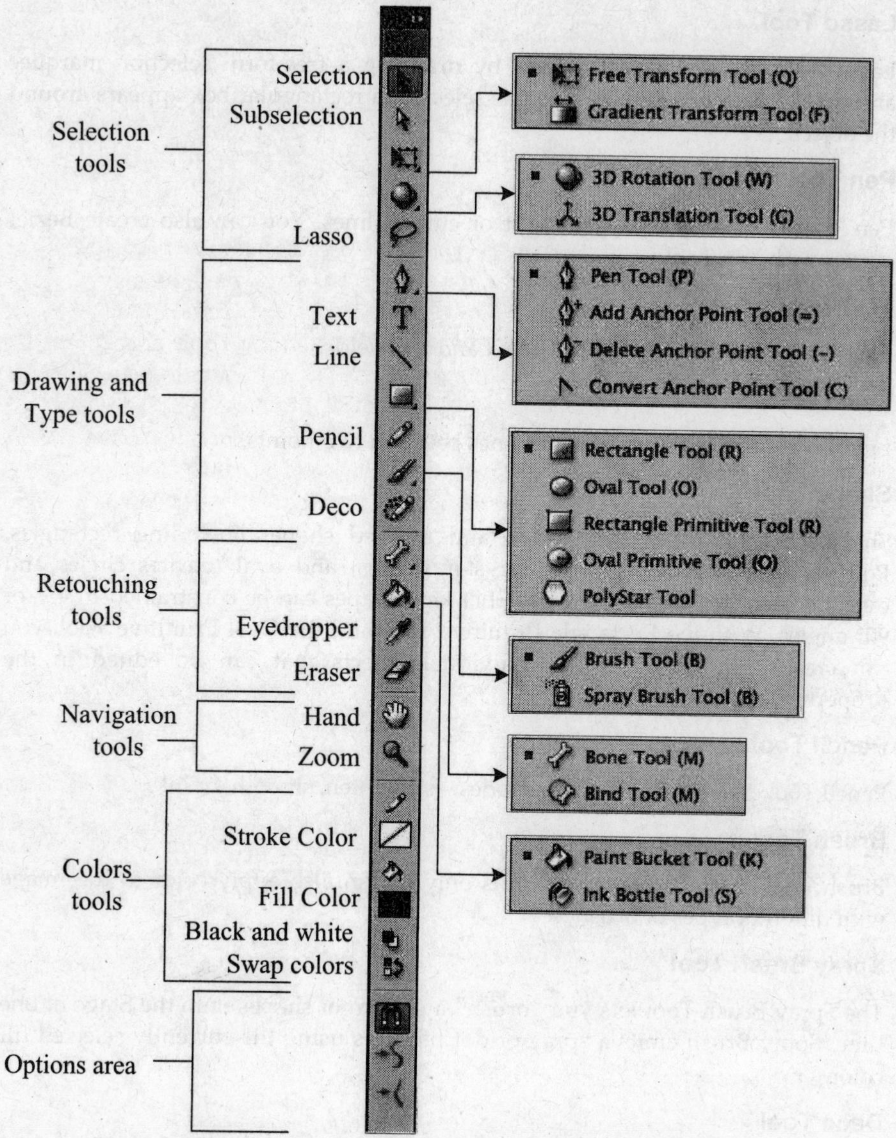

Figure 1.9 Tools panel with expanded Flyouts

3D Translation Tool

3D Translation Tool move movie clip instances in 3D space. When you select a movie clip with this tool, its three axes, X, Y, and Z, appear on the top of the object.

Lasso Tool

Lasso Tool lets you select objects by dragging a free-form selection marquee around the object. When an object is selected, a rectangular box appears around the object.

Pen Tool

Pen Tool is used to create straight or curved lines. You can also create Bezier curves with Pen Tool.

Text Tool

Text Tool is used to create or edit text and text fields.

Line Tool

Line Tool is used to draw straight lines between two points.

Shape Tool

Shape Tool can draw both filled and unfilled shapes, including rectangles, PolyStar (create either polygon or star shapes) and oval (creates circles and ovals). When you hold down the Shift key, shapes can be constrained to 45° or 90° angles. With the Rectangle Primitive Tool and the Oval Primitive Tool, you can create primitive shapes (individual objects that can be edited in the Properties Inspector).

Pencil Tool

Pencil Tool creates lines in three modes—straighten, smooth, or ink.

Brush Tool

Brush Tool creates shapes with fills only. It can also apply color to the image with different types of brushes.

Spray Brush Tool

The Spray Brush Tool lets you "brush" a pattern of shapes onto the Stage at one time. Spray Brush emits a spray of dot particles using the currently selected fill color.

Deco Tool

Deco Tool lets you create complex, geometric shapes and patterns to give the banner ad more punch, and floral decorations to adorn the edges. It is used to apply an effect to a selected object.

Bone Tool

Bone Tool is providing a method for animating an object or a set of objects in relation to each other using an articulated structure of bones.

Bind Tool

Bind Tool allows you to click a control point or a bone and display the connections between the bones and control points. You can then change the connections in a variety of ways.

Paint Bucket Tool

Paint Bucket Tool is used to fill inside closed objects or change the fill color.

Ink Bottle Tool

This Tool is used to modify the colour of the strokes of lines or shape.

Eyedropper Tool

This Tool is used to select colour from an object, swatches or anywhere on the screen and apply the same to another object.

Eraser Tool

Eraser Tool erase parts of an image, i.e., fills or stroke.

Hand Tool

Hand Tool move the view of the Stage. When the Stage is magnified, you may not be able to see all of it. To change the view without having to change the magnification, use the Hand Tool to move the Stage. In the Tools panel, select the Hand Tool and drag the Stage. To temporarily switch between another Tool and the Hand Tool, hold down the Spacebar and click the Tool in the Tools panel.

Zoom Tool

Zoom Tool is used to see enlarged or reduced view of graphic or object. To zoom out, hold down the Alt key.

Stroke Color

Stroke Color is used to choose a stroke color.

Fill Color

Fill Color is used to choose a fill color.

Properties Inspector or Properties Panel

The Properties Inspector provides an easy access to the most commonly used attributes of the currently selected object, either on the Stage or in the Timeline (See Figure 1.10). You can make changes to the object's attributes in the Properties Inspector without accessing the menus or panels.

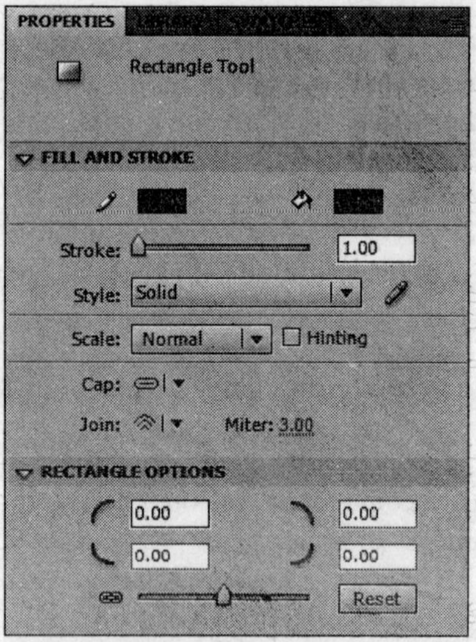

Figure 1.10 Properties Inspector for Rectangle Tool

Depending on what you have selected, appears on the Properties Inspector. The Properties Inspector displays information and settings about the current document, text, symbol, shape, bitmap, video, group, frame, or tool. When two or more different types of objects are selected, the Properties Inspector displays information about the objects you have selected. For example, if nothing is selected, the Properties Inspector includes options for the general Flash document including changing the Stage color or dimensions. If an object on the Stage is selected, the Properties Inspector shows its X and Y coordinates and its width and height, among other information (See Figure 1.10). By default, the Properties Inspector is visible. You can also hide or show it.

To hide or show Properties Inspector, do this:

1. Click the Windows menu and click on **Properties**. Or *alternatively*, press **Ctrl +** F3 keys together.

Library Panel

The Library panel is accessible from a tab just to the right of the Properties Inspector. The Library panel is a place to store and organize symbols created in Flash Professional CS6, as well as imported files, including bitmaps, graphics, sound files, and video clips (See Figure 1.11). Symbols are often-used graphics used for animation and for interactivity.

The Library panel lets you organize library items in folders, see how often an item is used in a document, and sort items by type. When you import items into Flash Professional CS5, you can import them directly onto the Stage or into the library. However, any item you import onto the Stage is also added to the library. You can then easily access the items to add them to the Stage again, edit them, or see their properties.

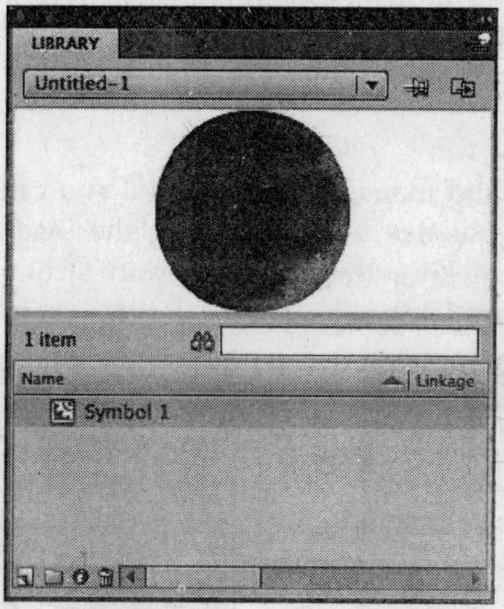

Figure 1.11 Library Panel

Info Panel

The Info panel lets you see and manipulate visual properties of objects like height and width, the location of its registration point; its Red (R), Green (G), Blue (B), and Alpha (A) values and the location of the pointer. See the change in the X: and Y: coordinates in Info panel, as you move the cursor on the Stage. Apart from this, attributes for stroke and fill properties of objects can be set or modified from here (See Figure 1.12).

Align Panel

The Align panel enables you to control the alignment of objects on the Stage. It provides you with tools to line up two or more objects vertically and horizontally and equally space among three or more objects (See Figure 1.13).

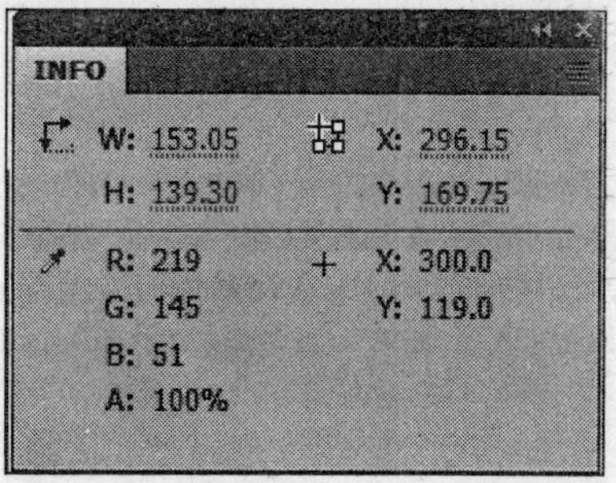

Figure 1.12 Info Panel

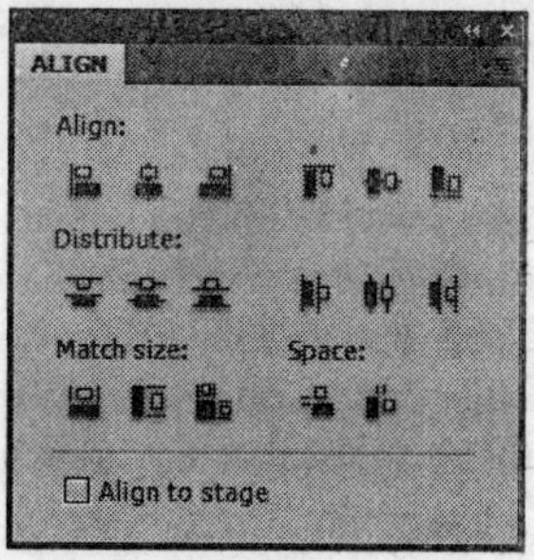

Figure 1.13 Align Panel

Transform Panel

Transform panel enables you to scale, rotate and skew the objects and symbols that you create on Stage. This panel also lets you remove the transformations you applied and restore the original values (See Figure 1.14).

Swatches Panel

It is used for selecting and managing the colors. You can import, export, delete and modify the color palettes for a file using the Swatches panel. The Color palette displayed on clicking the Fill color and stroke color buttons for all drawing tools (See Figure 1.15).

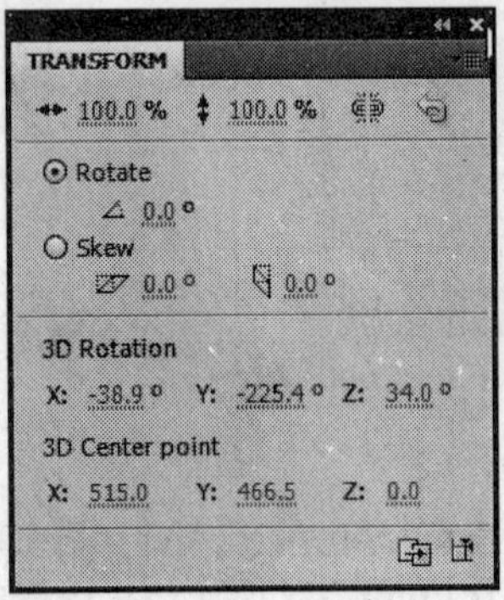

Figure 1.14 Transform Panel

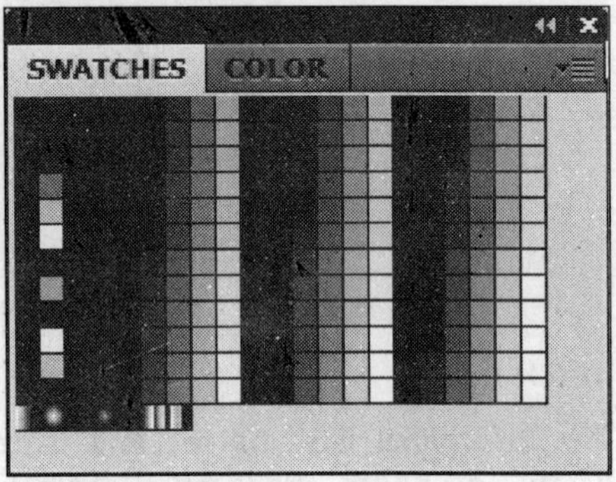

Figure 1.15 Swatches Panel

Color Panel

It is used to create and edit solid colors and gradient fills, using the Color Mixer. If an object is selected on the Stage, the color modifications you make in the Color Mixer are applied to the selection. You can choose between the RGB (Red, Green, Blue) and HSB (Hue, Saturation, Brightness) mode of color specification or simply type in the hexadecimal value of the color. You have the control over the opacity/transparency of color using Alpha slider. The slider controls the lightness/darkness of the color (See Figure 1.16).

Scene Panel

It displays a list of all the scenes you use to create a movie (See Figure 1.17). The Scene panel is also used to create, delete and arrange the order of scenes in your movie. You can display the Scene panel by clicking on the **Window** menu and choose the **Other panels** option, and then select **Scene** option from the sub-menu. Or press **Shift + F2** keys together.

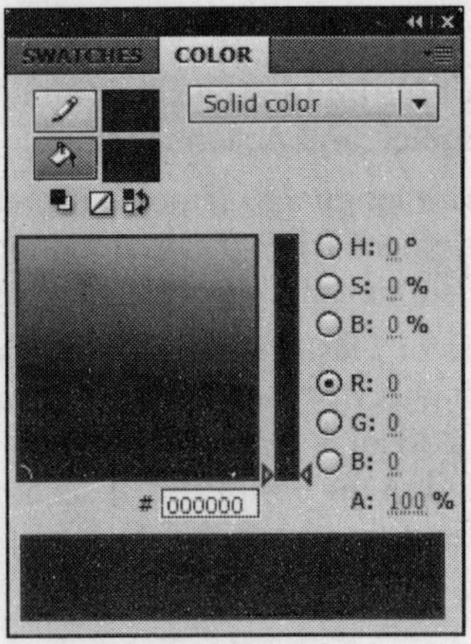

Figure 1.16 Color Panel

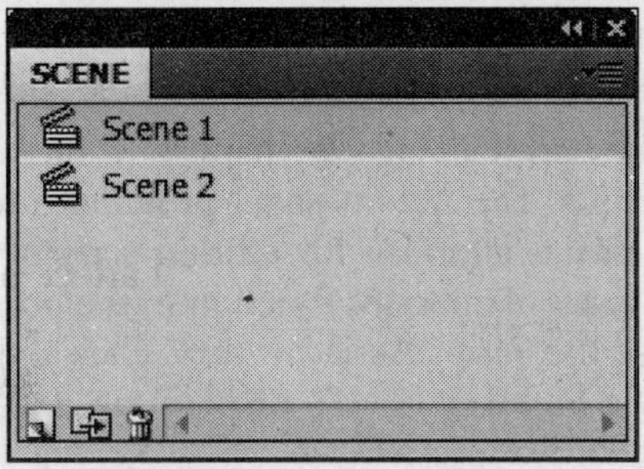

Figure 1.17 Scene Panel

Movie Explorer Panel

You can use the Movie Explorer panel to view and organize the contents of a document containing scenes. It also helps to interact with and perform a number of functions on the movie components like layers, frames, actions, sound, video etc. Some of the functions you can perform from the Movie explorer panel are:

1. Filter categories of items in the document.
2. Display the selected categories as scenes, symbol definitions, or both.
3. Expand and collapse the navigation tree.
4. Find an element in a document by name.
5. Find all the instances of a particular symbol or action.
6. Print the navigable display list that appears in the Movie Explorer.

Elements in the Movie Explorer are arranged in folder like hierarchy with scenes, layers, symbol definitions, and other titles acting as containers to organize elements in the movie (See Figure 1.18).

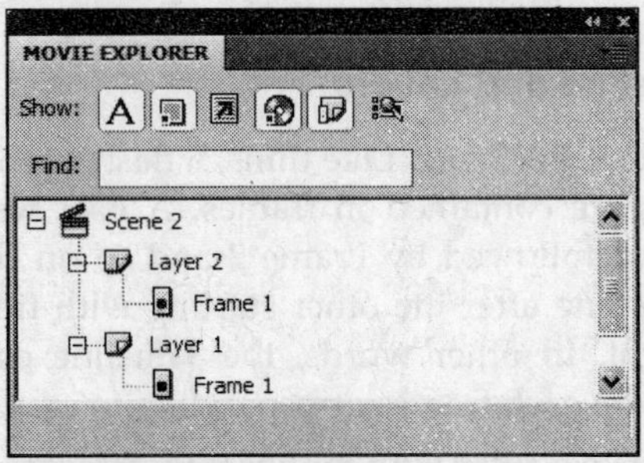

Figure 1.18 Movie Explorer Panel

Actions Panel

The Actions Panel is used to create ActionScript for buttons and keyframe. It is divided into three parts: **Script pane, Script navigator, and Actions toolbox.**

The Actions toolbox provides a list of ActionScript language elements (functions, classes, operators and types, etc.). To add an element from the Actions toolbox into the Script pane, either double click the element or drag it from the toolbox.

The Script navigator displays a hierarchical list of Flash elements that contain scripts. The Action panel provides a feature called Script Assist, which provides a visual interface for editing scripts. You can add or edit the parameters of a given ActionScript function in the boxes provided in the Script Assist section. To use the Script Assist feature, click the Script Assist button in the Actions panel. (See Figure 1.19). To display the actions panel, click **Window** menu and choose **Actions** or press **F9** key.

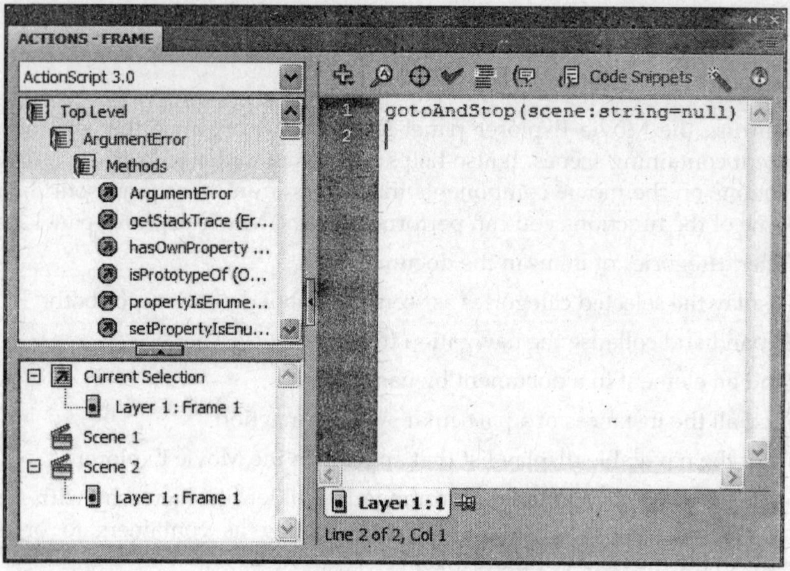

Figure 1.19 Actions Panel

Understanding Timeline and Layers

Timeline is located below the Stage. Like films, a flash movie consists of multiple images. These images are contained in frames. A user watching an animation sees images in Frame 1 followed by Frame 2 and so on. The timeline contains these image sequences one after the other starting with frame 1 on the left and last frame on the right. In other words, the Timeline covers a span of time divided into frames, with each frame corresponding to an action.

Timeline appears like a ruler with numbers incremented at regular intervals. The images in these frames are displayed in sequence as time passes. When these frames are viewed in quick succession, our brain interprets it as if an action is taking place continuously. The Timeline status displayed at the bottom of the Timeline indicates the selected frame number, the current frame rate (how many frames play per second), and the time that has elapsed so far in the movie (See Figure 1.20).

The Timeline also contains layers, which helps to organize the movie components. Layers can be defined as multiple film strips stacked on top of each other. Each layer contains a different image that appears on the Stage. Modifications or effects applied on graphics or images stored in a layer do not affect the components of other layers. The Layer area presents at the left of Timeline lists the different layers of the current movie. The selected layer with the pencil icon is the active layer. Whatever effects you apply on it will affect only this selected layer. You can Hide, Show, Lock, or Unlock Layers. Each layer's frames are unique, but you can drag them to a new location on the same layer or copy or move them to another layer.

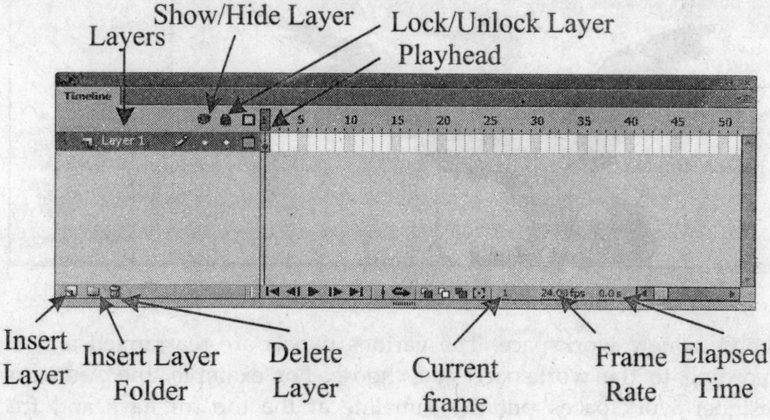

Figure 1.20 Timeline

Motion Editor

The Motion Editor is a special panel that is used to control the properties of fine tweening of individual objects (See Figure 1.21). The Motion Editor is helpful when multiple properties are changing at different times. Therefore, it also shows the animation property-by-property.

Creating or Choosing a New Workspace

Flash Professional CS6 provides a few preset workspaces, arranged for particular tasks or types of users. These workspace are listed in a pull-down menu at the top right of the Flash Professional CS6 workspace as shown in Figure 1.22 or you can access it from Window menu.

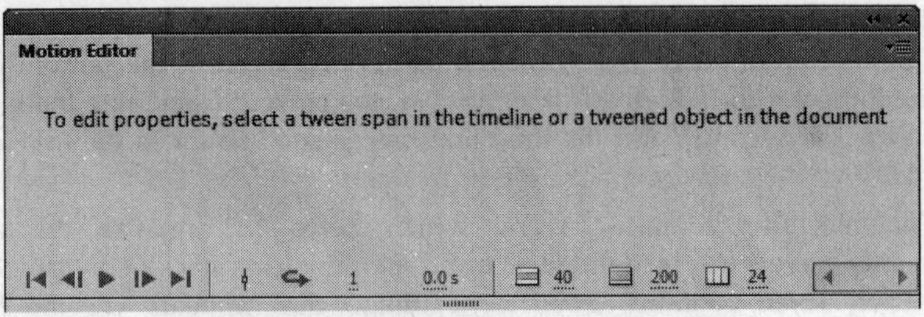

Figure 1.21 Motion Editor screen

To switch between workspace, do this:

1. Click on the Workspace switcher button at the top right of the Flash Professional CS6 workspace (See Figure 1.22).

Figure 1.22 Switching between workspace

2. Choose a new workspace. The various panels are rearranged and resized according to the workspace you choose. For example, the Animator and Designer workspaces put the Timeline at the top for easy and frequent access.

You can create a custom workspace by moving and manipulating panels, such as adding, removing, docking, grouping, or collapsing them. You can also save these custom workspaces.

To create a custom workspace, do this:

1. Make changes to an existing workspace, such as by moving panels, opening new panels or closing opened panels.
2. Click on the Window menu, highlight Workspace and then choose New Workspace… (or choose New Workspace… from Workspace switcher (See Figure 1.22)).
3. The New Workspace dialog box appears as shown in Figure 1.23.
4. In this dialog box, enter a name in the Name: box for the new workspace.

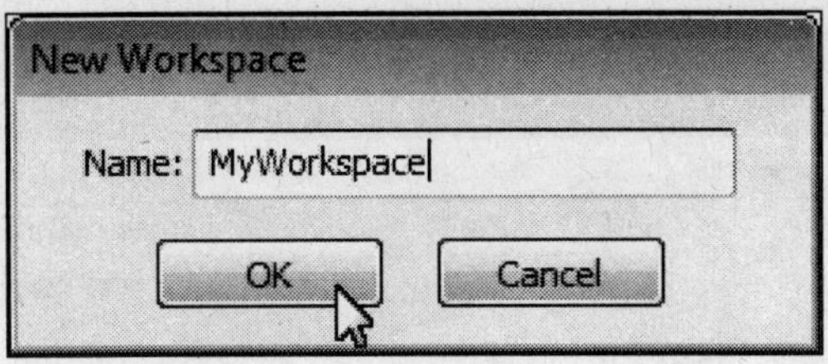

Figure 1.23 New Workspace dialog box

5. Then click OK.

The current arrangement of panels is saved. Your workspace is added in the options of the Workspace switcher pull-down menu, which you can access at any time.

Saving Flash Files

After you have created a file or made changes to an existing file, you need to save the file. You can save a file with its current filename, location, or with a different filename, location and options. You can also save a copy of a file while leaving the current file open on your desktop. Flash file is saved with .fla extension. When a flash file contains unsaved changes, an asterisk (*) appears after the filename in the document tab. When you save the document, the asterisk (*) is removed.

Flash Professional CS6 provides a new life-saving feature for files. When you create a new file you can turn on Auto-Save (See Figure 1.3). This feature saves your file periodically even if you forget. You even get to choose the period. Initially, the Auto-Save period is set to every 10 minutes. To change that, click the number and type a new value.

To save a Flash file in the default FLA format, do this:

1. Click the File menu and choose Save… . *Alternatively,* press Ctrl + S keys together. In Save As dialog box, provide the name of the file and then choose Save button.
2. Flash Professional CS6 saves your file and leaves it open for use.

To save a file with a different name and location, do this:

1. Click the File menu and choose Save As… . *Alternatively*, press Shift + Ctrl + S keys together. The Save As dialog box appears as shown in Figure 1.24.
2. In this dialog box, navigate to the file location where you want to save the file.
3. Double-click on the File name: text box, then type a new name for your file.
4. From the Save as type: drop-down list, choose Flash CS6 Uncompressed Document (*xfl).

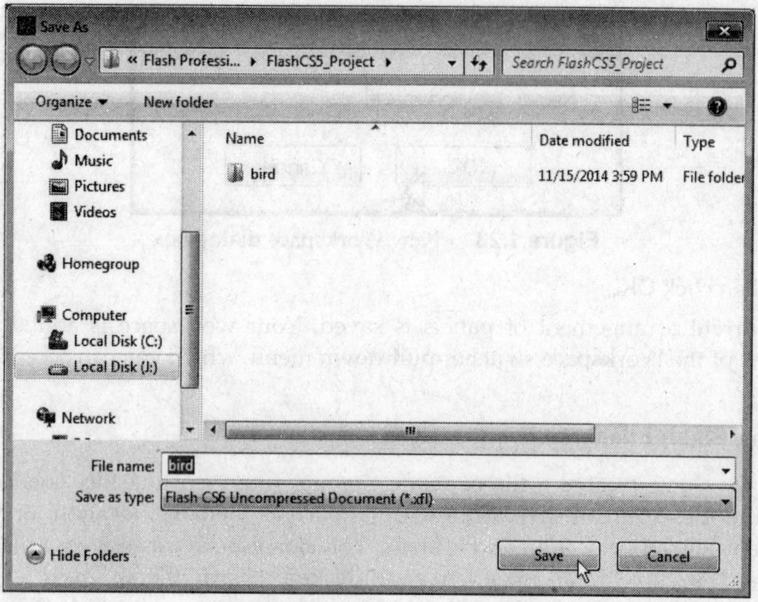

Figure 1.24 Save As dialog box

5. Click on **Save** button. The **Save As** dialog box will close. Flash Professional CS6 saves the file and leaves it open for use.

The XFL (eXtensible Form Language)format is actually a folder of files rather than a single document. This format exposes the contents of Flash movie so that other developers or animators can easily edit your file without having to open the movie in the Flash application. For example, all the imported photos in your Library panel appear in a Library folder within the XFL format. You can edit the library photos or swap them with new photos. Flash will make the substitutions in the movie automatically.

To revert to the last saved version of a document, do this:

1. Click the **File** menu and choose **Revert**.
2. Reverting is undoable. Therefore, a confirmation dialog box will display to confirm whether you want to revert a file or not. If you want to revert then click on **Revert** button otherwise click **Cancel** button (See Figure 1.25).

Figure 1.25 Revert confirmation dialog box

To save a document as a template, do this:

1. Click the File menu and choose Save as Template… . The Save as Template dialog box appears as shown in Figure 1.26.
2. In the Save as Template dialog box, enter a name for the template in the Name: box.
3. In the Category: drop-down list, select a category.
4. Enter a description of the template in the Description: box (up to 255 characters).
5. Then click Save button.

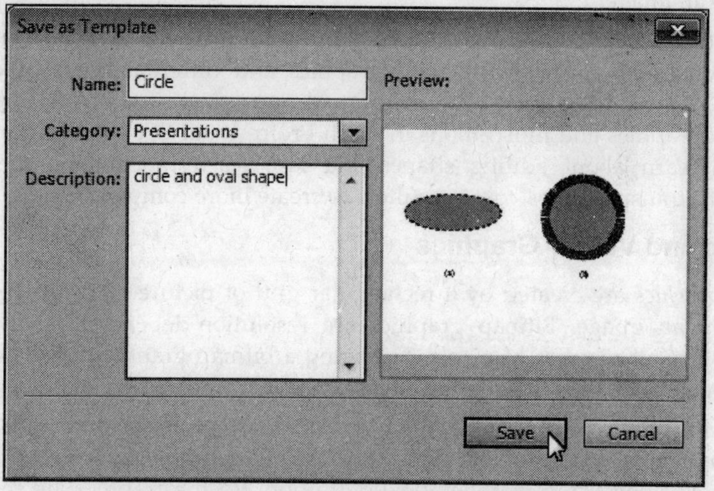

Figure 1.26 Save As Template dialog box

The written description about the template will appear in the New from Template dialog box, when the template is selected.

To close the Flash file, do this:

1. Click the File menu and choose Close. The Flash file is closed and the Welcome screen gets visible as shown in Figure 1.2.

CHAPTER 2

Working with Graphics

Introduction

When we talk about graphics, we can define graphics into two classes. One is bitmap (raster) and other is Vector and computers can display graphics either in a bitmap or in a vector format. The difference between these formats is how they describe an image.

In this Chapter, we will learn about the methods available in Flash Professional CS6 for working with graphics and different types of drawing modes. We will also learn how to draw various shapes to create interesting, complex graphics and illustrations in Flash Professional CS6. In addition to this, we will learn about editing shapes and also learn to combine them with gradients, transparencies, text and filters to create more complex visuals.

Bitmap and Vector Graphics

Bitmap graphics are created by a rectangular grid of picture elements (pixels) to represent an image. Bitmap graphics are resolution-dependent, that is, they contain a fixed number of pixels. Enlarging a bitmap graphic redistributes the pixels in the grid, thus making the edges of the image to appear jagged.

On the other hand, *vector graphics* are made up of objects like lines, curves, and shapes, placed on top of each other to create an image. A vector graphic can be described using mathematical definition. Vector graphics are resolution independent, that is, they can be displayed on output devices of varying resolutions without losing quality. Thus, moving, resizing or reshaping a vector graphic will not distort the image quality and therefore, user can easily modify these attributes. Also, the file size of a vector graphic is generally smaller than the file size of a bitmap graphic, which makes vector graphics particularly useful for a Website.

Figure 2.1 (a) is an example of a bitmap graphic and the Figure 2.1 (b) is an example of a vector graphic. They are shown at four times actual size to exaggerate the fact that the edges of a bitmap become jagged as it is scaled up.

(a) (b)

Figure 2.1 Concept of (a) Bitmap graphic (b) Vector graphic

However, vector graphics are not as effective as bitmap graphics for representing photo-realistic images. Even so, one of the most compelling features of Flash Professional CS6 is the ability to create and manipulate vector graphics. Flash images are vector graphics and they are referred to as *objects*. Flash provides you a number of drawing and color tools to create vector graphics.

Flash Professional CS6 Drawing Modes

Flash Professional CS6 provides three drawing modes called *models* that determine how objects interact with each other on the Stage and how you can edit them.

By default, Flash Professional CS6 uses Merge Drawing Mode, *but you can enable* Object Drawing Mode *or use the Rectangle Primitive or Oval Primitive Tool to use the* Primitive Drawing Mode.

Merge Drawing Mode

In Merge Drawing Mode, when you draw two shapes and one overlaps the other, a change in the top object may affect the object it overlaps. For example, if you draw oval on the top of a rectangle and then move or delete the oval off the rectangle, the portion of the rectangle covered by the oval is permanently removed (See Figure 2.2).

In the Merge Drawing Mode, the stroke and fill of an object are separate. Thus, as you draw an object such as a circle, the stroke and fill can be selected individually.

To convert an object to shapes (merge drawing mode), select it and press Ctrl+B *keys together. To convert a shape to an object (Object Drawing Mode), select it and choose* Modify > Combine Objects > Union.

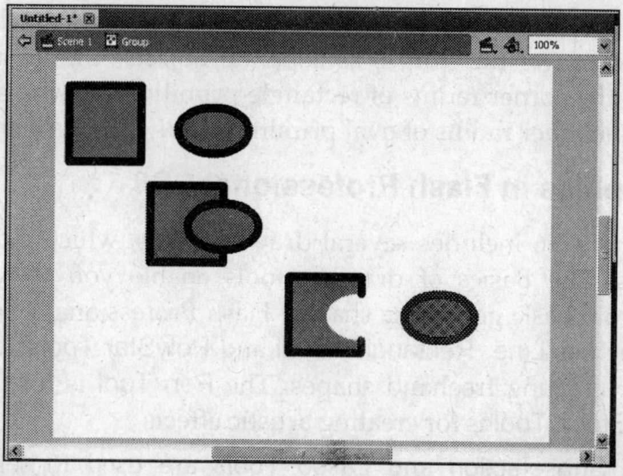

Figure 2.2 Illustration showing Merge Drawing Mode

Object Drawing Mode

In Object Drawing Mode, Flash Professional CS6 does not merge drawn objects. They remain distinct and separate, even when they overlap, so that the changes in one object do not affect another object (See Figure 2.3).

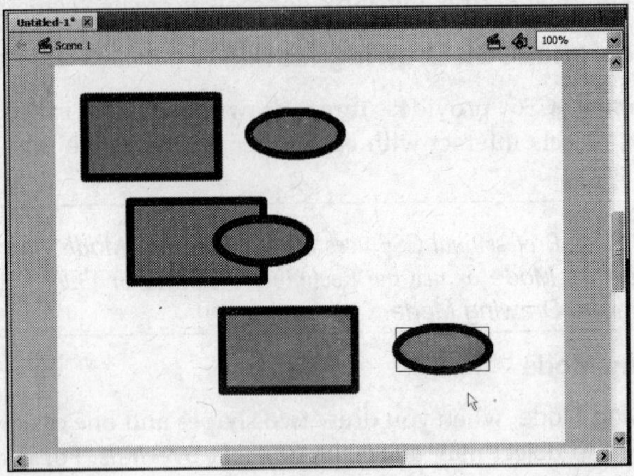

Figure 2.3 Illustration showing Object Drawing Mode

When using the Object Drawing Mode, the stroke and fill are combined and cannot be selected individually. However, you can use the Break Apart option from the Modify menu to separate the stroke and fill so that they can be selected individually.

You can toggle between the two modes by clicking Object Drawing icon in the Options area of the Tools panel.

Primitive Drawing Mode

When you use the Rectangle Primitive Tool or the Oval Primitive Tool, Flash Professional CS6 draws the shapes as separate objects. Unlike regular objects, you can modify the corner radius of rectangle primitives as well as the start and end angle, and the inner radius of oval primitives using the Properties Inspector.

Creating Graphics in Flash Professional CS6

Flash Professional CS6 includes several drawing tools, which work in different drawing modes. The Basics of drawing tools enable you to create and edit graphics. To create basic geometric shapes, Flash Professional CS6 provides you various tools such as Line, Rectangle, Oval and PolyStar Tools. The Pencil Tool can be used for creating freehand shapes. The Pen Tool is for drawing Bezier curves and the Brush Tool is for creating artistic effects.

Selection Tool, Subselection and Lasso Tools are used to select objects for editing and reshaping the objects. There is another set of tools called Ink Bottle,

Paint Bucket and Eyedropper Tools, which are used to modify fill and outlines of the objects.

Selecting Objects

To edit or modify an object, you must first select different parts of it. In Flash Professional CS6, you can select objects with the Selection, Subselection, or Lasso Tools. Flash provides you the following tools to select shapes and objects.

✍ *Typically, you can use the Selection Tool to select an entire object or a section of an object. The Subselection Tool lets you select a specific point or line in an object. With Lasso Tool, you can make a freeform selection.*

Using Selection Tool

Selection tools look like Arrow tool. You can use this tool to select a single or multiple objects on the Stage.

✍ *To select Selection Tool, you can also press V key. To temporarily switch to Selection Tool when another tool is active, hold down the Ctrl key.*

To select the objects with the Selection Tool, do this:

- To select a filled object, click the Selection Tool in the Tools panel and click in the fill area. On a merged object, the selected fill is highlighted as shown in Figure 2.4 (a).
- To select both fill and outline, double-click the fill area with the Selection Tool as shown in Figure 2.4 (b).
- To select the stroke of an object, click on the Object's stroke with the Selection Tool.

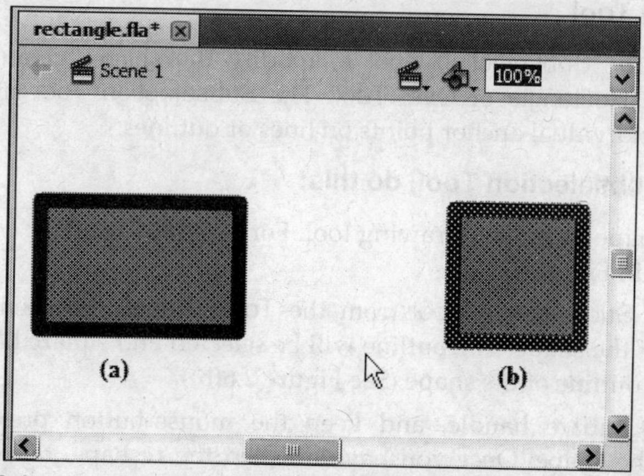

Figure 2.4 Using the Selection Tool for selecting both fill and stroke

- To select two or more objects together, click on the first object with the Selection Tool and then hold down the Shift key and click on all other objects. Or

You can also create a marquee selection to select multiple objects on the Stage.

The Selection Tool can be used to reshape objects on the Stage. You can modify the segments or move the endpoints to reshape the curve.

To reshape the object with the Selection Tool, do this:

1. Click the Selection Tool in the Tools panel.
2. Move the pointer around the segment, which you want to modify. The Selection Tool cursor will display with a curve under it (See Figure 2.5).
3. Click and drag the cursor to move the desired segment.

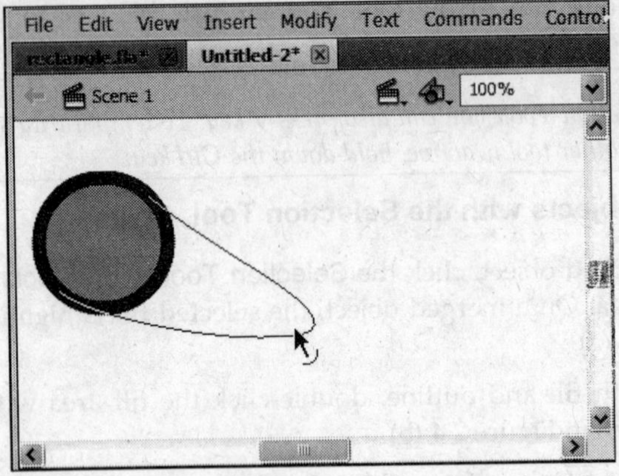

Figure 2.5 Reshape an object using the Selection Tool

Subselection Tool

You can use the Subselection Tool to modify the shapes created with Pen, Pencil, Brush, Rectangle or Oval Tool. The Subselection Tool enables you to move or edit individual anchor points on lines or outlines.

To use the Subselection Tool, do this:

1. Draw a shape using any drawing tool. For example, we have created a circle as shown in Figure 2.6 (a).
2. Click the Subselection Tool from the Tools Panel and then click on the Outline of the shape. The outline will be selected and square handles appear along the outline of the shape (See Figure 2.6(b)).
3. Click the square handle, and keep the mouse-button pressed. Drag to reshape the shape. Once you have finished the reshape, release the mouse button (See Figure 2.6(b)).

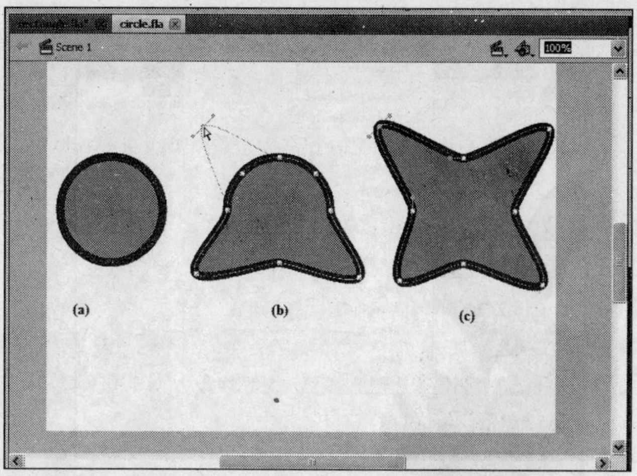

Figure 2.6 Using the Subselection Tool to reshape the circle

4. Reshape of the Circle object looks like a flower shape as shown in Figure 2.6(c)).

Lasso Tool

Another way to make a selection is to use the Lasso Tool. The Lasso Tool provides more flexibility than the Selection Tool when selecting object(s) or parts of an object on the Stage. The Lasso Tool lets you select an irregular part of a graphic, which you can then move, scale, rotate, reshape, or delete.

The Lasso Options area contains the following modifiers:

Magic Wand—Magic Wand Tool is useful for selecting areas of similar color in a bitmap graphic you have broken apart.

Polygon Mode—Polygon Mode option is useful for drawing straight lines and connect them to form a shape that will select any object(s) within the shape.

If you want to select different areas of graphic (with Selection Tool, Lasso Tool and Magic Wand Tool) to manipulate them separately from the graphic, you need to break apart a graphic. But, there is no need to break apart a bitmap graphic that you do not plan to manipulate.

Selection using a Lasso Tool

To make a selection using Lasso Tool, do this:

1. Open an image.
2. To break apart graphic, select the image and then click on the Modify menu and select Break Apart option (See Figure 2.7). *Alternatively*, press Ctrl + B keys together to work with Break Apart option.
3. Image after breaking apart look like Figure 2.8.

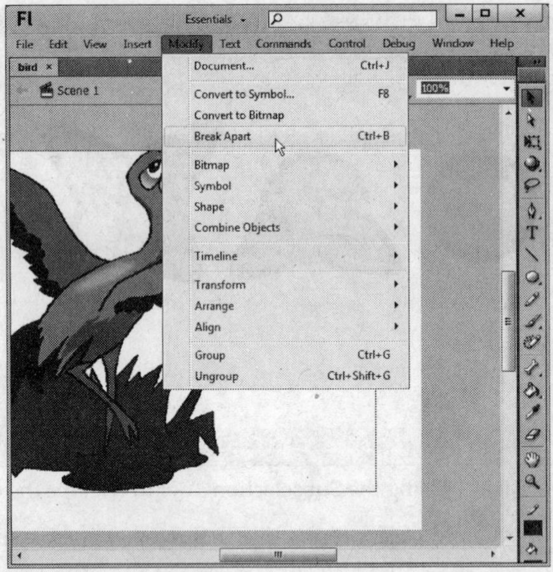

Figure 2.7 Break Apart option selected in Modify menu

Figure 2.8 Image after break apart

4. Click on the Lasso Tool from Tools panel. Place the mouse pointer over the image and drag it around the neck of the bird and end the loop approximately where you started (See Figure 2.9).

Figure 2.9 Selection using Lasso Tool

Lasso Tool with Polygon Modifier

Polygonal Lasso Tool draws straight segments.

To make a selection using Polygonal Lasso Tool, do this:

1. Select the Lasso Tool's Polygon Mode modifier from the Options area of the Tools panel.
2. Click to set the starting point.
3. Position the pointer where you want the first line to end, and click. Continue setting end points for additional line segments (See Figure 2.10).
4. To close the selection area, double-click.

The Lasso Tools with Magic Wand Modifier

The Magic Wand modifier of the Lasso Tool is used to select areas of bitmap that contain the same or similar colours in a bitmap graphic you have broken apart. After an image is broken apart, you can select individual areas of an image with Magic Wand option of the Lasso Tool.

To make a selection using Magic Wand Tool, do this:

1. Select the Lasso Tool's Magic Wand Settings from the Options area of the Tools panel. A Magic Wand Settings dialog box appears as shown in Figure 2.11.
2. In this dialog box, in Threshold: text box, enter a value between 1 and 200 to define how closely the color of adjacent pixels must match to be included in the selection.

Figure 2.10 Selecting flower using Polygon modifier of the Lasso Tool

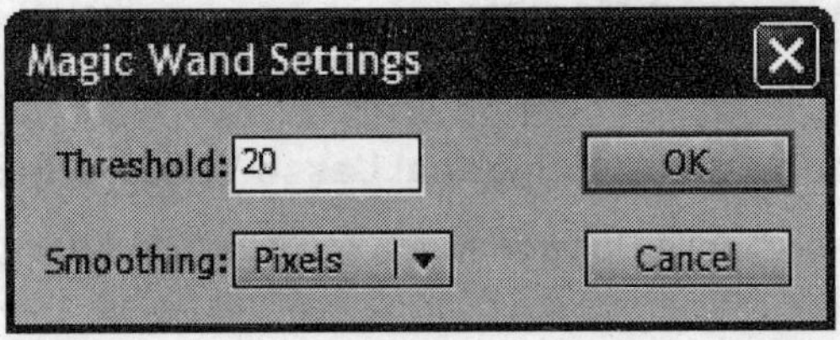

Figure 2.11 Magic Wand Settings dialog box

3. In Smoothing: drop-down list; select an option (for example, pixels) to define how much the edges of the selection are smoothened. Then click OK.
4. To select an area, click the bitmap. To add to the selection, continue clicking (See Figure 2.12).

Figure 2.12 Selecting area using Magic Wand modifier of Lasso Tool

5. To apply the new fill to the selected area, select the Paint Bucket Tool and click anywhere in the selected area.
6. The selected area now filled with new colour (See Figure 2.13).

Figure 2.13 Bird's wings after new fill

Line Tool

You can draw Straight lines using the Line Tool.

To draw straight lines, do this:

1. Click the Line Tool in the Tools Panel.
2. On the Stage, click the mouse button. The Cursor looks like a Plus sign. Keep the mouse button pressed, and drag the desired position you want to draw a line (See Figure 2.14).
3. If desired, change the stroke color, height and style from the Properties Inspector (See Figure 2.14).
4. Using the Shift key, you can draw straight lines at angles in increments of 15°. That is you can draw straight lines at angles 0°, 15°, 30°, 45°, etc. This is useful for drawing horizontal and vertical straight lines.

Draw Rectangles and Ovals

The Oval and Rectangle Tools let you create basic geometric shapes. In addition to the Merge and Object Drawing Modes, the Oval Tool and Rectangle Tool also provide the Primitive Object Drawing Mode as described earlier in this Chapter.

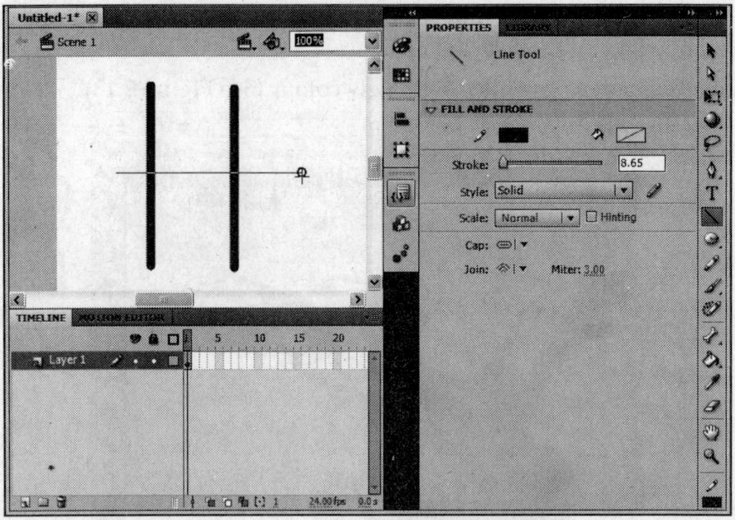

Figure 2.14 A straight line drawn with Line Tool

When you create rectangles or ovals using the Rectangle Primitive or Oval Primitive Tools, Flash draws the shapes as separate objects. After you create a primitive shape, you can alter the corners of rectangles, the start and end angle and the inner radius of ovals using controls in the Properties Inspector.

Rectangles and Squares

Rectangles and squares are the basic shapes available with most drawing software packages. Flash Professional CS6 lets you draw rectangles and squares with ease.

To draw rectangle and square, do this:

1. Click the Rectangle Tool in the Tools panel. Make sure the Object Drawing Mode icon is not selected in the Options area.
2. Click and drag the mouse on the Stage until the rectangle is of the size you want (See Figure 2.15 (a)). If you want to draw a square, press and hold down the Shift key, while dragging until the Square is of the size you want. (See Figure 2.15 (b)).

To draw rectangle using Rectangle Primitive Tool, do this:

1. Click on the small black arrow on the Rectangle Tool in the Tools panel. The Rectangle Tool flyout is activated as shown in Figure 2.16.
2. Click the Rectangle Primitive Tool.
3. Drag the mouse on the Stage until the rectangle is of the size you want.

Primitive objects (such as Primitive rectangles and ovals) are shapes that let you adjust their characteristics in the **Properties Inspector***. You can precisely control the size, corner radius, and other properties of the shape at any time after you have created it without having to draw it from scratch.*

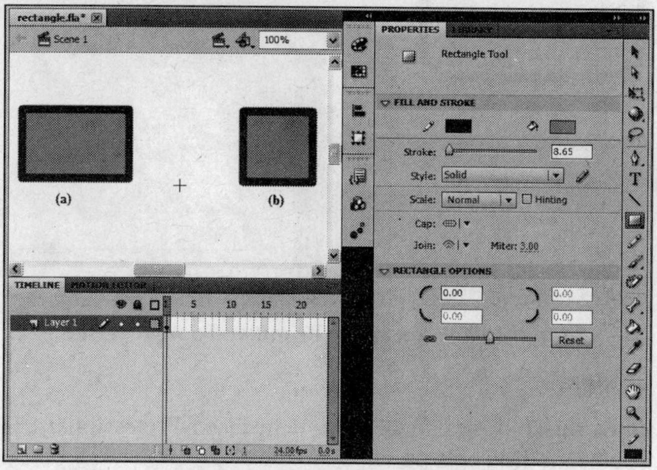

Figure 2.15 Using a Rectangle Tool to draw square and rectangle

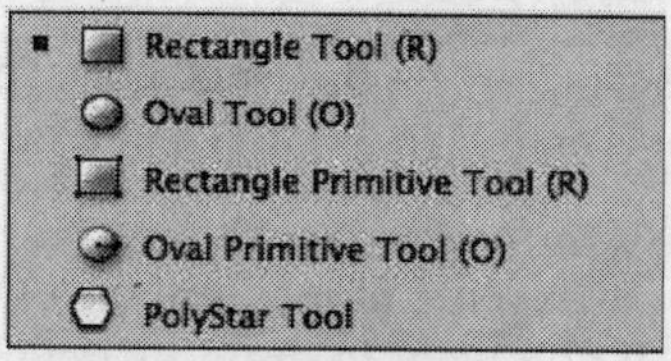

Figure 2.16 Rectangle Tool flyout (or hidden tools)

4. In the Properties Inspector, select the one of the following options:

   Rectangle Corner Radius Controls: To specify the corner radii for the rectangle, enter a numeric value for the inner radius in each text box. Entering a negative value creates an inverse radius. You can also deselect constrain corner radius icon, and adjust each corner radius individually.

   Reset: To reset all of the controls and restores the rectangle's initial size and shape.

   Lock Corner: To specify a different corner radius for each corner, deselect the Lock icon in the Rectangle Options area of the Properties Inspector (See Figure 2.17).

To change the corner radius while dragging with the **Rectangle Primitive Tool***, press the* **Up Arrow key** *or* **Down Arrow key***. When the corners achieve the desired roundness, release the key.*

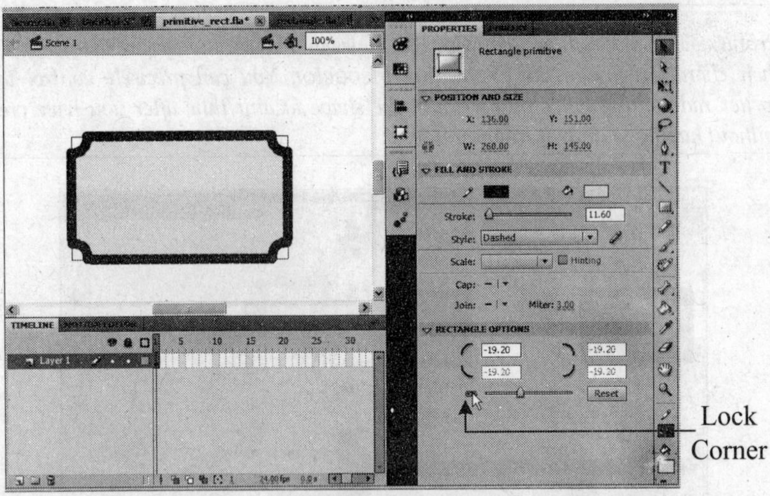

Figure 2.17 Rectangle Primitive Tool properties

Oval and Circles

Oval also known as Ellipse can be drawn in Flash Professional CS6 using the Rectangle Tool from the Tools panel.

To draw Oval and Circle, do this:

1. Click on the small black arrow on the Rectangle Tool in the Tools panel. The Rectangle Tool flyout is activated as shown in Figure 2.16.
2. Click the Oval Tool.
3. Click and drag the mouse on the Stage until the Oval is of the size you want. (See Figure 2.18 (a)). If you want to draw a Circle, press and hold down the Shift key while dragging until the Circle is of the size you want (See Figure 2.18 (b)).
4. If desired, change the stroke colour, fill color, height and style in the Properties Inspector (See Figure 2.18).

To draw oval using Oval Primitive Tool, do this:

1. Click on the small black arrow on the Rectangle Tool in the Tools panel. The Rectangle Tool flyout is activated as shown in Figure 2.16.
2. Click the Oval Primitive Tool.
3. Drag the mouse on the Stage until the oval is of the size you want.
4. In the Properties Inspector, select the one of the following options:

   Start Angle/End Angle: These controls are useful for easily modify the shape of ovals and circles into pie slices, half circles, and other creative shapes (See Figure 2.19).

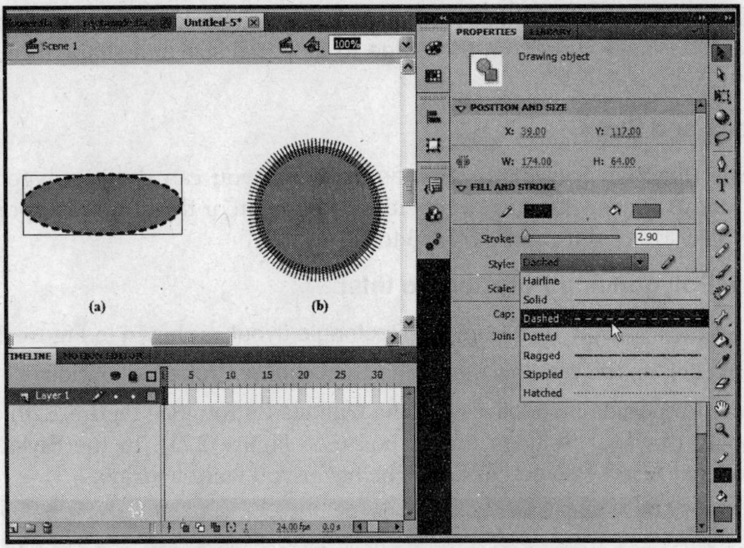

Figure 2.18 Drawing Oval and Circle

Inner Radius: It is an inner radius (or oval) within the oval. To set inner radius, you have to either enter a numeric value for the inner radius in the box or click the slider and interactively adjust the size of the inner radius.

Close Path: It determines whether the path of the oval is closed. If you specify an open path, Close path option is unchecked and no fill is applied to the resulting shape, only the stroke is drawn (See Figure 2.19). Close Path is selected by default.

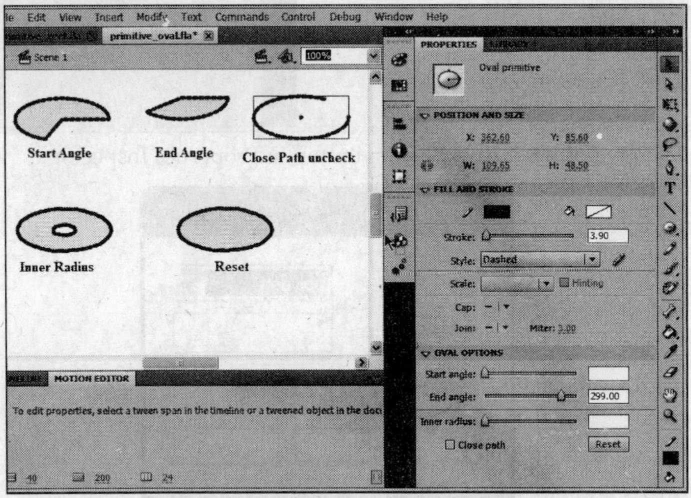

Figure 2.19 Oval primitive Tool properties

Reset: It resets all of the Oval Primitive Tool controls and restores the oval primitive shape drawn on the Stage to its initial size and shape (See Figure 2.19).

Polygons and Stars

Using the PolyStar Tool of the Rectangle flyout, you can draw polygons and stars. You can choose the number of sides of polygon or the number of points on the star. The size of star ranges from 3 to 32.

To draw Polygon and Polystar, do this:

1. Select the PolyStar Tool from the Rectangle flyout as shown in Figure 2.16.
2. Then click on the Window menu and then choose Properties option.
3. In the Properties Inspector, click the Options button (See Figure 2.20). It will display the Tool Settings dialog box (See Figure 2.21). In the Style: drop-down list, select Polygon or Star whichever you want to draw.

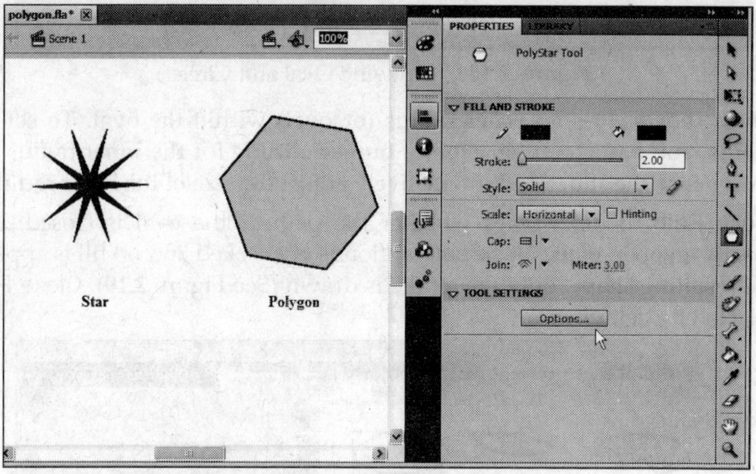

Figure 2.20 Option button in Properties Inspector

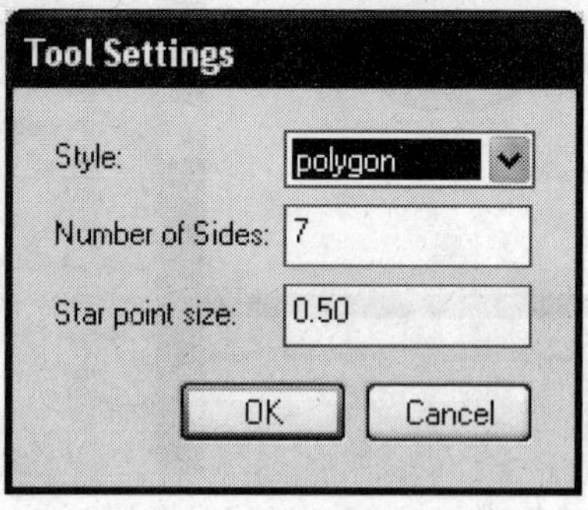

Figure 2.21 Tool Settings dialog box

4. In the Number of Sides: text box, enter a number from 3 to 32.
5. If you are drawing star, then in Star point size: text box, enter a number (from 0 to 1) to specify the depth of the star points. But, if you are drawing a polygon, leave this setting unchanged.
6. Click the OK button.
7. Drag on the Stage.

Pencil Tool

To draw lines and shapes, use the Pencil Tool, in much the same way as you would use a real pencil to draw. To apply smoothing or straightening to the lines and shapes as you draw, you can select a drawing mode for the Pencil Tool.

To draw with the Pencil Tool, do this:

1. Click the Pencil Tool in the Tools panel.
2. Select Window menu highlight Properties and select a stroke color, line weight, and style from the Properties Inspector.
3. Then select one of the following drawing modes under Options area of the Tools panel (See Figure 2.22).

   Straighten: To draw straight lines and convert approximations of triangles, ovals, circles, rectangles, and squares into these common geometric shapes (See Figure 2.22 (a)).

   Smooth: To draw smooth curved lines (See Figure 2.22 (b)).

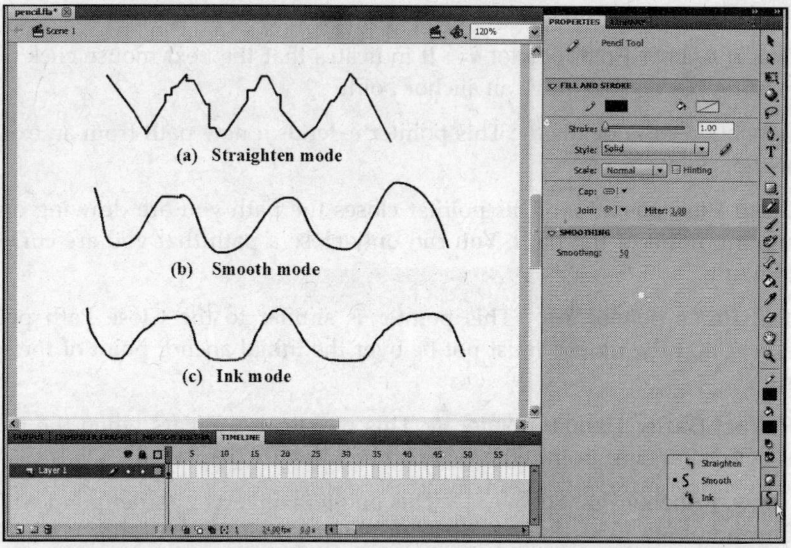

Figure 2.22 Different shapes of line drawn using Pencil mode options

Ink: To draw freehand lines with no modification applied. The Ink setting will not change shape (See Figure 2.22 (c)).

4. Click the Stage and drag to draw with the Pencil Tool. Shift-drag to constrain lines to vertical or horizontal directions. Figure 2.22 shows different shapes drawn with the three options for the Pencil Mode modifier.

Pen Tool

To draw precise paths as straight lines or smooth, flowing curves, you can use the Pen Tool. You can create straight or curved line segments, adjust the angle and length of straight segments, and the slope of curved segments.

Pen Tool Drawing States

The Pen Tool provides current drawing state by displaying different pointers. The various drawing states are indicated by the following pointers:

- Initial Anchor Point pointer: This is the pointer you see when you select the Pen Tool. It indicates that the next mouse click on the Stage will create an initial anchor point (beginning of a new path).
- Sequential Anchor Point pointer: This pointer is displayed during the creation of all user-defined anchor points except the initial anchor point of a path. It indicates that the next mouse click will create an anchor point with a line connecting it to the previous anchor point.
- Add Anchor Point pointer: It indicates that the next mouse click will add an anchor point to an existing path.
- Delete Anchor Point pointer: It indicates that the next mouse click on an existing path will remove an anchor point.
- Continue Path pointer: This pointer extends a new path from an existing anchor point.
- Close Path pointer: This pointer closes the path you are drawing on the starting point of the path. You can only close a path that you are currently drawing.
- Join Paths pointer: This pointer is similar to the Close Path pointer except that the mouse must not be over the initial anchor point of the same path.
- Retract Bezier Handle pointer: This pointer is appears when the mouse is over an anchor point whose Bezier handles are displayed.
- Convert Anchor Point pointer: This pointer converts a corner point without direction lines to a corner point with independent direction lines. To enable the Convert Anchor Point pointer, use the Shift+C keys together to toggle the Pen Tool.

Setting Pen Tool Preferences

There are certain options which control the appearance of the Pen Tool pointer, for previewing line segments as you draw, or for the appearance of selected anchor points. Selected line segments and anchor points are displayed using the outline color of the layer on which the lines and points appear. To access and change the settings of the Pen Tool preferences do the following steps:

To set Pen Tool Preferences, do this:

1. Select the Pen Tool from the Tools Panel.
2. Click the Edit menu and choose Preferences… . *Alternatively*, press Ctrl + U keys together. The Preferences dialog box appears as shown in Figure 2.23.
3. Select the Drawing option from the Category list of Preferences dialog box.
4. The Pen Tool has the following check box options (See Figure 2.23):

   Show pen preview: Flash displays a preview of line segments as you draw and as you move the pointer around the Stage. If this option is not selected, it does not display a line segment until you create the end point of the segment

   Show solid points: It displays selected anchor points as hollow (empty) and deselected anchor points as solid. If this option is not chosen, selected anchor points are solid, and deselected anchor points are hollow.

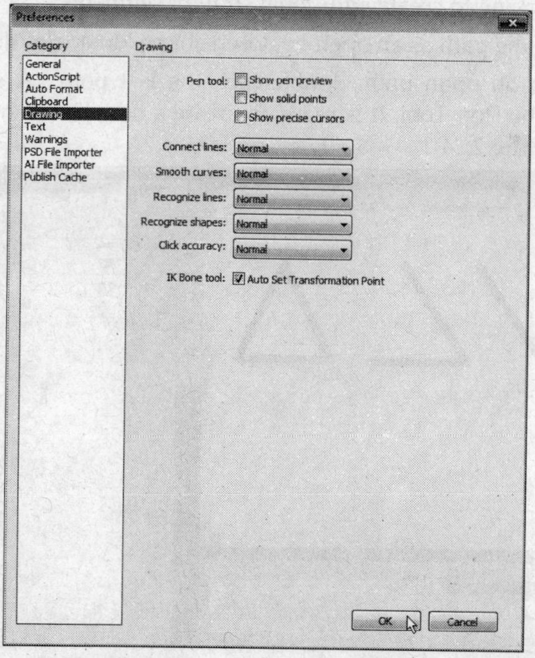

Figure 2.23 Preferences dialog box

Show precise cursors: It displays that the Pen Tool pointer appears as a cross-hair pointer, rather than the default Pen Tool icon, for more precise placement of lines. Deselect this option to display the default Pen Tool icon.

5. Click the OK button.

Press the CapsLock key while switching between the cross-hair pointer and the default Pen Tool icon.

Draw Straight Lines with the Pen Tool

The simplest path you can draw with the Pen Tool is a straight line. To draw straight line segments with the Pen Tool, you have to create anchor points on the line that determines the length of individual line segments.

To create a straight-line with the Pen Tool, do this:

1. Select the Pen Tool.
2. From the Properties Inspector, change *Stroke style, height, color* and *fill color*.
3. Position the pointer on the Stage where you want to define the first point of the path to appear and click to define the first anchor point.
4. Again click where you want the second point of the path to appear. A line segment connects the two points (See Figure 2.24).
5. Continue clicking to create additional straight segments.
6. To complete the path as an open or closed shape, do one of the following:

   To complete an open path, double-click the last point. A small x appears along with the Pen Tool. It is ready to create a new line segment of the new path (See Figure 2.24).

Figure 2.24 Using the Pen Tool to draw straight-line object

To close a path, position the Pen Tool over the first anchor point. A small circle appears next to the pen tip when it is positioned correctly. Click or drag to close the path.

Creating a Curved Path using Pen Tool

You can create curves by dragging the Pen Tool in the direction you want the curve to go to create the first anchor point, and then dragging the Pen Tool in the opposite direction to create the second anchor point. The length and slope of the direction lines determine the shape of the curve.

To create curved paths, do this:

1. Select the Pen Tool.
2. Position the Pen Tool where you want the curve to begin (See Figure 2.25).
3. The first anchor point appears. Hold down the mouse button. Click and drag the anchor point. The Pen Tool pointer changes to an arrowhead (See Figure 2.25).
4. Drag to set the slope of the curve segment and then release the mouse button (See Figure 2.25).

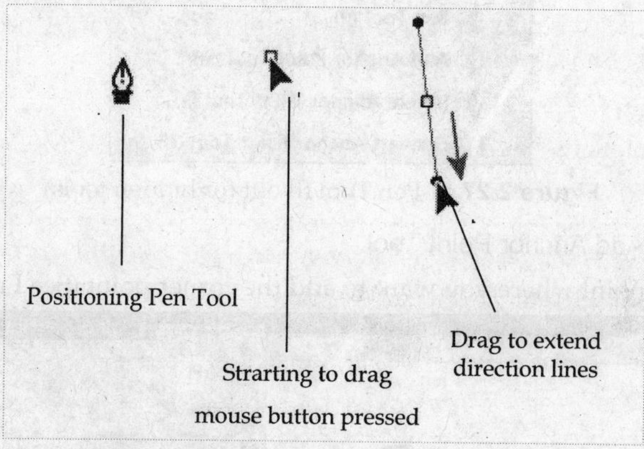

Figure 2.25 Steps to create curved path

5. Position the Pen Tool where you want the curve segment to end. For example, to create a C-shaped curve, drag in the opposite direction. Then release the mouse button.
6. Again click the anchor point continues the direction line. Drag the mouse to the opposite direction. Then release the mouse button. The S-shaped curve is drawn as shown in Figure 2.26.

Adding Anchor Points on Paths

When you draw a curve with the Pen Tool, you create curve points - anchor points on a continuous, curved path. By default, selected curve points appear as hollow circles, and selected corner points appear as hollow squares.

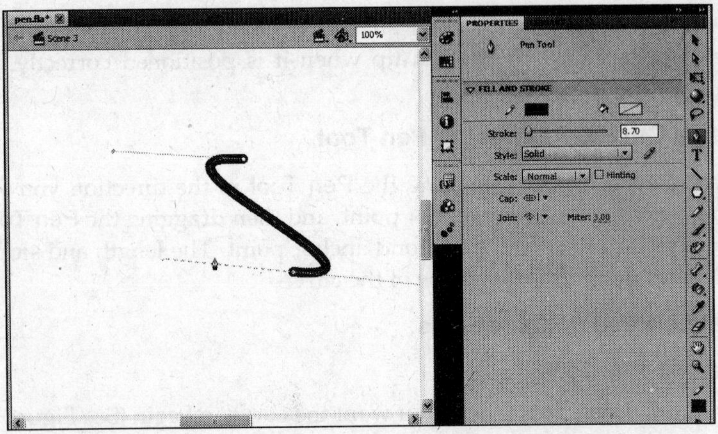

Figure 2.26 The S-shaped curve drawn using with Pen Tool

To add an anchor point on a path, do this:

1. Click on the small black arrow on the Pen Tool in the Tools panel. The Pen Tool flyout is activated as shown in Figure 2.27.

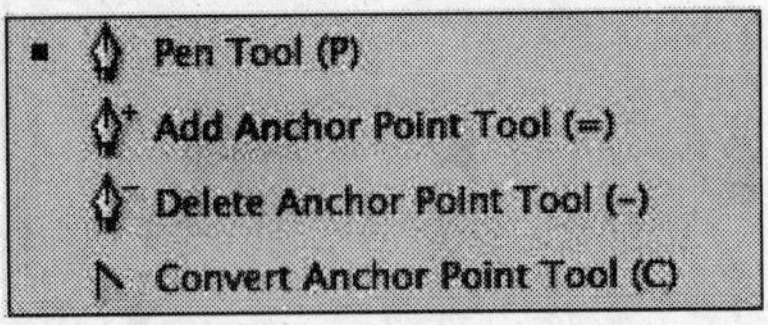

Figure 2.27 Pen Tool flyout (or hidden tools)

2. Select the Add Anchor Point Tool.
3. Click at a point where you want to add the corner point (See Figure 2.28).

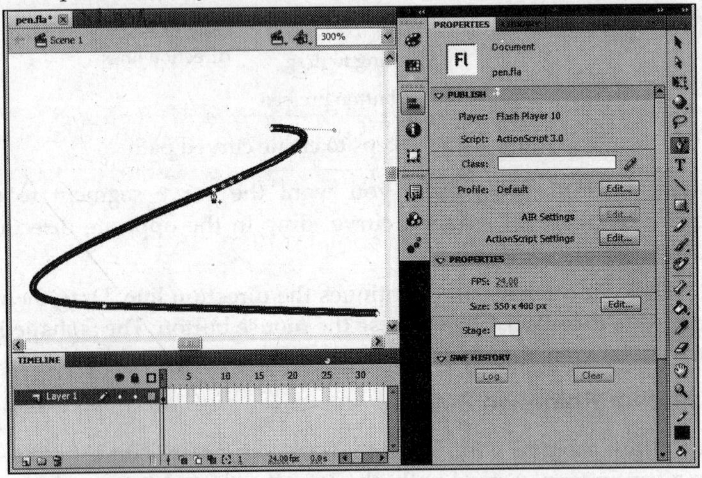

Figure 2.28 Adding an anchor point on a path

Deleting Corner and Curve Points

Deleting unneeded anchor points on a curved path optimizes the curve and reduces the resulting SWF (Small Web Format) file size.

To delete a corner and a curve point, do this:

1. Click on the small black arrow on the Pen Tool in the Tools panel. The Pen Tool flyout is activated as shown in Figure 2.27.
2. Select the Delete Anchor Point Tool.
3. To delete a corner point, click the point once with Pen Tool.

Conversion between Straight and Curved Segments

To convert segments in a line from straight segments to curve segments, convert corner points to smooth points. You can also do the reverse.

To convert a corner point to a smooth point, do this:

1. Click on the Subselection Tool to select the point.
2. Then press Alt key while you drag the point to place the tangent handles.

To convert a smooth point to a corner point, do this:

1. Click on the small black arrow on the Pen Tool in the Tools panel. The Pen Tool flyout is activated as shown in Figure 2.27.
2. Select the Convert Anchor Point Tool.
3. Click the point. Your point is turned into a corner point.

Painting with the Brush Tool

The Brush Tool draws brushlike strokes, as if you were painting. It lets you create special effects, including calligraphic effects. You can select a brush size and shape using the Brush Tool modifiers.

Brush size for new strokes remains constant even when you change the magnification level of the Stage, so the same brush size appears larger when the Stage magnification is lower.

To Paint a Shape with the Brush Tool, do this:

1. Select the Brush Tool in the Tools panel.
2. In the Properties Inspector, change *Stroke style, height, color* and *fill color*.
3. Click one of the following Brush Mode modifiers from the Options area of the Tools panel and select one of the following painting modes (See Figure 2.29):

   Paint Normal: It paints over lines and fills on the same layer.

   Paint Fills: It fills empty areas, leaving lines unaffected.

   Paint Behind: It paints behind existing lines and fills.

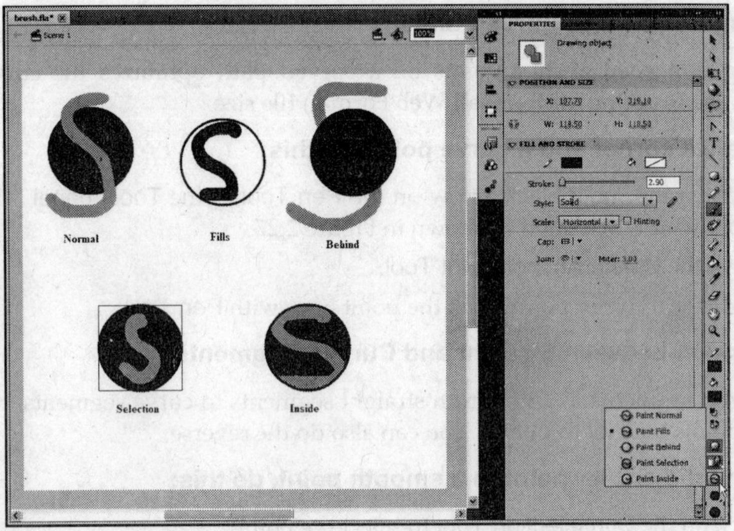

Figure 2.29 Different Brush Strokes applied in the object

Paint Selection: It applies paint within the selected filled shape leaving lines and blank areas of the Stage unaffected.

Paint Inside: It applies paint within the filled shape where you begin the stroke without affecting surrounding lines, fills and blank areas of the Stage.

4. Now, select a brush size from the Brush Size modifier from the Options area of the Tools panel (See Figure 2.30 (a)).
5. Select a brush shape from the Brush Shape modifier from the Options area of the Tools panel as shown in Figure 2.30 (b).

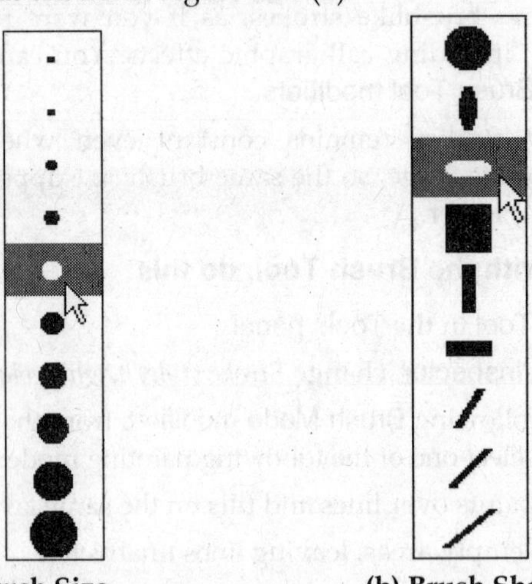

(a) Brush Size **(b) Brush Shape**

Figure 2.30 Selecting Brush Size and Shape from Options area

6. Choose the desired fill color from the Properties Inspector.
7. Enter a value between 0 to 100 in the Smoothing: text box in the Properties Inspector or use the Slider beside the textbox to specify the value.
8. Drag the mouse pointer on the Stage to apply a brush stroke on the Object as shown in Figure 2.29.

Spray Brush Tool

In Flash Professional CS6, Spray Brush Tool is like a particle sprayer. It lets you create a pattern of shapes onto the Stage at one time. By default, the Spray Brush Tool emits a spray of dot particles using the currently selected fill color. However, you can use the Spray Brush Tool to apply a movie clip or graphic symbol as a pattern.

To apply patterns with the Spray Brush Tool, do this:

1. Click on the small black arrow on the Brush Tool in the Tools panel. The Brush Tool flyout is activated as shown in Figure 2.31.

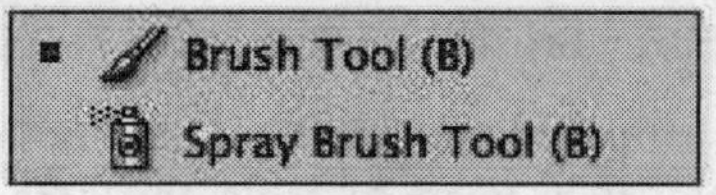

Figure 2.31 Brush Tool flyout (or hidden tools)

2. Select the Spray Brush Tool.
3. Select one of the following Spray Brush Tool options from the Properties Inspector of the Tools panel (See Figure 2.33).

   Edit... : It opens the Select Symbol dialog box as shown in Figure 2.32. Select symbol from the list as a spray brush particle and then press OK button (See Figure 2.32). When a symbol in the library is selected, its name appears next to the edit button (See Figure 2.33).

   Color selector: Select a fill color for the default particle spray. The color selector is disabled when you use a symbol in the library as a spray particle.

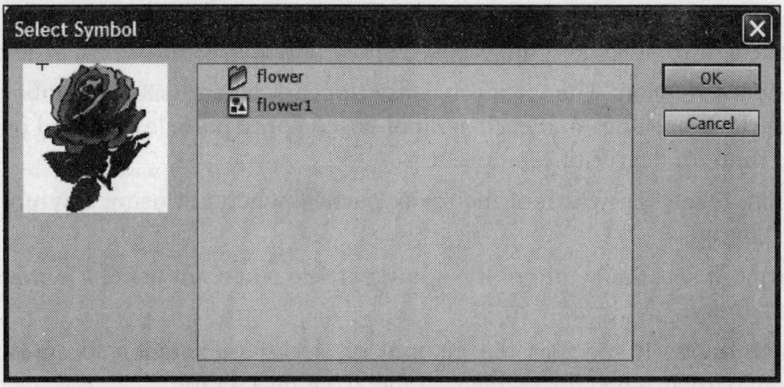

Figure 2.32 Select Symbol dialog box

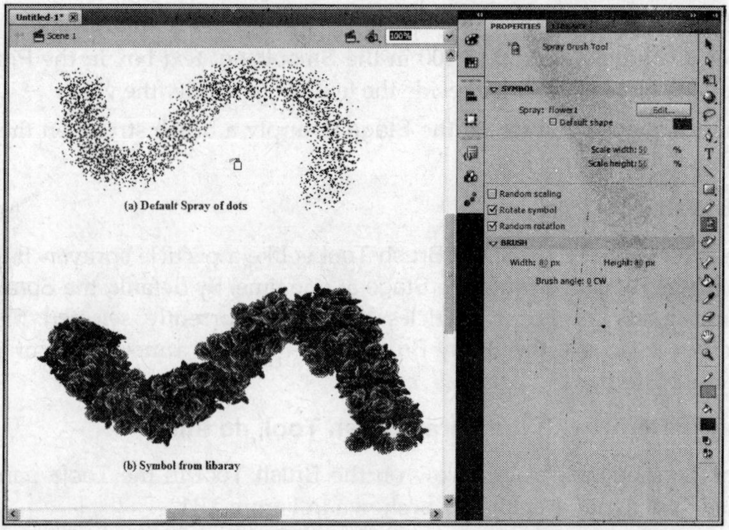

Figure 2.33 Spray Brush Tool Options in Properties Inspector

Scale: This property only appears when you are not using a symbol from the Library as the particle. It is used to scale the default spray dots as spray particles.

Scale width: This property only appears when using a symbol as the particle. It scales the width of a symbol used as a spray particle. This property is measured in terms of percentage (%).

Scale height: This property only appears when using a symbol as the particle. It scales the height of a symbol used as a spray particle. This property is measured in terms of percentage (%).

Random scaling: This option appears when using a symbol from the Library. It specifies that each symbol-based spray particle is placed on Stage at a random scale, altering the size of each particle.

Rotate symbol: This property only appears when using a symbol as the particle. It rotates the symbol-based spray particle around a center point.

Random rotation: This property only appears when using a symbol as the particle. It specifies that each symbol-based spray particle is placed on Stage at a random degree of rotation.

Width: It sets the width of the spray particle when not using a symbol from the Library.

Height: It sets the height of the spray particle when not using a symbol from the Library.

Brush angle: It specifies the amount of clock-wise rotation to apply to the spray particle when not using a symbol from the Library.

4. Click or drag on the Stage where you want the pattern to be appeared. Figure 2.33 (a) shows default spray dots and Figure 2.33 (b) shows spray symbol selected from the **Library**.

You can use any movie clip or graphic symbol in the library as a "particle." These symbol-based particles give you a great deal of creative control over artwork you create in Flash Professional CS6.

Drawing Patterns with the Deco (Decorative) Tool

The **Deco** (Decorative drawing) **Tool** provides a variety of drawing effects that can be used to quickly create environments and to create various animations. In addition, the **Deco Tool** can be used to create decorative patterns. These patterns can be animated and added to a movie to create special effects. Flash Professional CS6 has a number of **Deco Tool brushes and effects**.

One drawback of using the **Deco Tool** is that animations created with the **Deco Tool** results in large file sizes. This is because the images created with the brush Tools are made up of small segments and the animations are frame-by-frame animations.

Any effect created using the **Deco Tool** *can be selected, converted to a graphic or movie clip symbol, and animated by inserting a motion tween or used in another animation process in Flash Professional CS6.*

There are thirteen types of drawing effects available with the **Deco Tool**. These drawing effects are available in the **Properties panel** when the **Deco Tool** is selected from the **Tools panel** (See Figure 2.34).

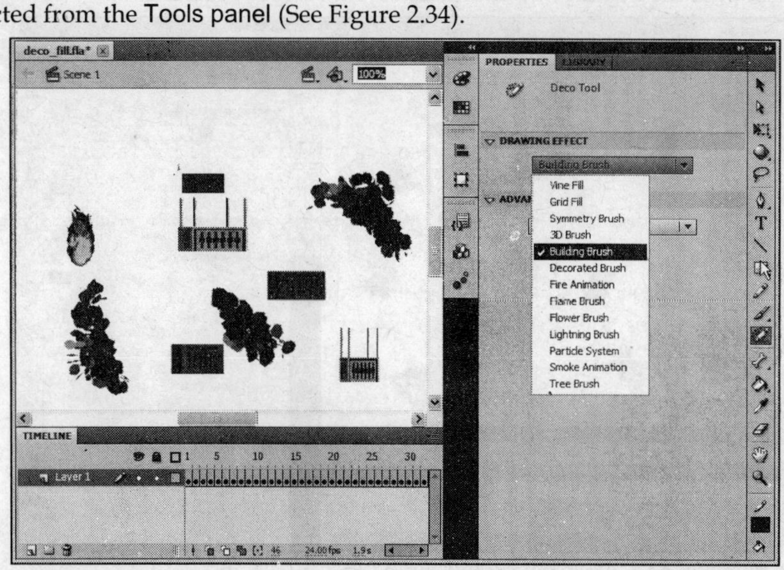

Figure 2.34 Different drawing effects available with the Deco Tool

They are grouped into three basic types. These are as follows:

- Fills – Vine Fill, Grid Fill and Symmetry Brush create patterns that can be used as fill for graphics or as a backdrop for a movie. Flash Professional CS6 allows you to create your own fill using an image of your choice, such as a logo. In addition, you can set various properties such as the pattern scale.
- Brushes – Brushes, such as Building, Lightning, Tree, and Flower can be used to create drawings that can be combined to construct environments.
- Animations – Animation, such as Fire Animation, Smoke Animation, and Particle System, create animations as they are used.

Apply the Vine Fill Effect

The Vine Fill Effect lets you create a simple pattern with the default symbol. You can substitute your own artwork for the leaves and flowers by selecting symbols from the library.

To apply Vine Fill Effect, do this:

1. Select the Deco Drawing Tool.
2. Then select Vine Fill from the Drawing Effect section in the Properties Inspector as shown in Figure 2.34.
3. In the Deco Drawing Tool Properties Inspector, select a fill color for the default flower and leaf shapes. Or,
4. Click Edit… button to select a custom symbol from the library to replace one or both of the default flower and leaf symbols (See Figure 2.35).

Figure 2.35 Vine Fill Effect with their options in Properties Inspector

5. Select one of the following Deco Tool Advanced Options from the Properties Inspector of the Tools panel (See Figure 2.35).

   Branch angle: To specify the angle of the branch pattern.

   Branch color: To specify the color to use for the branch.

   Pattern scale: It scales an object to enlarge or reduce it both horizontally (along the x-axis) and vertically (along the y-axis).

   Segment length: It specifies the length of the segments between leaf and flower nodes.

   Animate Pattern: It specifies that each iteration of the effect is drawn to a new frame in the timeline. This check box option creates a frame-by-frame animated sequence of the flower pattern as it is drawn.

   Frame step: It specifies how many frames to span per second of the effect being drawn.
6. Now click on the Stage or within the shape or symbol where you want the Vine Fill pattern to be appeared as shown in Figure 2.35.

✍ *After you apply the Vine Fill effect, you cannot change the Advanced Options in the Properties Inspector afterward to alter the fill pattern.*

Apply the Decorated Brush Effect

The Decorated Brush Effect lets you draw decorative lines, such as dotted lines, wavy lines, circle, rope and others.

To apply Decorated Brush effect, do this:

1. Select the Deco Tool in the Tools panel.
2. Then select Decorated Brush from the Drawing Effect menu in the Properties Inspector as shown in Figure 2.34.
3. In the Properties Inspector, from the Advanced Options menu, set the following properties for the Decorated Brush effect (See Figure 2.36):

   Line style: Select the style of line to draw Cartoon Stars, Shiny Stars, etc.

   Pattern color: Specify the color of the line.

   Pattern size: Specify the size of the selected pattern.

   Pattern width: Specify the width of the selected pattern.
4. Now drag the cursor on the Stage.
5. Decorated Brush with styled line that follows the path of the cursor is shown in Figure 2.36.

Apply the Fire Animation Effect

The Fire Animation automatically creates stylized frame-by-frame fire animation

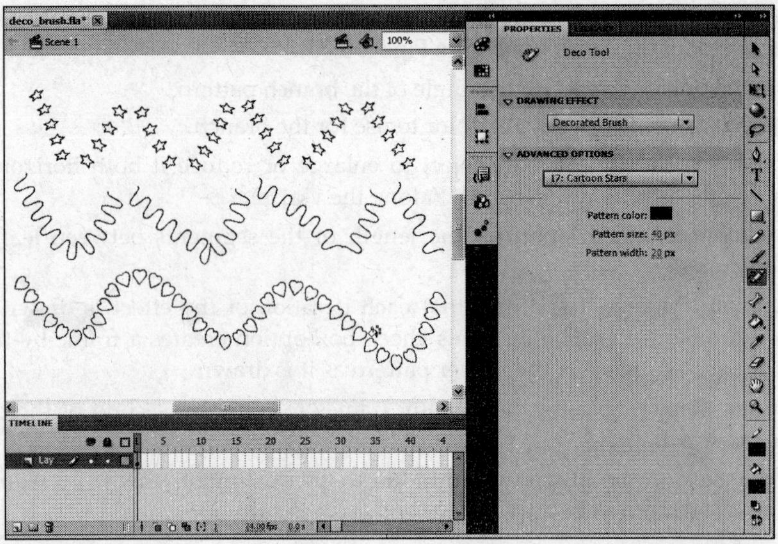

Figure 2.36 Different line styles available with Decorated Brush

of fire burning. The colours of the fire can be controlled through the Properties Inspector.

To apply Fire Animation effect, do this:

1. Select the Deco Tool in the Tools panel.
2. Then choose Fire Animation from the Drawing Effect menu in the Properties Inspector as shown in Figure 2.34.
3. In the Properties Inspector, from the Advanced Options menu, set the following properties for the Fire Animation effect (See Figure 2.37):

   Fire size: It sets the width and height of the flames. Higher values create larger flames.

   Fire speed: It sets the speed of the animation. Larger values create faster flames.

   Fire duration: Specify the number of frames created in the timeline during the animation.

   End animation: Select this check box option to create an animation of the fire burning out instead of burning continuously. If you want to loop the finished animation to create a continuous burning effect, do not select this option.

   Flame color: It sets the color of the tips of the flames.

   Flame core color: It sets the color of the base of the flames.

   Fire spark: It sets the number of individual flames at the base of the fire.

4. Now drag on the Stage to create the animation.
5. Flash Professional CS6 adds frames to the timeline while you hold the mouse button as shown in Figure 2.37.

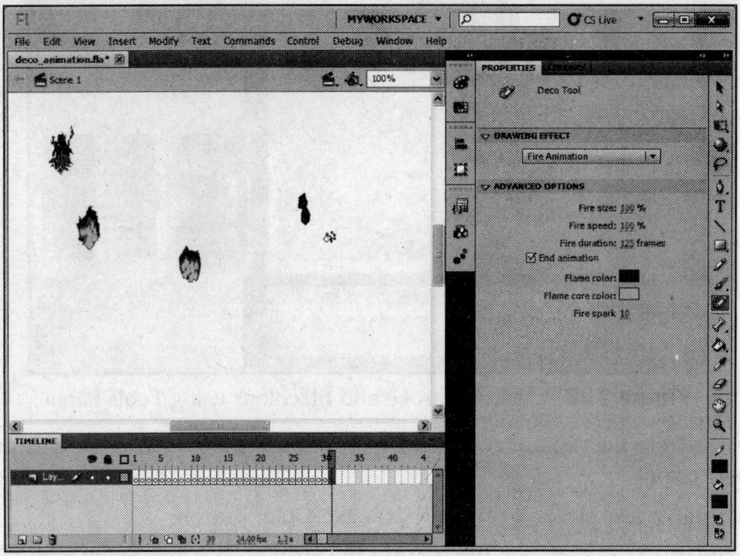

Figure 2.37 Fire Animation using Deco Tool

Understanding Fills and Strokes

Every graphic in Flash Professional CS6 starts with a shape. A shape is made of two components. These components are:

- Fill (inside a shape)
- Stroke (outline of the shape)

The fill and the stroke are independent of each other, so you can modify or delete either without affecting the other.

There are two ways to specify the fill and stroke colour of graphic objects and shapes:

1. Using Tools panel
2. Using Properties Inspector

To adjust Fill and Stroke colour using the Tools panel, do this:

1. Select the object on the Stage.
2. Click the Stroke or Fill Color control, and select a color swatch (See Figure 2.38).
3. Select a colour through Color Picker button from the pop-up window. Or type a color's hexadecimal value in the box (See Figure 2.38).

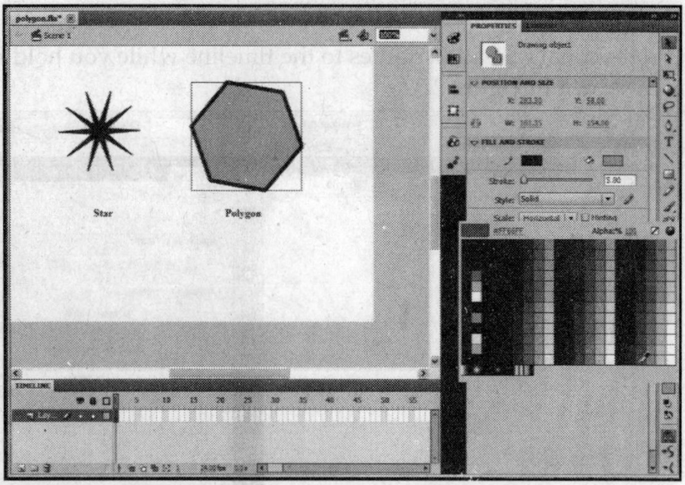

Figure 2.38 Setting Stroke and fill colour using Tools Panel

4. To return to the default color settings, click the Black and White button in the Tools panel.
5. To remove any stroke or fill, click the No Color button.
6. To Swap colors between the fill and the stroke, click the Swap Colors button in the Tools panel.

Selecting Stroke Color, Style and Weight using the Properties Inspector

To change the stroke color, style and weight for a selected object, use the Stroke Color control in the Properties Inspector.

Stoke Color: The Stroke Color is the color of the outline of an object. You can set the Stroke color for objects drawn with the Line, Rectangle, PolyStar, Pen and Pencil Tool.

1. If you want to change the Stroke color for an existing object, select the outline of the object on the Stage using the Selection Tool.
2. In the Properties Inspector, click the Stroke color box icon from the Fill and Stroke Option. And then select the desired color of the Outline (See Figure 2.39).

Fill Color: The Fill Color is the color that fills the inside area of closed objects, such as rectangle or an oval. You can also set the fill color for the objects created with the Oval, Rectangle, Brush Tool, etc.

1. Select the object on the Stage by clicking on the object with the Selection Tool.
2. In the Properties Inspector, click the Fill color box icon from the Fill and Stroke Option. And then select the desired color of the object (See Figure 2.39).

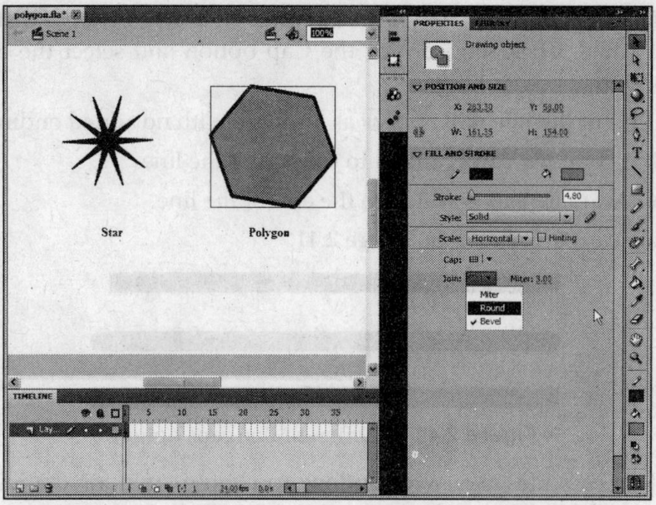

Figure 2.39 Setting fill colour using Properties Inspector

Stroke Height: You can set the thickness of the lines and outlines of the shapes, drawn with the Pen, Line and Pencil Tools.

1. If you want to modify the thickness of an existing line or an outline of an existing object, select the line or the outline with the Selection Tool.
2. In the Properties Inspector, enter the value in the Stroke height: text box or drag the slider of Stroke to specify a value (See Figure 2.39).

Stroke Style: The Stroke style offers you seven line styles to use for the lines and outlines. The Hairline style draws a line with thickness of 1 pixel, which does not visually change at different zoom levels.

1. Select a tool to draw a new line or a shape with an outline. To modify an existing line or the shape of an existing object, select the line or the outline of the object.
2. In the Properties Inspector, from the Style: drop-down list, select a desired line style (See Figure 2.40).

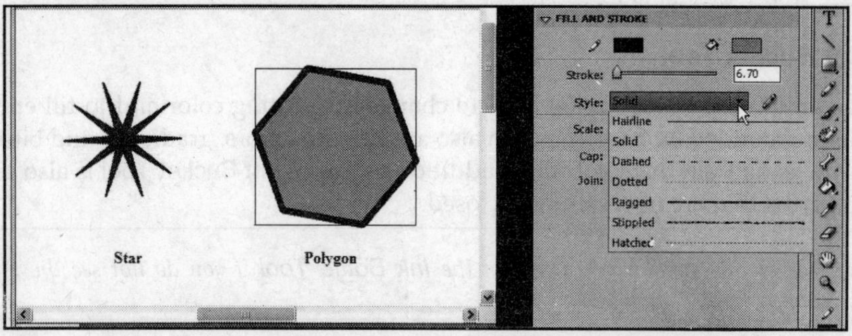

Figure 2.40 Setting Stroke color using Properties Inspector

3. Cap: The Cap provides you with the three options to choose a style for the end of a line. Click the icon for the Cap option and select the desired cap style option.

   None: End of the line will appear as a square with no added ending.

   Round: A rounded cap is added to the end of the line.

   Square: A square cap is added to the end of the line.

Different line caps are shown in Figure 2.41.

Figure 2.41 Different line caps option

Join: The Join provides you with options to choose style for the joining point which appears when two path segments meet. Click the Join icon to display a list of options as follows (See Figure 2.39):

Miter: The joining points will appear as pointed corner.

Round: The joining points will appear as rounded corner.

Bevel: The joining points will appear as squared-off corner.

The Rectangle corner joins with the three settings for the Join attributes (See Figure 2.42).

Figure 2.42 Rectangles corner joins with the three setting of Join options

Stroke Hinting: The Stroke Hinting option is useful for clearing the blurry horizontal and vertical lines.

Paint Bucket Tool

You can use the Paint Bucket Tool to change an existing color and to fill empty areas surrounded by lines. You can also apply solid colors, gradients, and bitmap fills by using Pain Bucket Tool. In addition to this, Paint Bucket Tool is also used to fill areas that are not entirely enclosed.

✍ *Click on the small black arrow of the Ink Bottle Tool if you do not see the Paint Bucket Tool.*

To use the Paint Bucket Tool to fill area, do this:

1. Click the Paint Bucket Tool in the Tools Panel.
2. Choose the color or gradient from Fill color option in the Color modes in the Tools Panel or Properties Inspector.
3. Then click on the object. The selected color automatically applied in the object as shown in Figure 2.43.
4. Click the Gap Size modifier that appears at the bottom of the Tools panel and select the desired gap size option as shown in Figure 2.43.
5. Then Click the shape or enclosed area to fill.

The Paint Bucket Tool has a lock modifier that can be used to apply a bitmap fill or gradient across multiple graphics. You can toggle the lock OFF and ON using the Lock Fill option, which is available in the Options area at the bottom of the Tools panel when the Paint Bucket Tool is selected. Usually, you toggle the lock OFF if you are filling only one object.

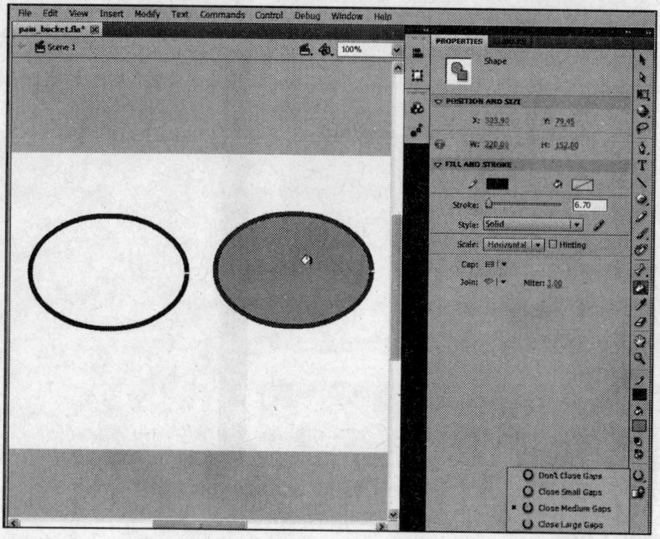

Figure 2.43 Using the Paint Bucket Tool to fill the colour in the oval

Ink Bottle Tool

To change or modify the stroke color, width, and style of lines or shape outlines, you can use the Ink Bottle Tool. You can apply only solid colors, not gradients or bitmaps, to lines or shape outlines.

Using the Ink Bottle Tool, rather than selecting individual lines, makes it easier to change the stroke attributes of multiple objects at one time.

To use the Ink Bottle Tool, do this:

1. Select the object using the Selection Tool.
2. Click on the small black arrow on the Paint Bucket Tool in the Tools panel. The Paint Bucket Tool flyout is activated as shown in Figure 2.44.

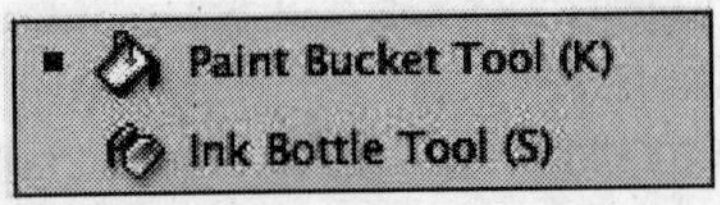

Figure 2.44 Paint Bucket Tool flyout (or hidden tools)

3. Click on the Ink Bottle Tool.
4. Select the Stroke color, height and style from the Properties Inspector.
5. Click on the object. The selected stroke color, height and style applied to the object using the Ink Bottle Tool as shown in Figure 2.45.

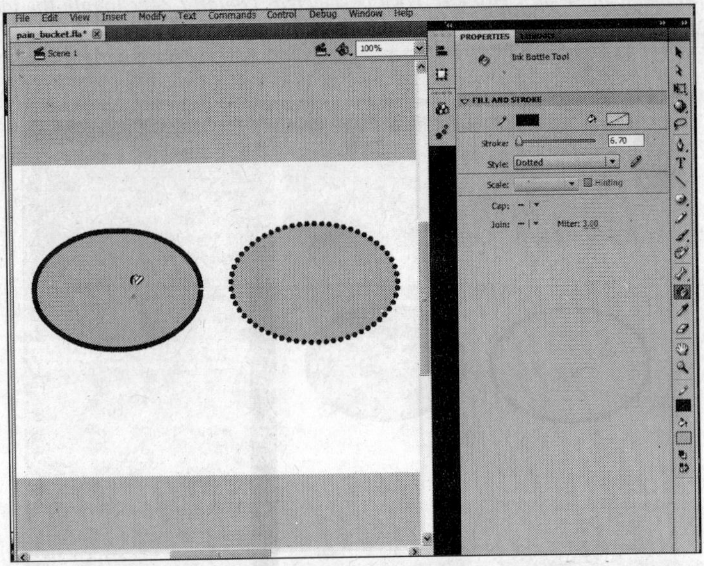

Figure 2.45 Using the Ink Bottle Tool to change the stroke color, height and style

Eyedropper Tool

You can use the Eyedropper Tool to copy fill and stroke attributes from one object and immediately apply them to another object.

To use the Eyedropper Tool to copy and apply stroke or fill attributes to the other object, do this:

1. Create an oval shape using the Oval Tool and its attributes which you want to apply in the rectangle shape.

2. Select the Eyedropper Tool and click the stroke or filled area whose attributes you want to apply in the rectangle shape.
3. You can notice Eyedropper Tool cursor turning into the Ink Bottle Tool cursor, if you click a stroke (See Figure 2.46). But, when you click a filled area, the tool automatically changes to the Paint Bucket Tool with the Lock Fill modifier turned ON.

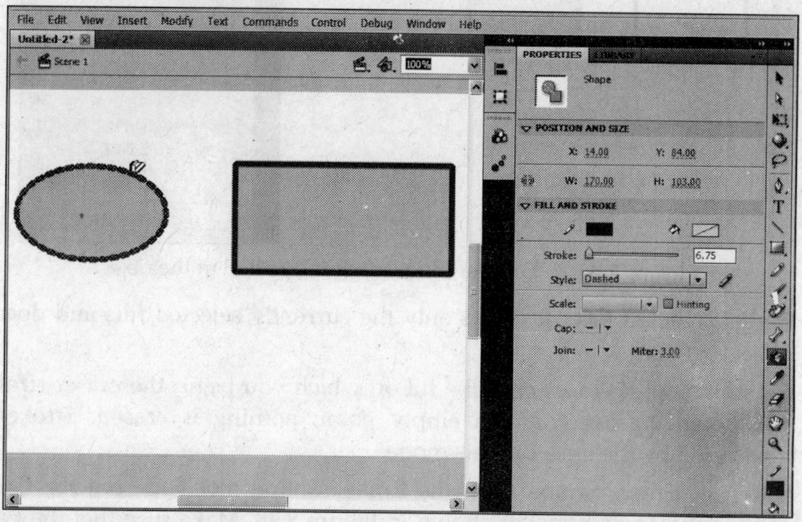

Figure 2.46 Eyedropper Tool to copy and apply stroke or fill attributes

4. Click inside the Rectangle. You can notice that the color and style of the rectangle stroke is exactly same as the Oval.

Using the Eraser Tool for Erasing Fill and Strokes

Erasing with the Eraser Tool removes strokes and fills. You can quickly erase everything on the Stage. You can remove the fill or the stroke of an object by selecting the appropriate Eraser mode. You also have the choice for selecting an Eraser shape. Apart from this, you can also use Eraser Tool to delete parts of the bitmap image that has been broken apart.

To erase fills and strokes using the Eraser Tool, do this:

1. Click the Eraser Tool in Tools panel.
2. Click one of the following Eraser Mode modifiers from the Options area of the Tools panel (See Figure 2.47).

   Erase Normal: It erases strokes and fills on the same layer.

   Erase Fills: It erases only the fill of an object.

   Erase Lines: It erases only the stroke of an object but not fill.

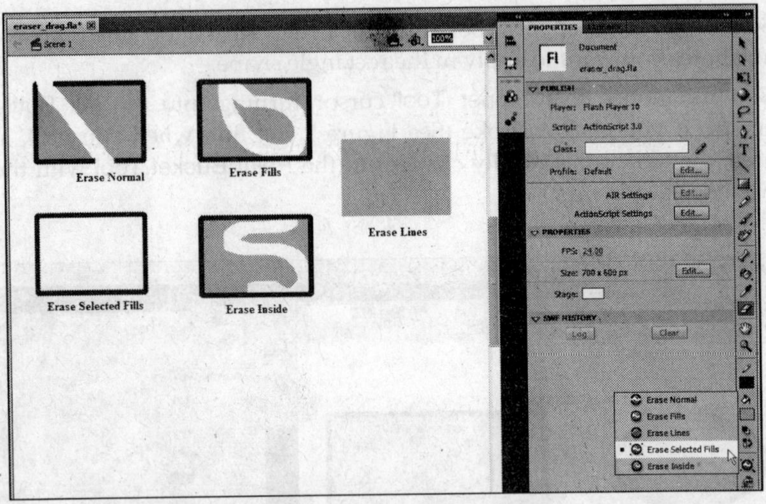

Figure 2.47 Different Eraser mode applied in the object

Erase Selected Fills: It erases only the currently selected fills and does not affect strokes.

Erase Inside: It erases only the fill on which you begin the eraser stroke. If you begin erasing from an empty point, nothing is erased. Strokes are unaffected by the eraser in this mode.

3. Select an Eraser shape from the Eraser Shape modifier from the Options area of the Tools panel as shown in Figure 2.48. Make sure that the Faucet modifier is not selected.

To erase a line or a fill in one fell swoop, click the Faucet modifier, *and then click the line or fill.*

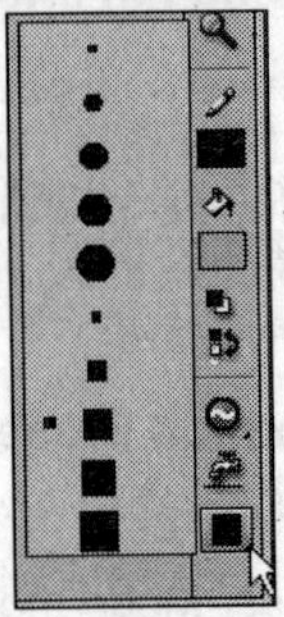

Figure 2.48 Selecting Eraser shape from Options area

4. Drag over the object you want to delete. Different parts of objects being removed using the Erase Tool with five brush mode types as shown in Figure 2.47.

> ✍ *To erase all types of content from the stage and pasteboard, double-click the* Eraser Tool *in the* Tools Panel.

To remove stroke segments or filled areas using Faucet modifier of Eraser Tool, do this:

1. Select the Eraser Tool from the Tool panel.
2. Then click the Faucet modifier from the Options area of the Tools panel as shown in Figure 2.49.
3. Click the stroke segment or filled area of an object to delete as shown in Figure 2.49.

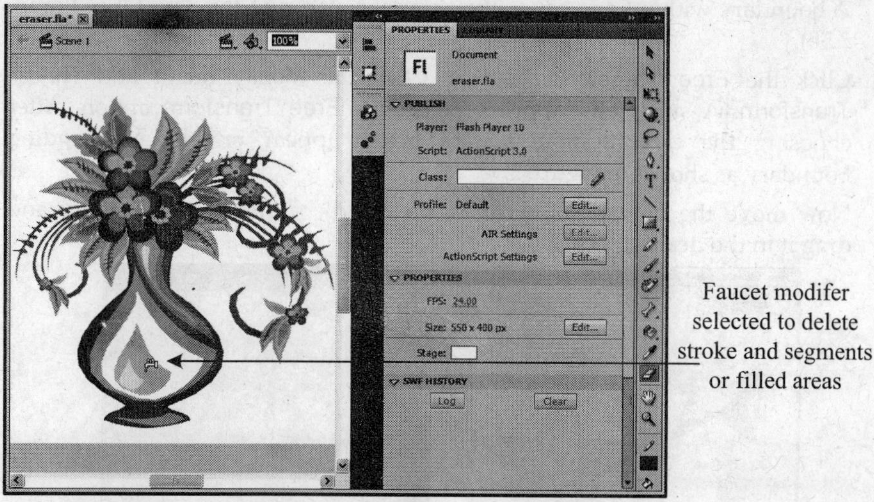

Figure 2.49 Delete stroke segments or filled areas using Faucet modifier

Transforming Objects

You can transform drawing objects, grouped objects, symbols and text blocks either by using the Free Transform Tool or by the Transform options of the Modify menu. Depending on the type of element you select, you can freely *transform, rotate, skew, scale*, or *distort* the element. You can change or add a selection during a transformation operation. Before transforming an object, you need to select it with the Selection Tool. When an object is selected, a boundary with small squares boxes appears around the object. You can drag the square handle to transform the object.

Use the Free Transform Tool

You can use the Free Transform Tool to freely transform objects, groups, instances, or text blocks. You can perform individual transformations or combine several transformations, such as *moving, rotating, scaling, skewing,* and *distortion* by dragging control points around a bounding box.

Free Transform Tool cannot transform symbols, bitmaps, video objects, sounds, gradients, or text. If a multiple selection contains any of these items, only the shape objects are distorted. To transform a text block, first convert the characters to shape objects.

To transform freely, do this:

1. Select a graphic, object group, instance, or text block with the Selection Tool on the Stage.
2. A boundary without any square boxes appears around the object (See Figure 2.50).
3. Click the Free Transform Tool or Click the Modify menu and choose Transform. A sub menu appears. Select the Free Transform option. After choosing the option small square boxes appear on the surrounding boundary as shown in Figure 2.50.
4. Now move the mouse pointer over the handle around the boundary and drag it in the desired location.

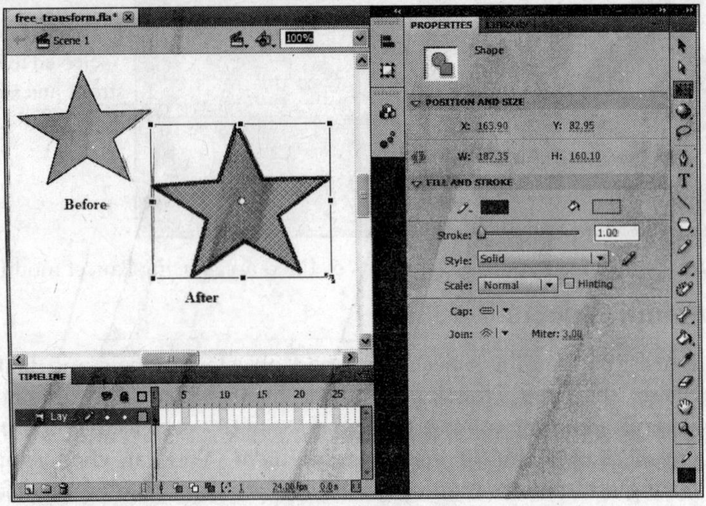

Figure 2.50 Transforming object using Free Transform Tool

5. After releasing the mouse button you see the effect of the object (See figure 2.50).

To move both corners of the object at the same distances simultaneously press Ctrl + Shift keys together while dragging.

Distorting Objects

Distortion is another way to transform an object. When you apply a Distort transformation to a selected object, dragging a corner handle or an edge handle on the bounding box moves the corner or edge and realigns the adjoining edges. The Distort option cannot modify *symbols, shape primitives, bitmaps, video objects, sounds, gradients, object groups,* or *text.* You can distort graphic objects by using the Distort command or while performing a free transform on them. You can use the Distort option with editable objects or shapes that you create in Flash Professional CS6.

To distort an object, do this:

1. Select the object with the Selection Tool on the Stage.
2. Click the Modify menu and choose Transform. A sub-menu appears. Select the Distort option.
3. Place the pointer on one of the transformation handles and drag.
4. Now release the mouse button and click outside the image to see the result as shown in Figure 2.51.

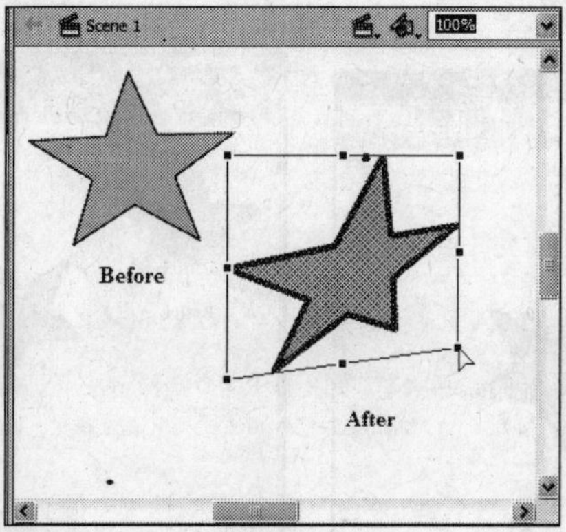

Figure 2.51 Distort option is applied to the object

Rotating and Skewing Objects

Rotating an object turns it around from its transformation point. You can rotate an object by using the Rotate command, by dragging with the Free Transform Tool, or by specifying an angle in the Transform panel. *Skewing* an object transforms it by slanting it along one or both axes.

You can skew an object by dragging or by entering a value in the Transform panel.

To rotate and skew an object, do this:

1. Select an object using the Selection Tool on the Stage.

2. Click the Modify menu and choose Transform. A sub-menu appears. Select either of the Rotate or Skew option.
3. Choose one of the following options:
   Drag a corner handle to rotate the object (See Figure 2.52).
   Drag a center handle to skew the object.

   Or

   You can choose from the Transform Panel. If you want to rotate the object, click the Rotate radio button and give the rotation angle in the text box. Or if you want to skew the object, click the Skew radio button and specify the angle of horizontally and vertically value in corresponding text box (See Figure 2.53).
4. Now release the mouse button and click outside the selected object. You can see a shaded outline following the movement.

To restore a transformed object to its original state, select it and click Remove Transform button from the Transform panel or select Modify > Transform > Remove Transform.

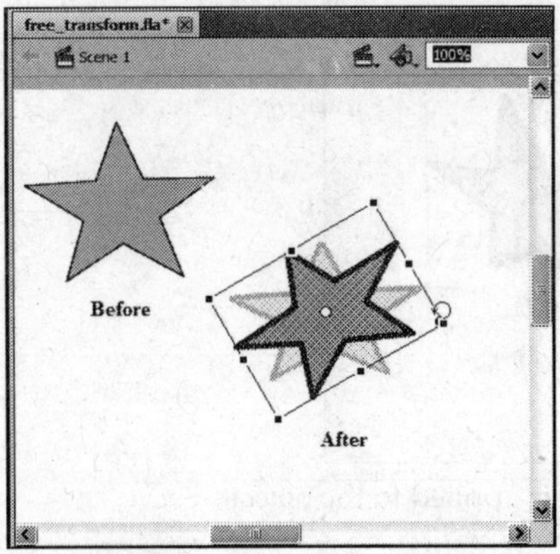

Figure 2.52 The object to be rotated

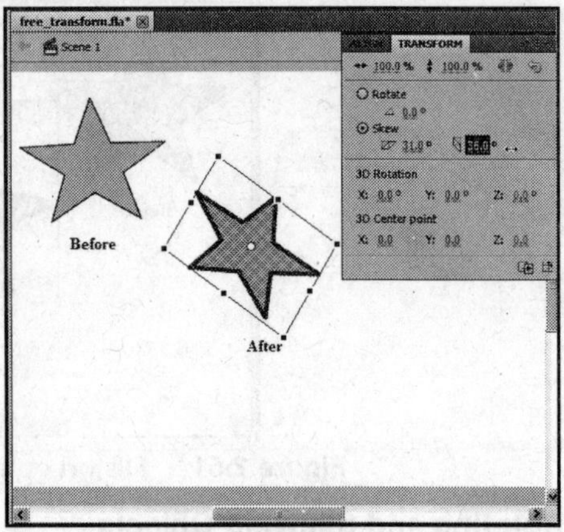

Figure 2.53 The object to be skewed

Using the Envelope Modifier

The Envelope modifier lets you warp (twist) and distort objects. An envelope is a bounding box that contains one or more objects. Changes made to an envelope's shape affect the shape of the objects contained within the envelope. You edit the shape of an envelope by adjusting its points and tangent handles.

To modify a shape with the Envelope modifier, do this:

1. Select an image using the Selection Tool on the Stage.

2. Click the Modify menu and choose Transform. A sub-menu appears. Select Envelope option.
3. You can see the several handlers surrounded by the image/object or graphic (See Figure 2.54).
4. Place the pointer over the desired handler and drag the mouse-pointer in the desired direction. After transforming the object, click outside the object to see the result. (See Figure 2.54)

Stacking Objects

The stacking order of objects determines how they appear when they are overlapped. If you place a drawing object, grouped object, or a symbol on top of another drawing object, the object created first will be hidden by the object created. You can also place the objects on different layers and reorder the layers to arrange the objects on one another.

To change the stacking orders of an object, do this:

1. Select the object with the Selection Tool.
2. Click Modify menu highlight Arrange. A sub-menu option appears. Choose one of the following options (See Figure 2.55):

   Bring to Front—Selected object moves to the top of the other object.

   Bring Forward—Selected object moves up one position of the other object.

   Send Backward—Selected object moves down one position of the other object.

   Send to Back— Selected object moves to the bottom of the other object.
3. Figure 2.55 shows different types of stacking order of objects.

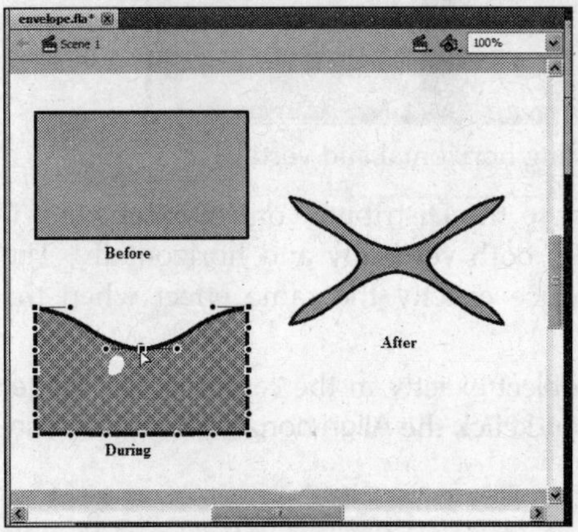

Figure 2.54 The objected to be enveloped

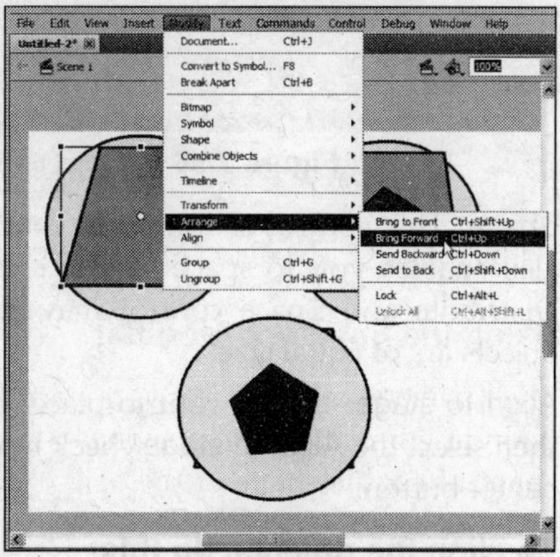

Figure 2.55 Different types of stacking order of objects

Aligning the Objects

The Align panel enables you to align selected objects along the horizontal or vertical axis. Using the Align panel, you can distribute selected objects so that their centers or edges are evenly spaced.

Align: The Align set of controls has six buttons. The first three buttons control the horizontal alignment (left, center, right) between two or more elements and the last three buttons in the Align set control over the vertical alignment (top, center, bottom) (See Figure 2.56).

Distribute: The Distribute control is used for placing three or more objects equally spaced. The first three buttons are set for vertical spacing and the next three are for horizontal spacing.

Match Size: The Match Size control makes two or more objects of different sizes, equal. The three buttons are set to have equality in terms of width, height or both.

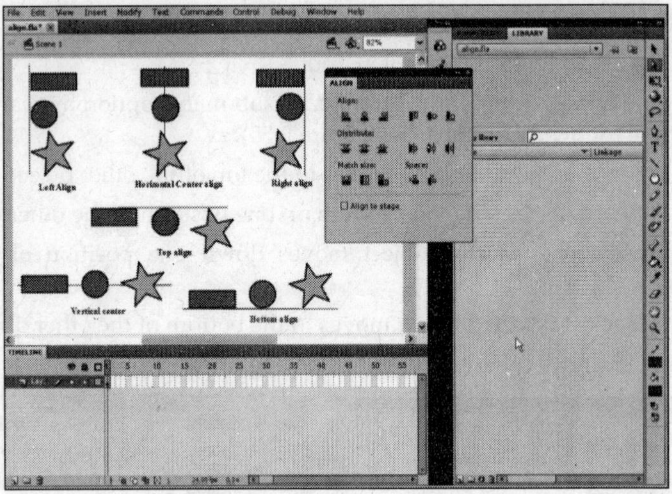

Figure 2.56 Object aligning horizontal and vertical

Space: This control is similar in concept to the Distribute control except that it also enables you to space objects evenly, both vertically and horizontally. The Distribute and Space control may produce exactly the same effect when the objects are of equal size.

Align to stage: If you want to place an object exactly in the center of the Stage, then select the Align to stage check box, and click the Align horizontal and Vertical center button.

To align the objects, do this:

1. Using the Oval Tool and the Pentagon Tool, draw oval and pentagon on the Stage (See Figure 2.57).

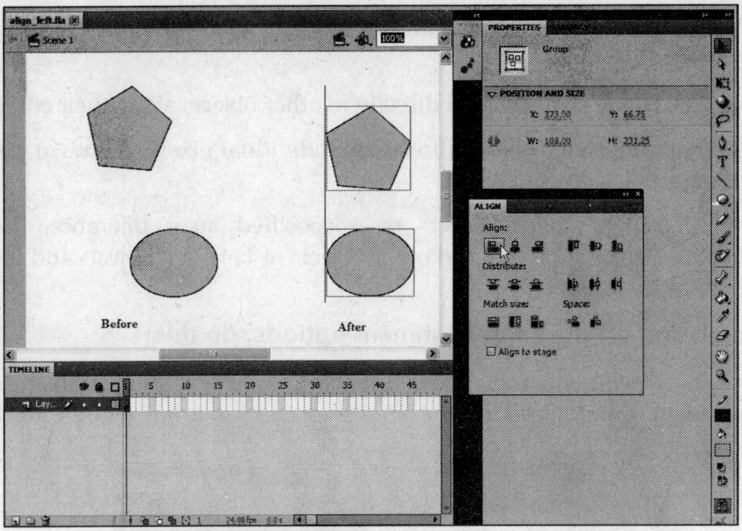

Figure 2.57 Selecting left edge alignment

2. After drawing shapes, click the Selection Tool in the Tools panel. Keep the left mouse button pressed; drag the mouse pointer over shapes. The objects get highlighted.
3. In the Align panel, click the Align left edge button. The selected shapes on the Stage appear aligned left edge position (See Figure 2.57).
4. Similarly, you can use other buttons to align objects, or shapes as per your requirement.

Using the Snap Align Option

The snap alignment option is useful to align an object around the edges of the Stage or align the object around other elements on the Stage. As you move the object, a dotted line appears when the edge of the element is 10 pixels from the next closet fixed element (See Figure 2.58).

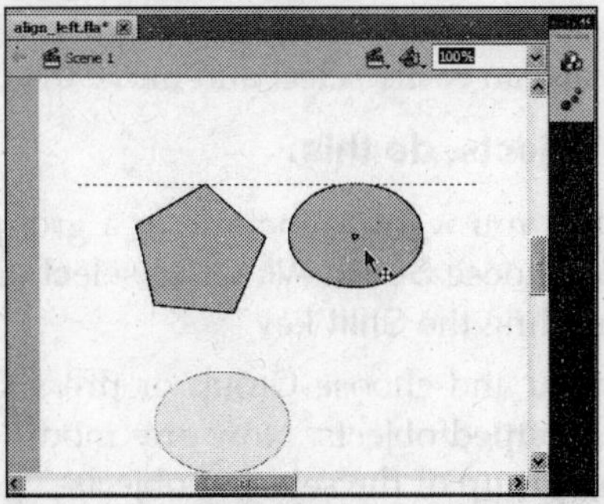

Figure 2.58 A dotted line appears as you move to the object

Flash Professional CS6 provides following three ways to align objects on the Stage:

- Object snapping snaps objects directly to other objects along their edges.
- Pixel snapping snaps objects directly to individual pixels or lines of pixels on the Stage.
- Snap alignment snaps objects to a specified snap tolerance, a preset boundary between objects and other objects or between objects and the edge of the Stage.

To turn on and off the snap alignment options, do this:

1. Click the View menu and choose Snapping. A sub-menu appears. Select the Snap Align option (See Figure 2.59). When check mark is there it means it is ON otherwise OFF.

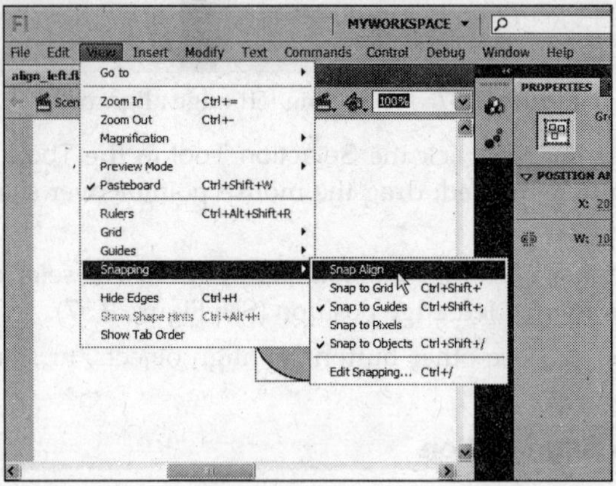

Figure 2.59 Selecting Snap alignment option from the View menu

Grouping and Ungrouping Objects

To manipulate elements as a single object, you need to group them. For example, after creating a drawing, such as a star or polygon, you might group the elements of the drawing so that you can easily select and move the drawing as a whole.

To create a group of objects, do this:

1. Select the objects that you want to include in a group. To select all objects, click Edit menu and choose Select All. Or to select particular objects, select each object while holding the Shift key.
2. Click the Modify menu and choose Group or press Ctrl + G keys together. Figure 2.60 shows grouped objects. Now any modifications you do will be applied to the entire group of the selected objects.

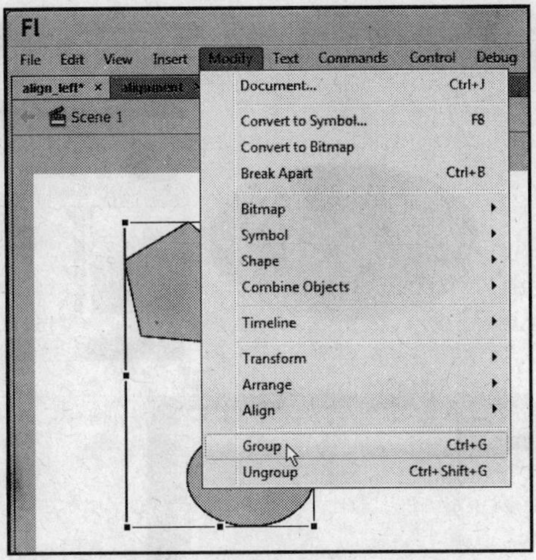

Figure 2.60 Grouping the objects

To ungroup the grouped objects, do this:

1. Select the group of objects you want to ungroup.
2. Click Modify menu and choose Ungroup or press Ctrl+Shift+G keys together (See Figure 2.60).

Using Gradient and Bitmap Fills

The *fill* is the interior of the drawn object. Till now you have been applying only solid colours to objects, but Flash Professional CS6 allows you to apply a gradient or bitmap fill to any drawn shape (such as a JPEG or Joint Photographic Experts Group file). A *gradient* is a multicolor fill in which one color gradually changes into another color. Flash Professional CS6 lets you apply up to 15 color transitions to a gradient. Applying a gradient is a good way to create a smooth color gradation across one or more objects. You can save a gradient as a swatch to make it easy to apply the gradient to multiple objects. Flash Professional CS6 can create two types of gradients:

- Linear gradient – It changes color horizontally, vertically or diagonally.
- Radial gradient – It changes color in an outward direction starting from a central focal point. You can adjust the direction of a gradient, its colors, the location of the focal point, and many other properties of the gradient.

To apply a gradient fill to existing object, do this:

1. Select the object or objects with the Selection Tool.
2. Then click on the Window menu and then choose the Color option or press Alt+Shift+F9 keys together to open the Color panel (See Figure 2.61).

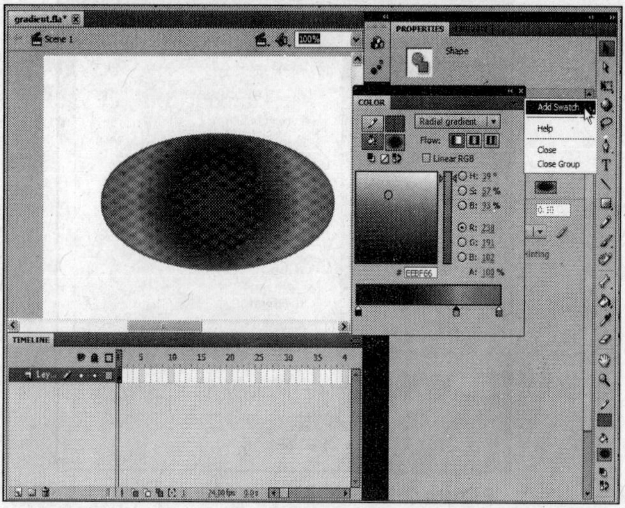

Figure 2.61 Gradient fill applied using Color panel

3. In the Color panel, select one of the following gradient type from Color Type: drop-down list.

   Linear: It creates a gradient that shades from the starting point to the end point in a straight line.

   Radial: It produces a gradient that blends outward in a circular path from a central focal point.

4. From Flow: area, select an overflow mode to apply to the gradient. i.e.. Extend (the default mode), Reflect, or Repeat (See Figure 2.61).
5. To create an (Scalable Vector Graphics) SVG-compliant linear or radial gradient, select the Linear RGB: check box. This will allow the gradient to look smooth when scaled to different sizes after it was first applied.
6. To change a color in the gradient, select one of the color pointers below the gradient definition bar.
7. Then click in the color space pane that appears above the gradient bar. Drag the Brightness slider to adjust the lightness of the color.
8. To add a pointer to the gradient, click on or below the gradient definition bar. Select a color for the new pointer.
9. To reposition a pointer on the gradient, drag the pointer along the gradient definition bar. Drag a pointer down and off the gradient definition bar to remove it.
10. To save gradient, click the triangle in the upper-right corner of the Color panel, and select Add Swatch from menu (See Figure 2.61).
11. The gradient is added to the Swatches panel for the current document.

Apply a Bitmap as a Fill

To apply a bitmap as a fill to a graphic object, use the Color panel. Applying a bitmap as a fill tiles the bitmap to fill the object. The Gradient Transform Tool allows you to *scale, rotate*, or *skew* an image and its bitmap fill.

To apply a bitmap fill to an existing object, do this:

1. Select the object or objects with the Selection Tool.
2. In the Color panel, select Bitmap fill from the Color Type: drop-down list (See Figure 2.62).
3. An Import to Library dialog box appears. Here, navigate a bitmap image (.bmp or .jpg file) from your local computer, and add it to the library. The .bmp represents Bitmap file and .jpg or .jpeg represents Joint Photographic Experts group file.

✍ *To import additional image files to use as fills, in the Color panel, click the button marked Import. Then, with the fill on the stage selected, click the image you want to use.*

---

4. Select a bitmap file and then click Open button.
5. The bitmap becomes the current fill color in the object or objects whatever you selected.

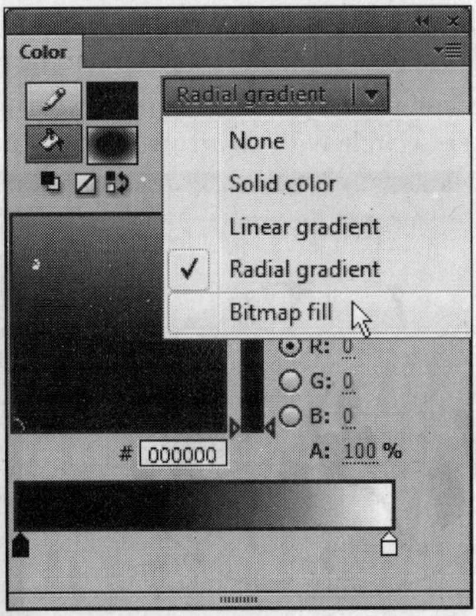

Figure 2.62 Bitmap fill using Color panel

✍ *You can also use the Gradient Transform Tool to change the way a bitmap fill is applied.*

Using the Gradient Transform Tool to Transform Gradient and Bitmap Fills

In addition to choosing colors and positioning the color pointers for a gradient or bitmap, you can adjust the size, direction, or center of a gradient or bitmap fill. To squeeze the gradient in the front surface and reverse the gradient in the back surface, you have to use the Gradient Transform Tool.

To transform gradient and bitmap fills, do this:

1. Click on the small black arrow on the Free Transform Tool in the Tools panel. The Free Transform Tool flyout is activated as shown in Figure 2.63.

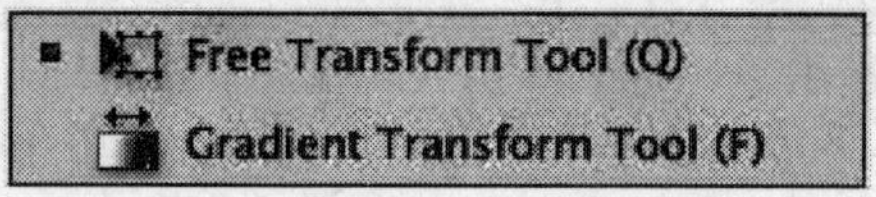

Figure 2.63 Free Transform Tool flyout (or hidden tools)

2. Click the Gradient Transform Tool.
3. Click an area filled with a gradient or bitmap fill. A bounding box with editing handles appears. When the pointer is over any one of these handles, it changes to indicate the function of the handle (See Figure 2.64).

   Center point: The rollover icon for the center point handle is a four-way arrow.

   Focal point: The focal point handle appears only when you select a Radial Gradient. The rollover icon for the focal point handle is an inverted triangle.

   Size: The rollover icon for the size handle (middle handle icon on the edge of the bounding box) is a circle with an arrow inside of it.

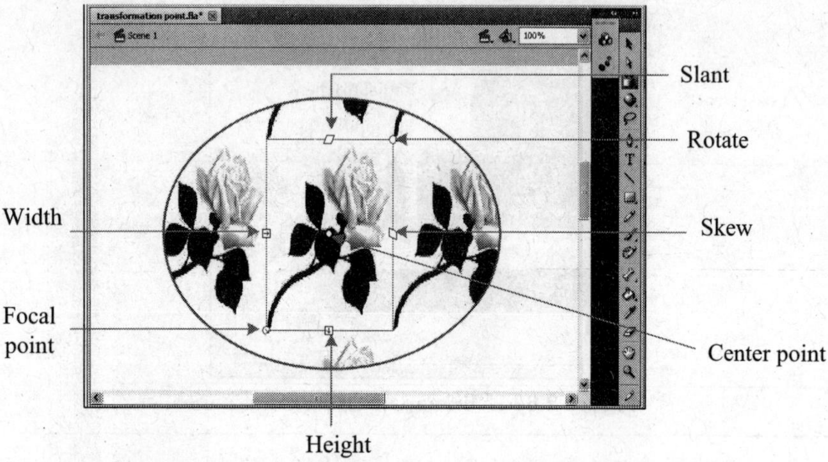

Figure 2.64 Editing handles of Gradient Transform Tool

Rotation: It adjusts the rotation of the gradient. The rollover icon for the rotation handle (the bottom handle icon on the edge of the bounding box) is four arrows in the shape of a circle.

Width: It adjusts the width of the gradient. The rollover icon for the width handle (the square handle) is a double-ended arrow.

4. Reshape the gradient or fill in any of the following ways (See Figure 2.65):
   (a) To reposition the center point of the gradient or bitmap fill, drag the center point.
   (b) To change the width of the gradient or bitmap fill, drag the square handle on the side of the bounding box. (This option resizes only the fill, not the object containing the fill).
   (c) To change the height of the gradient or bitmap fill, drag the square handle at the bottom of the bounding box.
   (d) To rotate the gradient or bitmap fill, drag the circular rotation handle at the corner. You can also drag the lowest handle on the bounding circle of a circular gradient or fill.
   (e) To change the focal point of a circular gradient, drag the middle circular handle on the bounding circle.
   (f) To skew or slant a fill within a shape, drag one of the circular handles on the top or right side of the bounding box.
   (g) To tile a bitmap inside a shape, scale the fill.

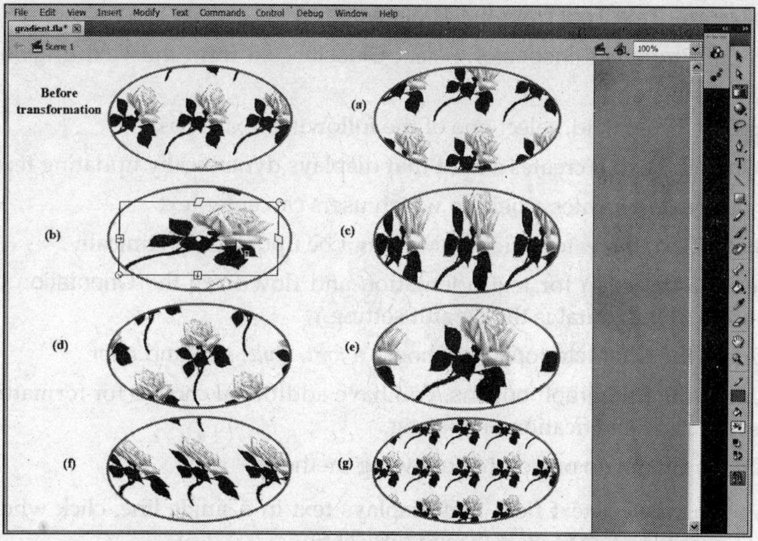

Figure 2.65 Different types of transformation

✍ *To see all the handles when working with large fills or fills close to the edge of the Stage, select* View > Pasteboard.

Using the Text Tool

Text is horizontal by default. However, static text can also be aligned vertically. Flash Professional CS6 has two text options. These are:

Classic Text: Classic text is the name for the older text engine. The classic text engine is still available in Flash Professional CS6. It may be preferable for certain types of content, such as for mobile devices, where SWF (Small Web Format) file size must be kept to a minimum.

Text Layout Framework (TLF): TLF supports a wide variety of rich text layout features and fine control of text attributes. TLF text allows greater control of text than the previous text engine, called *Classic text*.

In this Chapter, we will discuss only about the simpler classic text but, TLF (Text Layout Framework) Text will be discussed in detail in Chapter 6.

✍ *When you create text on the Stage and publish your project, Flash Professional CS6 automatically includes all the necessary fonts to display the text correctly. That means you do not have to worry about your audience having the required fonts to see the text as you intended it.*

To add a text on the stage, do this:

1. Select the Text Tool from the Tools panel.
2. In the Properties Inspector, Select Classic Text from the Text Engine drop-down list.
3. In Text Type: field, select one of the following text types:

   Dynamic Text: It creates a field that displays dynamically updating text.

   Input Text: It creates a field in which users can enter text.

   Static Text: It creates a field that cannot be updated dynamically.
4. Select a direction for text orientation and flow from the Orientation of Text button. (Horizontal is the default setting.)
5. Under the Character options, choose a *font, style, size,* and *color*.
6. Under the Paragraph options, you have additional choices for formatting the text such as justification or spacing.
7. On the Stage, do one of the following methods:
   - To create a text field that displays text in a single line, click where you want the text to start (See Figure 2.66).

- To create a text field with a fixed width or fixed height, position the pointer where you want the text to start and drag to the desired width or height (See Figure 2.66).

8. Exit the Text Tool by choosing the Selection Tool.

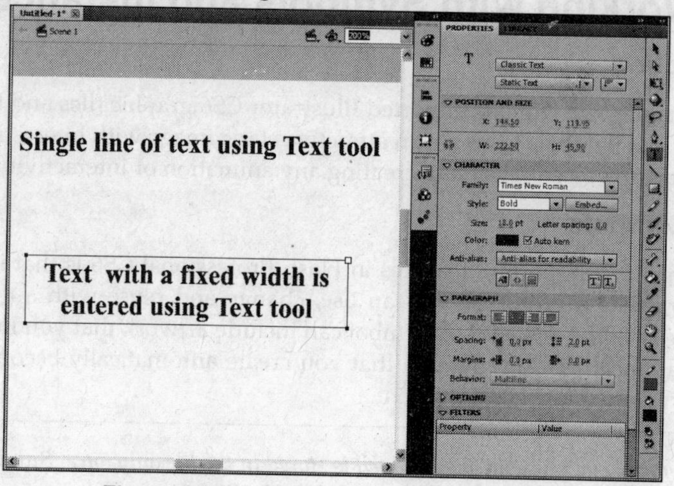

Figure 2.66 Entering text using Text Tool

If you create a text field that extends past the edge of the Stage as you type, the text is not lost. To make the handle accessible again, add line breaks, move the text field, or select View > Pasteboard.

CHAPTER 3

Working with Symbols and Instances

Introduction

In this Chapter, we will use imported Illustrator CS6 graphic files and Photoshop CS6 files, and Symbols to create an attractive static image with interesting effects. Symbols are the essential step to creating any animation or interactivity.

Using Symbols

One of the most important features in Flash Professional CS6 is that it gives the ability to create a prototype we can use, change and reuse with a movie. This prototype is called a *Symbol*. A Symbol can include artwork that you import from another application. Any Symbol that you create automatically becomes part of the library for the current document.

✍ *A* **Symbol** *is a reusable image which is stored in the file only once. But, an* **instance** *of a Symbol is an occurrence of a Symbol on the* **Stage**.

An *instance* is a copy of a Symbol which is either located on the **Stage** or inside another Symbol. An instance can be different from original Symbol in size, colour, etc. While we edit the Symbol, it will update all the instance cf Symbol. But, editing one instance of Symbol can change only that instance, not all the instances of the Symbol. Flash Professional CS6 uses four types of Symbols. These are:

(a) **Graphic Symbols**: These Symbols are used for static images. Therefore, sound will not work in graphic Symbols. Graphic Symbols add less to the **FLA** (Flash) file size than buttons or movie clips because they have no **Timeline**.

(b) **Button Symbols**: These Symbols are used to respond with the mouse clicks, rollovers, or other actions.

(c) **Movie clips**: These Symbols are used to create reusable piece of information. It can contain interactive controls, sound and even other movie clip instances. Movie clip Symbols contain their own independent **Timeline**. You can have an animation inside a movie clip Symbol just as easily as you can have an animation on the main **Timeline**.

(d) **Font Symbols**: These Symbols are created from font files to make them available for use in dynamic text fields.

The **Library** is a collection of Symbols and other media assets, such as *video clips, sound clips, bitmaps* that you create or import to use in a Flash Professional CS6 document. If the **Library** is not displayed, click the **Window** menu and choose **Library**. A **Library panel** appears.

Process of converting text/graphic into a Symbol and placing it into Library and dragging it from library to the **Stage** is a meaningless process but it has a valuable benefit. Advantages of converting any graphic/text into Symbols are as follows:

(a) **Reduce file size:** The *graphic, movie clip* or *button Symbol* is the master Symbol contributes to the file size. Therefore if any graphic having 10 KB size, it stores or reserves 10 KB for the graphic. No matter how many times it is used, graphic stored in memory only once. We drag only the instance of the Symbol to **Stage**. In this way, Symbol can reduce the file size and consume less memory.

(b) **Reduce the amount of work:** Suppose we want to insert block of text in many places in movie. If we put that block of text in **Library** and drag it from the **Library**, when we need it. In this way, there is no need to write the same block of text every time.

(c) We can make a visual change to the master Symbol and that change will be reflected in each instance. This is like using styles in MS Word. Make a change to the style and each instance where we used that style will reflect the change.

Creating a Symbol

You can create a Symbol from selected objects on the **Stage** or create an empty Symbol and make or import the content in Symbol-editing mode, and create font Symbols in Flash Professional CS6. Symbols can contain all the functionality that Flash Professional CS6 can create, including animation.

Converting an existing object into Symbol, do this:

1. Select the object on the **Stage** that you want to convert into Symbol.
2. Click the **Modify** menu and choose **Convert to Symbol**. Or press **F8** Function key.
3. **Convert to Symbol** dialog box appears as shown in Figure 3.1.
4. Enter a name for the Symbol in the **Name:** text box.
5. Choose a behavior type for the Symbol from the **Type:** drop-down list.
6. Click in the **Registration:** to position the registration point for the Symbol. Registration point of the Symbol refers to the point of reference on the Symbol. The registration point is the axis around which the Symbol rotates, and the point along which the Symbol aligns.
7. Click **OK** button. The object is now converted to a Symbol and appears in the **Library panel**. The selected object becomes instance of the Symbol in the **Library** and a registration point placed in it (See Figure 3.1).

✍ *Once you have created a Symbol, you can edit it in Symbol-editing mode by choosing Edit > Edit Symbols.*

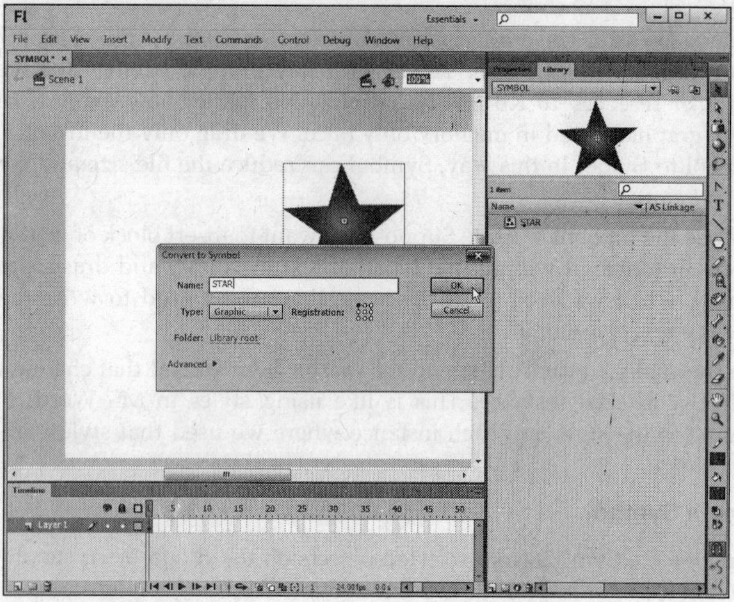

Figure 3.1 Convert to Symbol Dialog box

Creating a New or an Empty Symbol

The new Symbol is created in the Symbol-editing mode.

To create new Symbol, do this:

1. Click the Insert menu and choose New Symbol... . Or press Ctrl+F8 keys together. The Create New Symbol dialog box appears as shown in Figure 3.2.

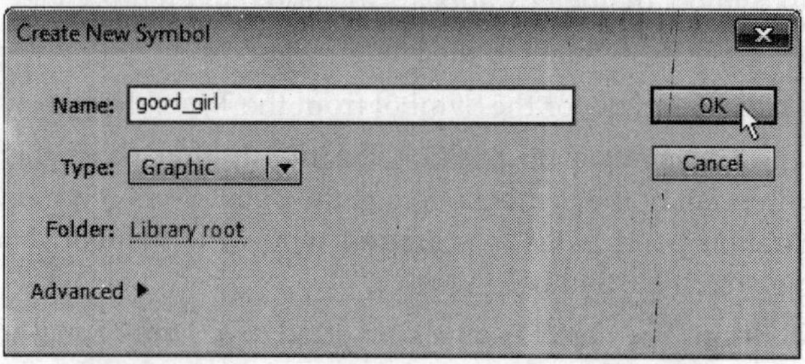

Figure 3.2 Create New Symbol Dialog box

2. Enter a Symbol name in the Name: text box. For example, we have given Symbol name as **good_girl**.

3. Select a behavior type for the Symbol in the Type: drop-down list box. For example, select **Graphic** as a type of Symbol.

4. Click OK button to close the dialog box. The dialog box will get closed, Symbol adds to the library and you will be moved to the *Symbol Editing mode*. In this mode, the name of the Symbol appears above the upper-left corner of the Stage, and a cross hair indicates the Symbol's registration point (See Figure 3.3).

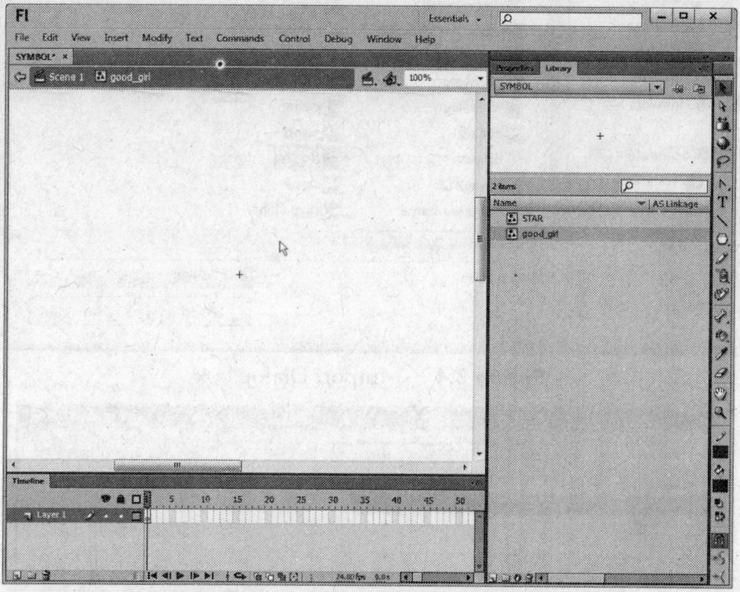

Figure 3.3 Symbol Editing Mode

5. Create a Symbol content using drawing tools, Timeline, import media. For example, we import a file from Illustrator.

6. To import an Illustrator CS6 file, click the File menu, choose Import and then select Import to Stage... . An Import dialog box appears as shown in Figure 3.4.

7. Here, navigate an Illustrator file (.ai file) from your local computer, and click Open (See Figure 3.4).

8. After that, in Import to Library dialog box as shown in Figure 3.5, make sure all layers are selected. A check mark should appear in the check box next to each layer.

9. In the Right pane, click the Import as Bitmap check box. The bitmap Symbol icon appears to the right of the layer, indicating that the imported layer will be made into a bitmap Symbol.

10. Choose Flash Layers from the onvert layers to: drop-down list box, and then click OK (See Figure 3.5).

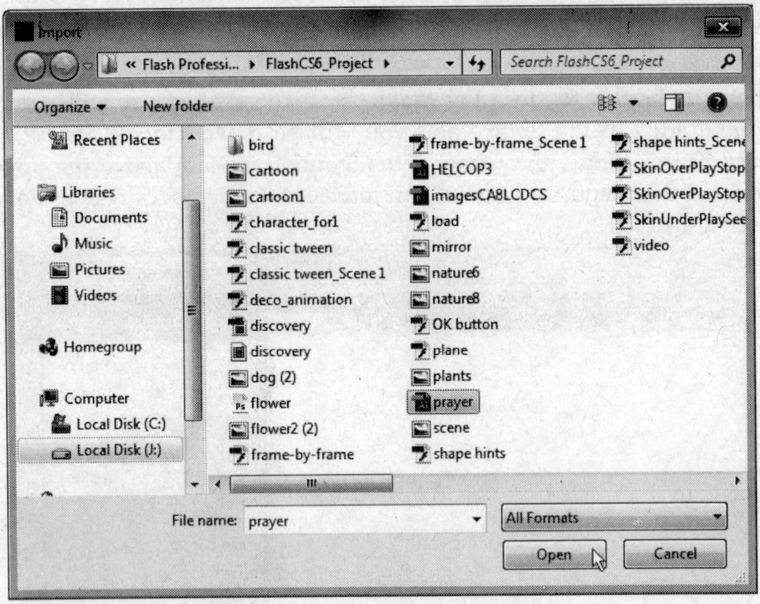

Figure 3.4 Import Dialog box

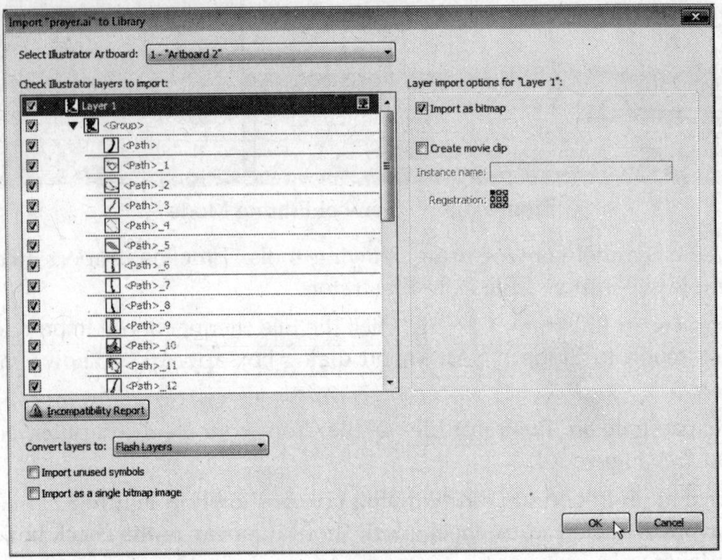

Figure 3.5 Import [File] to Library Dialog box

11. Flash Professional CS6 imports the Illustrator graphics to the **Stage** and **Library** simultaneously.

Flash Professional CS6 can import Illustrator files and automatically recognize layers, frames and Symbols.

12. Exit the Symbol-editing mode by clicking the current scene name in the Edit bar or click the Back button (See Figure 3.6).

Figure 3.6 Imported graphic appears on the Stage as well as in Library Panel

If an imported Illustrator file contains layers, you can convert Illustrator layers to Flash layers, Illustrator layers to Flash keyframes, each Illustrator layer to a Flash graphic Symbol and all Illustrator layers to a single Flash layer.

Duplicate Symbols

Duplicating a Symbol lets you use an existing Symbol as a starting point for creating a Symbol. It makes an exact copy of a Symbol, and the new copy becomes its own Symbol and is not associated with the original.

To duplicate a Symbol using the Library panel, do this:

1. Select a Symbol in the Library panel by clicking on it.
2. Right-click and select Duplicate... from the context menu or select Duplicate... from the Library Panel menu.
3. The Duplicate Symbol dialog box appears as shown in Figure 3.7, asking you to rename the Symbol and, if desired, change the Symbol type.
4. Then press OK button.

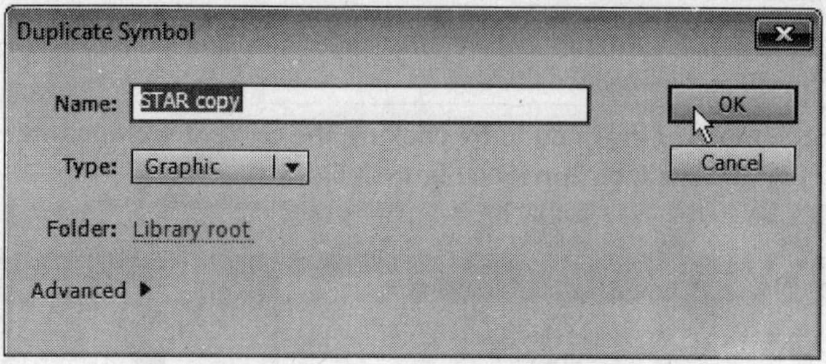

Figure 3.7 Duplicate Symbol dialog box

Flash adds the new Symbol to the Library. You can now use this Symbol like any other and it has no relationship to the original from which it was created.

Create Instances

After you have created a Symbol, you can place number of instances of the Symbol on the Stage, including inside other Symbols.

You can give names to instances from the Properties Inspector. To specify color effects, assign actions, set the graphic display mode, or change the behavior of new instances, use the Properties Inspector.

✍ *The behavior of the instance is the same as the Symbol behavior, unless you specify otherwise. Any changes you make in an instance affect only that instance and not the Symbol.*

To create an instance of a Symbol on the Stage, do this:

1. Select a layer in the Timeline.
2. Click the Symbol name or the Symbol image in the Library and drag it on the Stage (See Figure 3.8).
3. Release the mouse at location on the Stage where you want to place the instance. Figure 3.8 shows the instance of the Star Symbol placed on the Stage.

✍ *Flash Professional CS6 can place instances only in keyframes and always on the current layer. If you do not select a keyframe, Flash Professional CS6 adds the instance to the first keyframe to the left of the current frame.*

To apply a custom name to an instance, do this:

1. Select the instance on the Stage.
2. In the Properties Inspector, enter a name in the Instance Name box (See Figure 3.18).

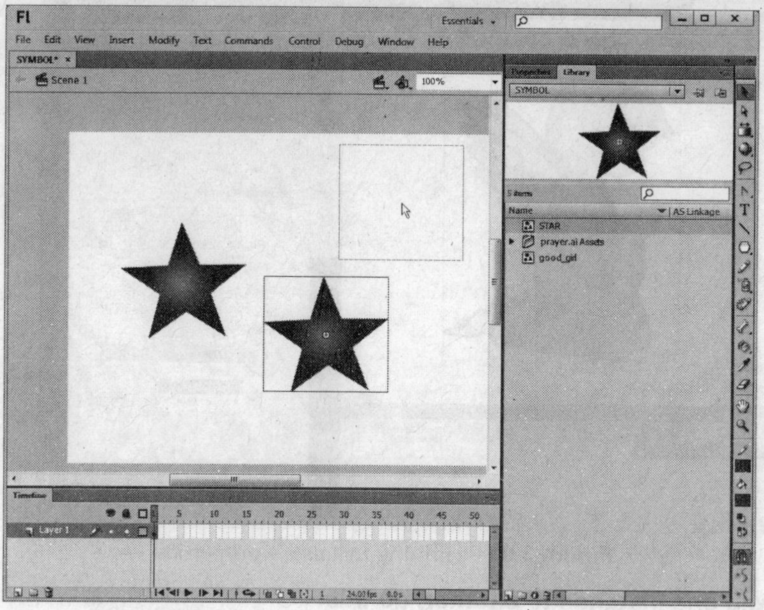

Figure 3.8 Instances of Symbol placed on the Stage

Editing Instance Properties

Each instance on the Stage has its own properties that are saved with it and every instance's properties are separate from the Symbol's properties. You can change instance's properties, such as *tint, transparency,* and *brightness,* redefine how the instance behaves and much more. You can also *skew, rotate,* or *scale* an instance without affecting the Symbol.

Each instance of a Symbol can have its own color effect. To set color and transparency options for instances, use the Properties Inspector. *Settings in the* Properties Inspector *also affect bitmaps placed in Symbols.*

To change the color and transparency of an instance, do this:

1. Select the instance of a Symbol on the Stage.
2. In the Properties Inspector, select one of the following options from the Style drop-down list of the Color Effect section (See Figure 3.9):

   Brightness: It adjusts the relative lightness or darkness of the image. Click the triangle and drag the slider or enter a value in the box.

   Tint: It colors the instance with the same hue.

   Advanced: It separately adjusts the red, green, blue and transparency values of an instance.

   Alpha: It adjusts the transparency of the instance.

Figure 3.9 Editing Instance's properties

To swap one instance to another, do this:

1. Select the instance on the Stage.
2. In the Properties Inspector, click the Swap... button (See Figure 3.9). A Swap Symbol dialog box appears as shown in Figure 3.10.
3. In Swap Symbol dialog box, select a new Symbol to replace the Symbol currently assigned to the instance and click OK (See Figure 3.10).

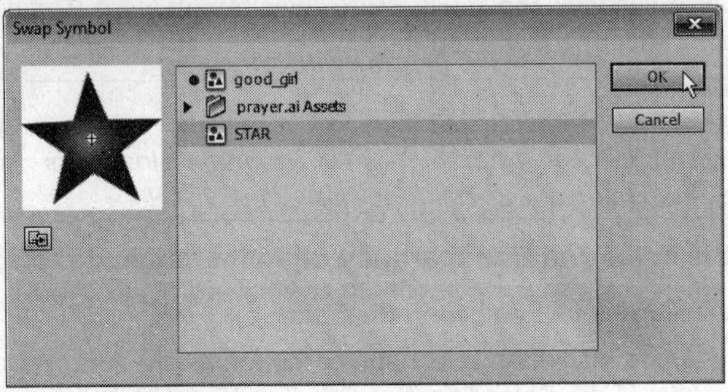

Figure 3.10 Swap Symbol dialog box

To change an instance's type, do this:

1. Select the instance on the Stage.
2. Select Graphic, Button, or Movie Clip from the Instance behavior drop-down list in the Properties Inspector (See Figure 3.9).

To change the size and position of Instances, do this:

1. Select the instance on the Stage.
2. In the Properties Inspector, select the options according to your requirement from the Position and Size section (See Figure 3.9).
3. Then drag the slider or double click to change the value.

If you edit a Symbol or relink an instance to a different Symbol, any instance properties you have changed still apply to the instance.

Breaking Apart a Symbol Instance

If you no longer want an object on the Stage to be as a Symbol instance, you can use the Break Apart command to return it to its original form. This command is useful for changing the instance substantially without affecting any other instance.

To break apart a Symbol instance, do this:

1. Select the instance on the Stage.
2. Click Modify menu and then select Break Apart. *Alternatively,* press Ctrl + B keys together to select Break Apart. It will break the instance into its component graphic elements (See Figure 3.11).

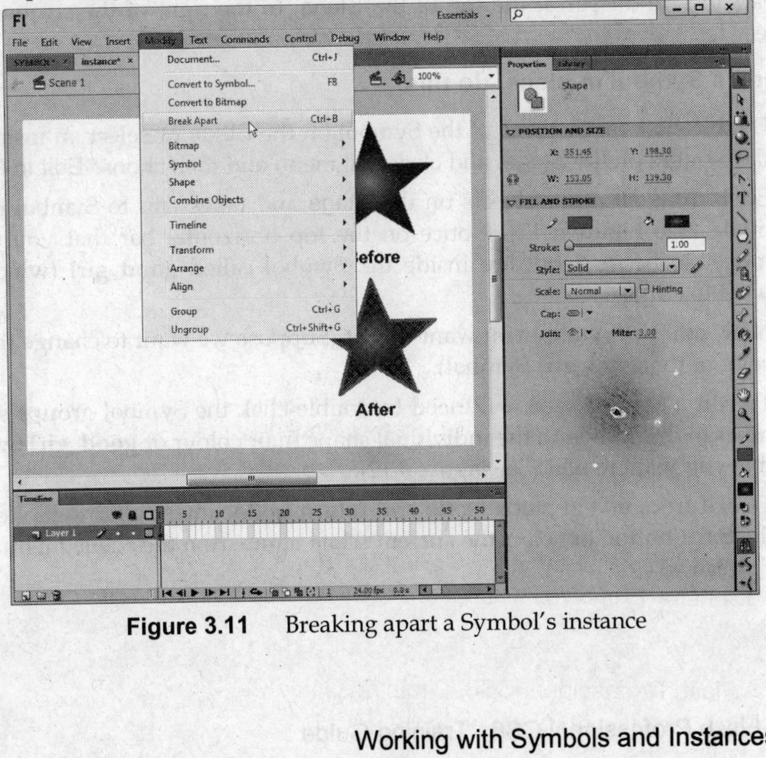

Figure 3.11 Breaking apart a Symbol's instance

To break the link between an instance and a Symbol and make the instance into a collection of ungrouped shapes and lines, break apart the instance. *After broken apart, changes to the source Symbol for an instance do not affect the instance.*

Editing Symbols

When you edit a Symbol, Flash Professional CS6 updates all instances of the Symbol throughout the document to reflect your edits because every instance of a Symbol is linked to the original Symbol. There are several ways to edit a Symbol. These are:

1. In context with the other objects on the Stage by using the Edit In Place command.
2. In a separate window, using the Edit In New Window command.
3. You can edit a Symbol by changing the window from the Stage view to a view of only the Symbol, using Symbol-editing mode.

Editing a Symbol in Place

When you want to edit a Symbol in context with the other objects on the Stage, you can use Edit In Place command. You can do so by double-clicking an instance on the Stage. In this method, other objects are dimmed to distinguish them from the Symbol you are editing. The name of the Symbol you are editing appears in an Edit bar at the top of the Stage, to the right of the current scene name.

To edit a Symbol in place, do this:

1. Double-click an instance of the Symbol on the Stage or select an instance of the Symbol on the Stage, and click Edit menu and then choose Edit In Place.
2. Flash dims all other objects on the Stage and takes you to Symbol editing mode (See Figure 3.12). Notice on the top horizontal bar that you are no longer in Scene 1 but are inside the Symbol called **good_girl** (which you want to edit).
3. Now, edit the Symbol you want to edit (Suppose we want to change the hair color of the **good_girl** Symbol).

   To edit a Symbol, you will need to double-click the Symbol groups several times to drill down to the individual shape (hair colour of **good_girl** Symbol) that you want to edit (See Figure 3.12).
4. To exit from edit-in-place mode and return to document-editing mode, click the Back button or select the current scene name from the Scene menu in the Edit bar.

Figure 3.12 Editing a Symbol in place

Edit a Symbol in a New Window

Editing a Symbol in a separate window lets you see the Symbol and the main Timeline at the same time. The name of the Symbol you are editing appears in the Edit bar at the top of the Stage.

To edit a Symbol in a separate window, do this:

1. Select an instance of the Symbol on the Stage, and right click and then choose Edit in New Window.
2. The selected Symbol will now appear in a separate window (See Figure 3.13).
3. Edit the Symbol. Suppose, you want to change the wings colour of the **good_girl** Symbol, then double click and select the wings and change its colour from the Properties Inspector.
4. Click the Close box in the upper-right corner to close the new window, and click in the main document window to return to editing the main document.

Edit a Symbol in Symbol-Editing Mode

You can also edit the Symbol by changing the window from the Stage view to a view of only the Symbol, using Symbol-editing mode. The name of the Symbol you are editing appears in the Edit bar at the top of the Stage, to the right of the current scene name.

To edit a Symbol in Symbol-Editing mode, do this:

1. Double-click the Symbol's icon in the Library panel.

Figure 3.13 Editing a Symbol in New Window

2. Edit the Symbol.
3. To exit Symbol-editing mode and return to editing the document, click the Back button at the left of the Edit bar at the top of the Stage.
4. The Symbol in the Library panel reflects the changes you made. The instance on the Stage also reflects the changes you made to the Symbol as shown in Figure 3.14.

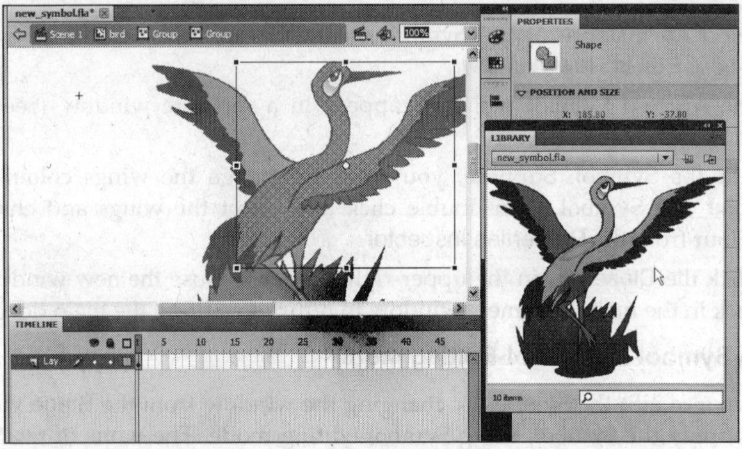

Figure 3.14 Editing a Symbol in Symbol-Editing mode

Using Rulers

Earlier, you had learned about the Align panel to align several objects with each other. But, sometimes, you may want to be more precise in placement of Symbol instances. For this, you can use rulers and guides to position objects on the Stage.

Rulers appear on the top and left side of the Pasteboard to provide measurement along the horizontal and vertical axes. You can change the unit of measurement used in the rulers from the default of pixels to another unit. When you move an element on the Stage with the rulers displayed, lines indicating the element's dimensions appear on the rulers.

To show or hide rulers, do this:

1. Click View menu.
2. Then choose Rulers or press Ctrl + Alt + Shift + R keys together.
3. Rulers will appears or disappear according to your need.

To change the ruler's unit of measurement, do this:

1. Click Modify menu.
2. Then select Document... .
3. A Document Settings dialog box appears and select a unit from the Ruler units drop-down list and press OK button.

Using Guides

Guides are vertical or horizontal lines that appear on the Stage but do not appear in the final published movie (See Figure 3.15). When rulers show, you can drag horizontal and vertical guides from the rulers onto the Stage.

Figure 3.15 Horizontal and vertical guides shown on the Stage

When you create nested timelines, draggable guides appear on the Stage only when the Timeline in which they were created is active.

To display or hide the drawing guides, do this:

1. Click View menu.
2. Then select Guides and then choose Show Guides.

To turn snapping to guides on or off, do this:

1. Click View menu.
2. Then select Snapping and then choose Snap to Guides.

✍ *Snap to guides feature, when turned on, makes the guides behave like magnets. That is when you move the object near the guides, it sticks to the guide.*

To move a guide, do this:

1. Click Selection Tool and drag the guide to the desired place on the Stage.

To remove guides, do this:

1. Click the Selection Tool and drag the guide to the horizontal or vertical ruler.

To lock guides, do this:

1. Click View menu.
2. Then select Guides and then choose Lock Guides.

To clear guides, do this:

1. Click View menu.
2. Then select Guides and then choose Clear Guides.

To set guide preferences, do this:

1. Click View menu.
2. Then select Guides and then click Edit Guides or press Ctrl + Alt + Shift + G keys together.
3. The Guides dialog box appears as shown in Figure 3.16.

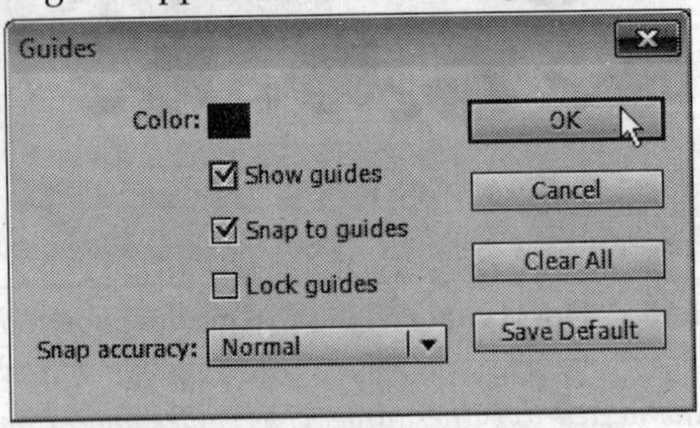

Figure 3.16 Guides dialog box

4. In this dialog box, select one of the following options to set guide preferences:

   Click the Color: box to set the different colour for the guide line. The default guide color is green.

   Click Show guides check box to display or hide guides.

   Select or deselect Snap to guides check box to turn snapping to guides on or off.

   Select or deselect Lock guides check box to lock or unlock guides.

   To set Snap Accuracy, select an option from the Snap accuracy: drop-down menu.

   To remove all guides, click Clear All button. It will remove all guides from the current scene.

   To save the current settings as the default, click Save Default.

5. Then click OK button to save the setting.

Using Grids

The grid appears in a document as a set of lines behind the artwork in all scenes. Working with the grid is like working on graph paper. The gridlines can be used to position an object. The grids are not printed but you can modify the grid. Figure 3.17 shows the Stage with gridlines displayed.

To display or hide the gridlines, do this:

1. Click View menu.

Figure 3.17 Using gridlines to position an object

2. Then select Grid and then choose Show Grid or press Ctrl + ' (quote) keys together.

To turn snapping to gridlines on or off, do this:

1. Click View menu.
2. Then select Snapping and then choose Snap to Grid.

Snap to Grid feature will make the grid coordinates act like magnets that attract the object you are moving. If you want to move an object to a location not on a grid coordinate, you will find it difficult with Snap to Grid turned on.

Understanding Display Options

The Display section in the Properties Inspector for movie clips offers options for controlling the instance's visibility, blending, and rendering.

About Visible Property for Movie Clips

The Visible property makes objects either visible or invisible to the audience. You can directly control the Visible property of movie clip instances on the Stage by selecting or deselecting the option in the Properties Inspector (See Figure 3.18).

About Blending Effects

Blending refers to how the colors of an instance interact with the colors below it. Blending modes let you create composite images. Compositing is the process of varying the transparency or color interaction of two or more overlapping objects. It creates unique effects by blending the colors in overlapping movie clips.

There are many types of Blending options. Some have surprising results, depending on the colors in the instance and the colors in the layers below it.

To apply blends to selected movie clips, use the Properties Inspector.

To apply a blend Effects, do this:

1. Select the movie clip instance on the Stage.
2. In the Properties Inspector, under the Color Effect section, click the drop-down arrow of Style: to adjust the color and transparency of the movie clip instance.
3. Under the Display section, select one of the following blend modes for movie clips from the Blending drop-down list (See Figure 3.18):

   Normal: To apply color normally, without any interaction with the base colors.

   Layer: To stack movie clips on top of each other without affecting their color.

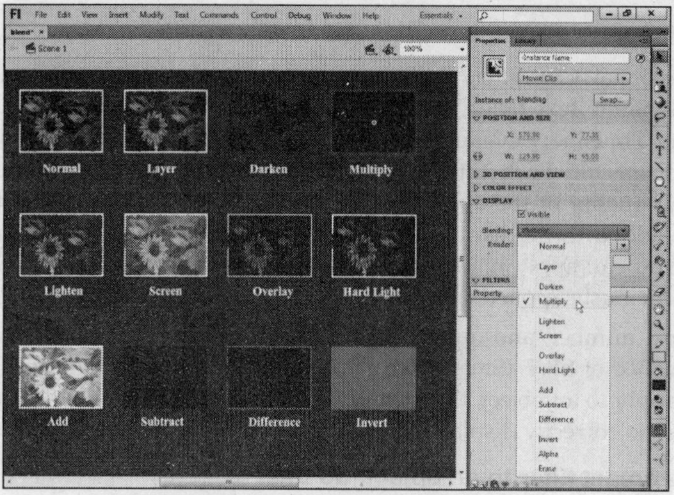

Figure 3.18 Different blending modes applied to the movie clip instances

Darken: To replace only that areas which are lighter than the blend color. Darker areas will not change.

Multiply: To multiply the base color by the blend color.

Lighten: To replace only pixels that are darker than the blend color. Lighter areas will not change.

Screen: To multiply the inverse of the blend color by the base color to give a bleaching effect to instance.

Overlay: To multiply the colors, depending on the base colors.

Hard Light: To multiply or screen the colors, depending on the blend mode color.

Add: To create an animated lightening dissolves effect between two images.

Subtract: To create an animated darkening dissolve effect between two images.

Difference: To subtract either the blend color from the base color or the base color from the blend color, depending on which has the greater brightness value.

Invert: To invert the base color.

Alpha: To apply an alpha mask.

Erase: To remove all base color pixels, including those in the background image.

4. Blending mode is applied to the selected movie clip instance. Figure 3.18 shows how different blend modes affect the appearance of an image. The resulting effect of a blend mode might be considerably different, depending on the color of the underlying image and the type of blend mode you apply.

About Filters

Flash Professional CS6 filters (graphic effects) let you add interesting visual effects to dynamic text fields, buttons and movie clips. You can also animate filters in the Timeline. Several filters are available in the Filters section of the Properties Inspector. Each filter has different controls that let you adjust the strength and quality of the applied filter. Each time you add a new filter to an object, it is added to the list of applied filters for that object in the Properties Inspector. You can apply multiple filters to an object, as well as remove filters that were previously applied.

The type, number, and quality of the filters you apply to objects can affect the performance of SWF (Small Web Format) files as you play them. The more filters you apply to an object, the greater the number of calculations Flash Player must process to correctly display the visual affects you have created.

To apply a preset filter to an object, do this:

1. Select the object on the Stage.
2. In the Properties Inspector, under the Filters section, click the Add filter button (bottom left corner).
3. Select one of the following filter preset from the list of available presets (See Figure 3.19):

   Drop Shadow: To simulate the look of an object casting a shadow onto a surface.

   Blur: To soften the edges and details of objects.

   Glow: To apply a color around the edges of an object.

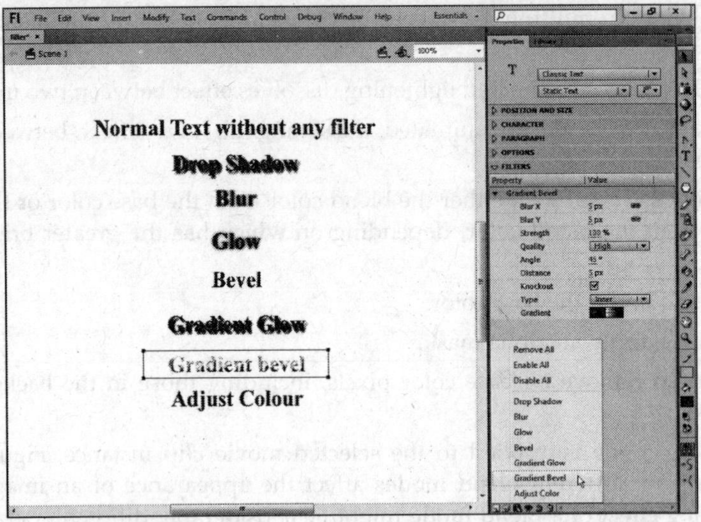

Figure 3.19 Different types of presets applied to text

Bevel: To highlight the object that makes it appear to be curved up above the background surface

Gradient Glow: To produce glow look with a gradient color across the surface of the glow.

Gradient Bevel: To produce a raised look that makes an object appears to be raised above the background, with a gradient color across the surface of the bevel.

Adjust Color: To control the color attributes of the selected object, including contrast, brightness, saturation, and hue.

When you apply a filter preset to an object, Flash Professional CS6 replaces any filter currently applied to the selected objects with the filters used in the preset.

To remove a filter, do this:

1. Select the filter to remove in the list of applied filters.
2. Then click the Delete Filter button from the Filters Section of the Properties Inspector.

To apply a drop shadow filter to an object, do this:

1. Select the object on the Stage.
2. In the Properties Inspector, under the Filters section, click the Add filter button and select Drop Shadow (See Figure 3.19).
3. Edit the Drop Shadow filter settings according to your requirement (See Figure 3.20):

   Blur X and Blur Y: To set the width and height, respectively of the Drop Shadow.

   Strength: To set the darkness of the shadow. The higher the numerical value the darker the shadow.

   Quality: To set the quality level for the drop shadow.

   Angle: Enter a value or drag the slider to set the angle of the shadow.

   Distance: To set the distance of the shadow from the object.

   Knockout: Select Knockout check box to knock out (or visually hide) the source object and display only the Drop Shadow on the knockout image.

   Inner shadow: To apply the shadow within the boundaries of the object, select Inner shadow check box.

   Hide object: To hide the object and display only its shadow.

   Color: To set the shadow color, click the Color box.
4. Selected object will respond according to the settings you applied for the drop shadow as shown in Figure 3.20.

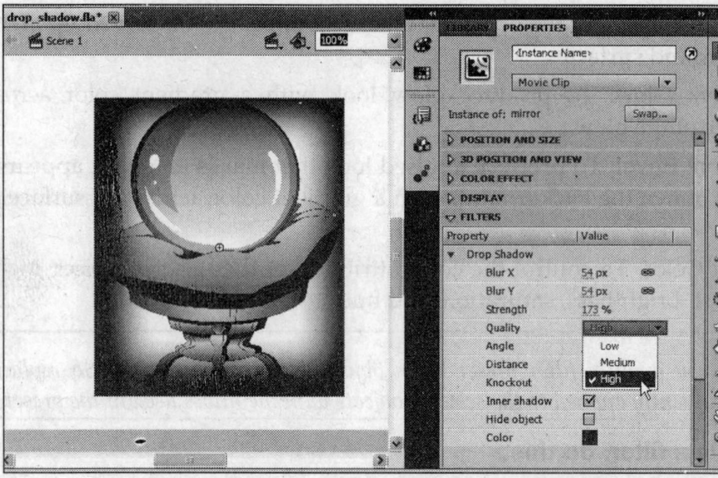

Figure 3.20 Object with the Drop Shadow filter applied

To apply a blur filter to an object, do this:

1. Select an object to apply a blur to.
2. In the Properties Inspector, under the Filters section, click the Add filter button and select Blur (See Figure 3.19).
3. Edit the blur filter settings according to your wish (See Figure 3.21):

   Blur X and Blur Y: To set the width and height of the blur.

   Quality: To set the quality level for the blur, click the drop-down arrow of Quality and select the quality level.

Figure 3.21 Cartoon instance with the blur filter applied

4. The instance on the Stage becomes blurry to give an atmospheric perspective to the Cartoon shown in Figure 3.21.

To apply a glow filter to an object, do this:

1. Select an object to apply a glow to.
2. In the Properties Inspector, under the Filters section, click the Add filter button and select Glow (See Figure 3.19).
3. Edit the glow filter settings according to your wish (See Figure 3.22):

   Blur X and Y: To set the width and height of the glow.

   Strength: To set the sharpness of the glow.

   Quality: To set the quality level for the glow, click the drop-down arrow of Quality and select the quality level.

   Color: To set the glow color, click the Color box.

   Knockout: Select Knockout check box to knock out (visually hide) the source object and display only the glow on the knockout image.

   Inner glow: To apply the glow within the boundaries of the object, select Inner shadow check box.

Figure 3.22 Object with the Glow filter applied

At the bottom of the Filters section, there is a row of options  *to help you manage and apply multiple filters.* ***Presets*** *button lets you save a particular filter and its settings so you can apply it to another instance. The* ***Clipboard*** *button lets you copy and paste any selected filter. The* ***Enable or Disable Filter*** *button lets you see your instance with or without the filter applied. The* ***Reset Filter*** *button resets the filter parameters to their default values and* ***Delete Filter*** *button lets you delete filter.*

Positioning in 3D Space

Flash Professional CS6 allows you to create 3D effects by manipulating objects (positioning and animating) in real 3D space on the **Stage**. However, objects need to be either movie clip Symbols, instances or TLF Text to move them in 3D. Flash Professional CS6 represents 3D space by including a z-axis in the properties of each movie clip instance. You can add 3D perspective effects to movie clip instances using the **3D Translation** and **3D Rotation tools**. Once you have applied these effects to a movie clip, Flash Professional CS6 considers it a 3D movie clip and a colored axes indicator appears overlaid onto the movie clip whenever it is selected.

✍ *In 3D terminology, moving an object in 3D space is called a* **translation** *and rotating an object in 3D space is called a* **transformation**.

Both the **3D Translation** and the **3D Rotation tools** allow you to manipulate objects in **global 3D space** (*Stage space* where global transformation and translations are relative to the **Stage**) or **local 3D space** (*movie clip space* where local transforms and translations are relative to the movie clip space). For example, if you have a movie clip containing several nested movie clips, local 3D transforms of the nested movie clips are relative to the drawing area inside the container movie clip. Understanding the 3D coordinate space is essential for successful 3D placement of objects. Flash Professional CS5 divides space using three axes:

- **X-axis**: It runs horizontally across the **Stage** with X = 0 at the left edge.
- **Y-axis**: It runs vertically with y = 0 at the top edge.
- **Zz-axis**: It runs into and out of the plane of the **Stage** (toward and away from the viewer) with z = 0 at the plane of the **Stage**.

✍ *By default,* **3D Translation** *and* **Rotation Tools** *is in global mode. To use them in local mode, click the* **Global** *toggle button in the* **Options area** *of the* **Tools panel**.

Moving Objects in 3D Space

You can move movie clip instances in 3D space with the help of 3D Translation tool. When you select a movie clip with this tool, its three axes, X, Y, and Z, appear on the **Stage** on the top of the object. The X- axis is red, the Y-axis is green, and the Z-axis is blue.

To move a single object in 3D space, do this:

1. Click the **3D Translation Tool** in the **Tools panel**.
2. Set the tool to **Local** or **Global mode** by checking the **Global** toggle button in the **Options area** of the **Tools panel**.

3. Select movie clip Symbol or instance with the 3D Translation tool.

4. Move the object by dragging over the X-, Y-, or Z-axis controls or you can also move the object using the Properties Inspector by entering values for X, Y, or Z in the 3D Position and View section of the Properties Inspector (See Figure 3.23).

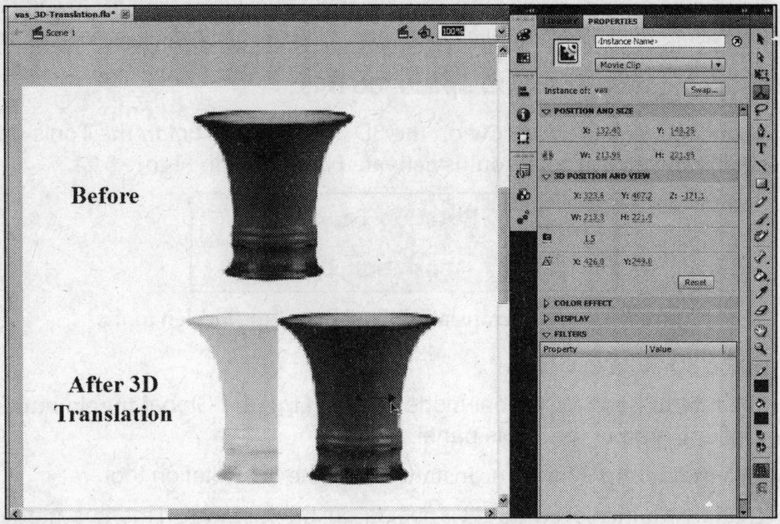

Figure 3.23 Moving single object in 3D space using 3D Translation Tool

---

The X- and Y-axis controls are the arrow tips on each axis. Drag one of these controls in the direction of its arrow to move the object along the selected axis (See Figure 3.23). The Z-axis control is the black dot at the center of the movie clip. Drag the Z-axis control up or down to move the object on the Z-axis.

When you select multiple movie clips, you can also move one of the selected objects with the 3D Translation tool and the others move in the same way.

To move multiple objects in 3D space, do this:

1. To move each object in the group in the same way in global 3D space, set the 3D Translation Tool to global mode and then drag one of the objects with the axis controls. Or

   To move each object in the group in the same way in local 3D space, set the 3D Translation tool to local mode and then drag one of the objects with the axis controls. Shift+ double-clicks one of the selected objects to move the axis controls to that object.

Rotating Objects in 3D Space

You can also rotate movie clip instances in 3D space with the 3D Rotation tool. A 3D rotation control appears on top of selected objects on the Stage. The X control is red, the Y control is green, and the Z control is blue. Use the orange free rotate control to rotate around the X- and Y-axes at the same time.

✎ *To make an object appear nearer or further away from the viewer, move it along its Z-axis with the 3D Translation Tool. To give the impression of an object that is at an angle to the viewer, rotate the movie clip around its Z-axis with the 3D Rotation tool. By using these tools in combination, you can create realistic perspective effects.*

To rotate a single object in 3D space, do this:

1. Click on the small black arrow on the 3D Translation Tool in the Tools panel. The 3D Translation Tool flyout is activated as shown in Figure 3.24.

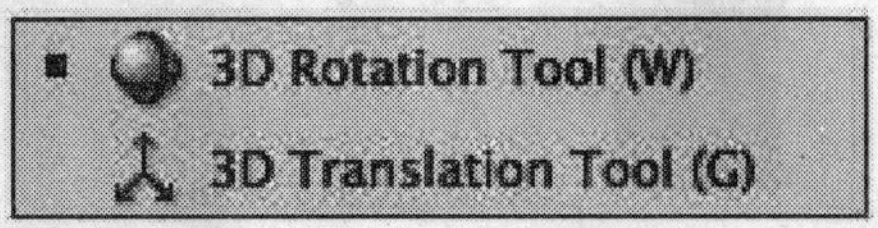

Figure 3.24 3D Translation Tool flyout (or hidden tools)

2. Click the 3D Rotation Tool.
3. Set the tool to Local or Global mode by checking the Global toggle button in the Options area of the Tools panel.
4. Select a movie clip Symbol or instance with the 3D Rotation tool.
5. A circular, multicolored target appears on the instance. This is a guide for the 3D rotation. The red longitudinal line rotates your instance around the X-axis. The green line along the equator rotates your instance around the Y-axis. The circular blue guide rotates your instance around the Z-axis.
6. Click on one of the guides—red for X, green for Y, or blue for Z—and drag your mouse in either direction to rotate your instance in 3D space (See Figure 3.25).
7. You can also click and drag the outer orange circular guide to freely rotate the instance in all three directions (See Figure 3.25).

To rotate a multiple objects in 3D space, do this:

1. Click the 3D Rotation Tool.
2. Set the tool to Local or Global mode by checking the Global toggle button in the Options area of the Tools panel.
3. Select multiple movie clips with the 3D Rotation Tool on the Stage. The 3D Rotation controls appear overlaid on the most recently selected object.
4. Place the pointer over one of the four rotation axis controls.
5. Drag one of the axis controls to rotate around that axis, or the free rotate control (outer orange circle) to rotate X and Y simultaneously (See Figure 3.26).

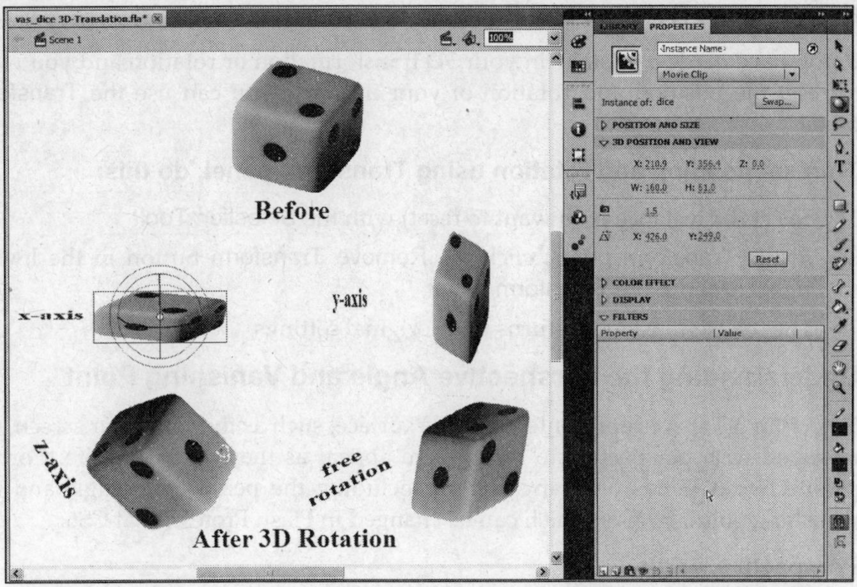

Figure 3.25 Rotating single object in 3D space using 3D Rotation Tool

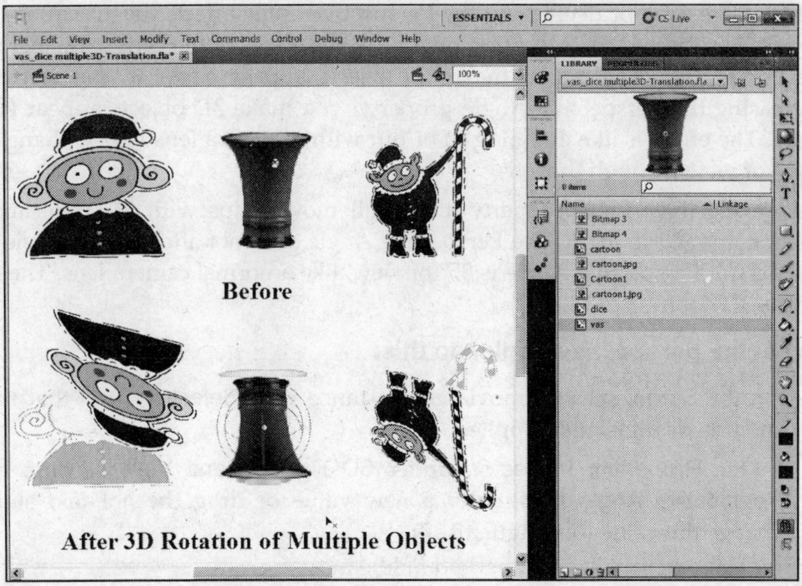

Figure 3.26 Rotating multiple objects in 3D space using 3D Rotation Tool

6. All of the selected movie clips rotate around the 3D center point which appears at the center of the rotation controls (See Figure 3.26).

Resetting the Rotation and Position

If you have made a mistake in your 3D transformation or rotation and you want to reset the position and rotation of your instance, you can use the Transform panel.

To reset position and rotation using Transform panel, do this:

1. Select the instance (you want to reset) with the Selection Tool.
2. In the Transform panel, click the Remove Transform button in the lower-right corner of the Transform panel.
3. The selected instance returns to its original settings.

Understanding the Perspective Angle and Vanishing Point

Objects in 3D space represented on a 2D surface, such as the computer screen, are rendered with perspective to make them appear as they do in real life. Correct perspective depends on many factors, including the perspective angle and the vanishing point, both of which can be changed in Flash Professional CS6.

Perspective Angle

Perspective Angle controls the apparent angle of view of 3D movie clips on the Stage. Increasing or decreasing the Perspective angle affects the apparent size of 3D movie clips and their location relative to the edges of the Stage. By increasing the Perspective Angle, you make 3D objects appear closer to the viewer. By decreasing the Perspective Angle property, you make 3D objects appear further away. The effect is like zooming in or out with a camera lens which changes the angle of view through the lens.

The Perspective Angle property affects all movie clips with 3D translation or rotation applied to them. The Perspective Angle does not affect other movie clips. The default Perspective Angle is 55° of view, like a normal camera lens. The range of values is from 1° to 180°.

To set the perspective angle, do this:

1. On the Stage, select a movie clip instance with Selection Tool that has 3D rotation or translation applied.
2. In the Properties Inspector, under 3D Position and View section, in the Perspective Angle field, enter a new value or drag the hot text slider to change the value (See Figure 3.27).

The Perspective Angle changes automatically when you change the Stage size so that the appearance of 3D objects does not change.

Figure 3.27 Object after setting perspective angle of 113°

Vanishing Point

The Vanishing Point controls the orientation of the Z-axis of 3D movie clips on the Stage. The Z-axis of all 3D movie clips diminishes toward the Vanishing Point.

The vanishing point determines where on the horizontal parallel lines of a perspective drawing meet. For example, in railroad tracks, parallel tracks converge (meet) to a single point as they move away into the distance. The vanishing point is usually at eye level in the center of your field of view, so the default settings are exactly in the middle of the Stage. You can, however, change the vanishing point setting so it appears above or below eye level, or to the right or left.

The Vanishing Point is a document property that affects all movie clips that have Z-axis translation or rotation applied to them. The Vanishing Point does not affect other movie clips. The default location of the Vanishing Point is the center of the Stage.

To adjust the Vanishing Point, do this:

1. On the Stage, select a movie clip instance with Selection tool that has 3D rotation or translation applied.
2. In the Properties Inspector, under 3D Position and View section, in the Vanishing point field, enter a new value or drag the hot text slider to change

the value. Guides indicating the location of the Vanishing Point appear on the Stage while dragging the hot text (See Figure 3.28).

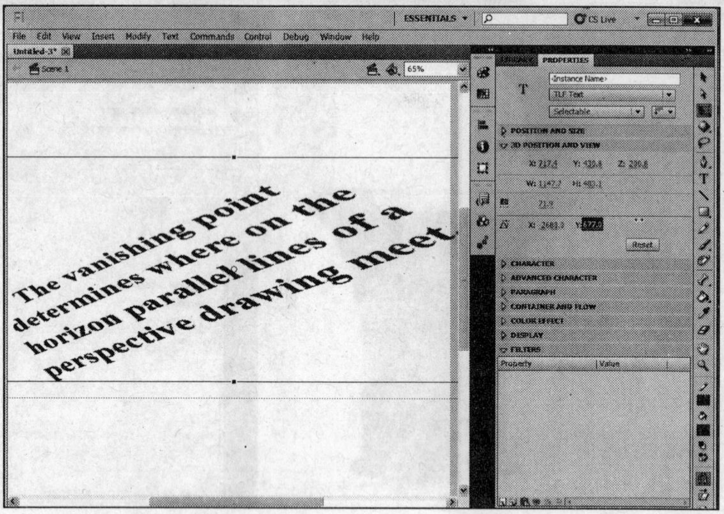

Figure 3.28 Object after applying vanishing point

3. To move the Vanishing Point back to the center of the Stage, click the Reset button in the Properties Inspector.

If you resize the Stage, the Vanishing Point does not update automatically. To maintain the 3D look created by Vanishing Point, you will need to reposition the Vanishing Point relative to the new Stage size.

CHAPTER 4

Timeline and Animation

Introduction

In this Chapter, we shall work with time-based contents, basic methods and tools to create animations as well as learn to create frame-by-frame animation and tweened animation. In addition to this, we shall also learn about the amazing (Inverse Kinematics) IK tools in Flash Professional CS6 that bring the power of inverse kinematics to the Flash authoring environment. Finally, we will introduce you about pinning, new feature of Flash Professional CS6 for inverse kinematics, which allows finer control for armatures.

Working with Timeline

The Timeline organizes and controls a movie's contents over time. With the help of Timeline, you can determine and change what will be happening in a movie, frame-by-frame. You can also determine which objects are animated, what types of animations are being used, when the various objects will appear in a movie, when changes are made to the properties of an object, which objects will appear on top of others, and how fast the movie will play. Features of the Timeline are shown in Figure 4.1 and further explained in this Chapter.

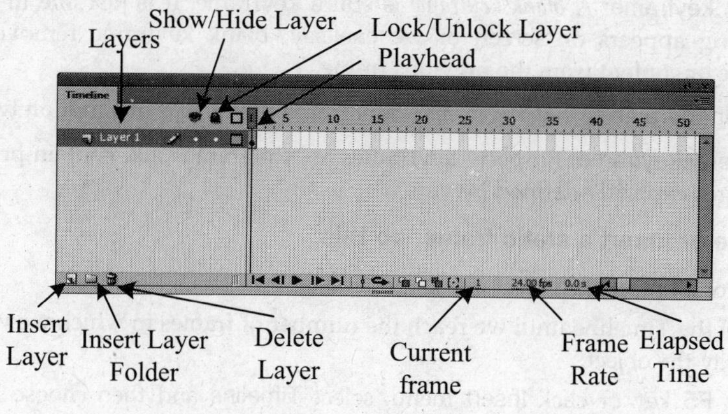

Figure 4.1 Timeline features

Using the Playhead

Playhead is a red vertical line. It indicates which frame is playing (See Figure 4.1). You can manually move the playhead by dragging it to left or right. This makes it easier to locate a frame that you may want to edit. Dragging the playhead also allows you to do a quick check of the movie without having to play it.

Concept of Frames

Like films, Flash Professional CS6 documents are divided into lengths of time and frames. In the Timeline, you work with these frames to organize and control the content of your document.

A *frame* is the little rectangular cell in a Timeline. Frames are numbered at the top of the Timeline. Every fifth frame is gray and rest is white with a gray outline. Timeline displays all the frames, but we can see only one frame's content at a time. Still images in an animation are kept in a frame.

When we create a Flash movie, one frame exists in a single layer. To display an object for more than one frame, we need to add more frames.

✎ *A frame is nothing more than a single segment of a movie. The more the frames in a movie, the longer the movie is shown.*

Flash Professional CS6 uses five types of frame. These are:

1. Regular or static frame: If we want to display an object or image across multiple frames without moving it, we need to add static or regular frame.
2. Keyframe: A *keyframe* is simply a frame in which we establish exactly what should appear on stage at particular point. It makes a change in an object's properties from the previous frame. When we associate a change in an object with a new frame, the frame must be a keyframe.
3. Blank keyframe: A *blank keyframe* is still a keyframe. It is just one in which nothing appears on screen or we can say, blank keyframe removes any image or content from the previous frame.
4. Tweened frame: A *tweened frame* is any frame that is part of a motion tween.
5. Property keyframe: Property keyframes are the frames that contain property changes explicitly defined by you.

To create or insert a static frame, do this:

1. First of all place the object in a stage.
2. Scroll the Timeline until we reach the number of frames in which we want to display the object.
3. Press F5 key or click Insert menu, select Timeline and then choose Frame. Range of static frames appears as solid bars (See Figure 4.2).

To create or insert a keyframe, do this:

1. First of all, locate or select an image or object in which we want a change to take place.

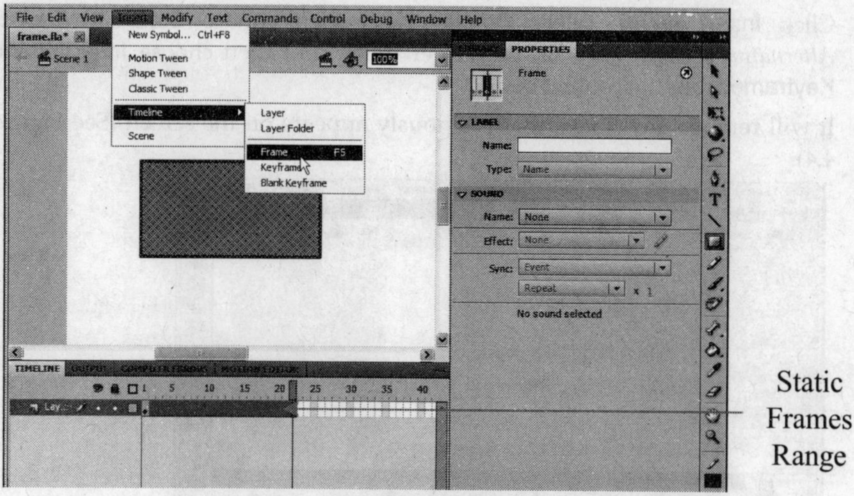

Figure 4.2 Creating a Static or Regular Frame

2. Press F6 key or click Insert menu, select Timeline and then choose Keyframe. Flash copies the object from the previous frame into the new keyframe (See Figure 4.3).

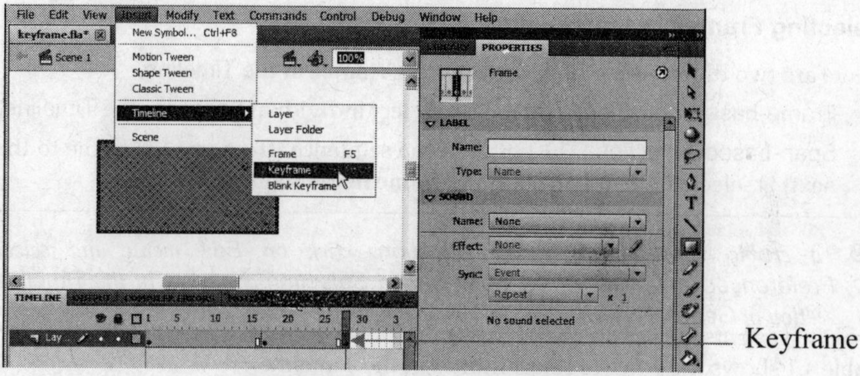

Figure 4.3 Creating a Keyframe

3. After that change the object as desired.

If you want to remove a keyframe, do not press the Delete key! Doing so will delete the contents of that keyframe on the Stage. Instead, select the keyframe and choose Modify > Timeline > Clear Keyframe or press Shift+F6 keys together. Your keyframe will be removed from the Timeline.

To create or insert a blank keyframe, do this:

1. Place the cursor at the target frame on the Timeline.

2. Click Insert menu, select Timeline and then choose Blank Keyframe. *Alternatively,* right click on the target frame and then choose Insert Blank Keyframe from the context menu.
3. It will remove any image that previously appears on the screen (See Figure 4.4).

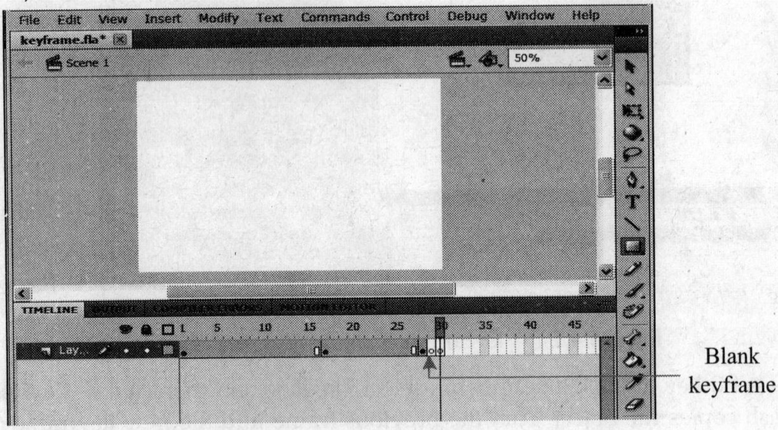

Figure 4.4 Inserting a Blank Keyframe

Selecting Frames in the Timeline

There are two different methods for selecting frames in the Timeline.

1. Frame-based Selection: You have to select individual frames in the Timeline.
2. Span-based Selection: The entire frame sequence (from one keyframe to the next) is selected when you click any frame in the sequence.

To enable span-based frame selection, click on Edit menu and select Preferences and then click on Span-based Selection check box in the Timeline section of General category.

Table 4.1 shows the ways to select frames in the Timeline.

Table 4.1 Selecting Frames

Various ways to select frames	Do this
To select one frame.	Click the frame.
To select multiple contiguous frames.	Drag the cursor over the frames, or Shift + click for additional frames.
To select multiple non-contiguous frames.	Ctrl + click for additional frames.

(Contd...)

Various ways to select frames	Do this
To select all frames in the Timeline.	Click Edit menu, select Timeline and then choose Select All Frames.
To select an entire span of static frames.	Double-click a frame between two keyframes. If you have Span-based Selection enabled, click any frame in the sequence.
To select a whole span of frames (motion tween or inverse kinematics).	Click on span once if you have Span-based Selection enabled, otherwise, double-click on the span.
To select multiple spans.	Shift + click on each span.

About Layers

Layers are like transparent sheets of plain glass placed one on the top of the other. With the help of layer, we can draw and edit objects on one layer without affecting objects of another layer.

Because layers do not increase the file size of the published movie therefore, we can create as many layers as we want but limited by computer's main memory.

We can also change the order of layers just by clicking on a layer and dragging it to a new position. In addition, special features of the layers are:

1. Guide layers (to make drawing and editing easier).
2. Mask layers (help in creating sophisticated effects).

We can perform different functions in a layer, such as adding layers, hiding layers, locking layers, dragging layers, deleting layers, etc. These functions are elaborated in detail in the following sections:

Layer Properties

If we want to set or change any property of layers, we have to use the Layers Properties dialog box.

To change layer's properties, do this:

1. Double-click the Layer Name icon of the layer whose properties you want to change. Layer Properties dialog box appears as shown in Figure 4.5.
2. To change the name or give the name of the layer, enter the name in the Name: text box.
3. If you want to show the layer, click on the check mark corresponding to the Show option otherwise uncheck it.

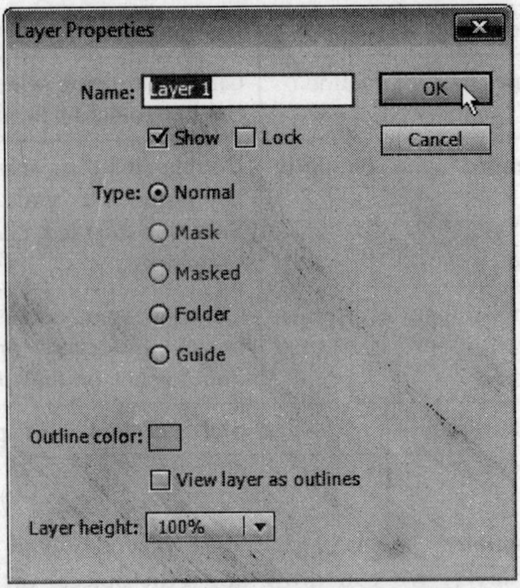

Figure 4.5 Layer Properties dialog box

4. To lock a layer to prevent editing, select Lock check box or deselect this check box to allow editing.
5. From the Type: section, select the type of the layer which you want to use.

   Normal: It is the default type in which you draw and animate objects. All the objects on these layers appear in the movie.

   Mask: A layer that hides and reveals portions of another layer. It contains objects used as masks to hide selected portions of layers below them. It is also used to create extra effects, such as spotlight. Several layers can be linked to a Mask layer.

   Masked: A layer beneath a Mask layer that is associated with the Mask layer. In this layer, only the portion of the masked layer revealed by the mask is visible.

   Folder: A layer that can contain other layers.

   Guide (Standard and Motion): It is mainly used to align the artwork. Standard Guide layer is used to set a reference point (such as a Guide line) for positioning objects on the Stage. Motion Guide layer is used to create a path for animated objects to follow.

   Outline color: This option is used to change the colour of outlines of the image of the layer.

   Check View layer as outlines to display all objects on the layer as outlines otherwise uncheck it.

   Layer height: This pull down option specifies the height of the layer in the Timeline.

6. After apply setting, click OK button.

Normal, Mask, Masked, and Guide layers can contain motion tweens or inverse kinematic bones. When these items are present in one of these layers, there are limitations to the types of content that can be added to the layer.

Create a Layer

A new Flash document contains only one layer in the initial Stage. You can add as many layers as you need on it. When you create a layer, it appears above the selected layer. The newly added layer becomes the active layer.

To create or add layer, do this:

1. Click Insert menu, select Timeline and then choose Layer (See Figure 4.6). Or click the New Layer button at the bottom of the Timeline.
2. A new layer appears above the selected layer (See Figure 4.6).

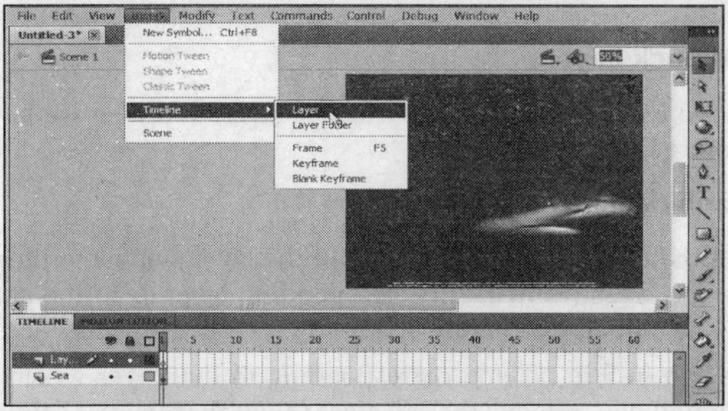

Figure 4.6 Creating a New Layer

To create a layer folder, do this:

1. Select a layer or folder in the Timeline.
2. Then click Insert menu, select Timeline and then choose Layer Folder. Or
3. Click the New Folder icon at the bottom of the Timeline.
4. The new folder appears above the layer or folder you selected as shown in Figure 4.7.

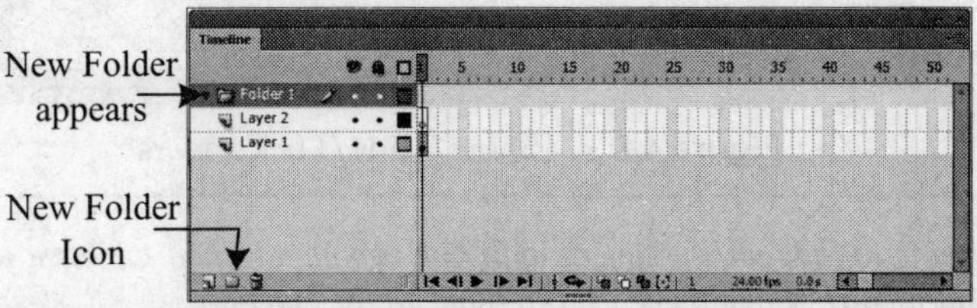

Figure 4.7 Creating Layer folder

Rename a Layer

Layer name is the name which is given to the particular layer. Always give a meaningful name to the layer, because when you use more layers named as Layer 1, Layer 2 and so on, it will be very difficult to find the needed layer.

To give a name or rename a layer, do this:

1. Double-click the layer name to rename a layer or enter the name in the Layer Properties dialog box as described in the above Section.

To delete a layer or layer folder, do this:

1. Select the layer or layer folder by clicking on its name in the Timeline.
2. Then click Delete Layer button in the Timeline. Or
   Drag the layer or layer folder to the Delete Layer button. Or
3. Right-click the layer or folder name and select Delete Layer from the context menu.

Show/Hide/Lock Layers

Sometimes we want to work on a particular layer, and then we have to hide or lock some other layer.

To show or hide a layer, do this:

1. Click in the Eye column to the right of the layer's name to hide it. This will show a red cross (×) mark in corresponding layer or to the particular layer which was hidden (See Figure 4.8).
2. Click again in Eye column corresponding to that layer which you want to show. It will now remove the red cross (×) mark from that column and it will be replaced by dot (•) (See Figure 4.8).

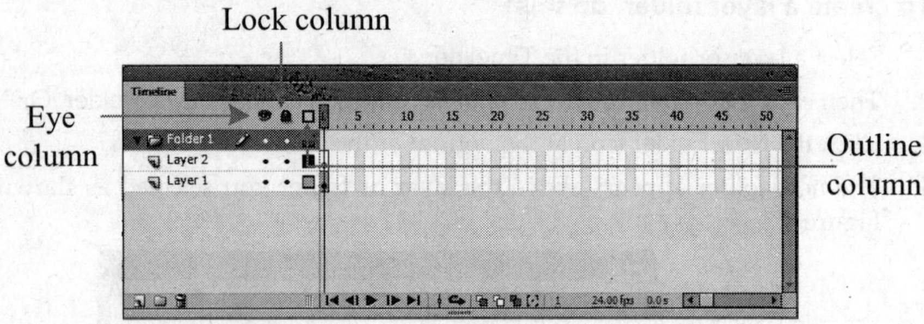

Figure 4.8 Show/Hide/Lock Layers

If we want to hide all the layers with one command, then we have to click the eye icon and then click again eye icon to show all the layers.

To lock a layer, do this:

1. Click in the Lock column to the right of the Eye Column to lock and it will show a lock to the particular layer which was locked.
2. Click again in Lock column to unlock the layer. It will remove the lock from that column and it will be replaced by dot (•).

   If we want to lock all the layers with one command, then we have to click the lock icon and then click again the lock icon to unlock all the layers.

Outline Color

Outline color is the color which we see when we click the option "View layer as outlines" of Layer Properties dialog box. We can change the outline color from Layer Properties dialog box.

To change layer's outline color, do this:

1. First of all, select the layer whose colour you want to change.
2. Click Modify menu, select Timeline and then choose Layer Properties. Layer Properties dialog box appears as shown in Figure 4.5.
3. Click the Outline color box, select new color and then click OK.

Viewing Layer as Outline

Viewing layer as outline means we want to see only the sketching part with colour (which we choose from the Outline color section of Layer Properties dialog box) without filling part (See Figure 4.9).

Figure 4.9 Contents of a layer as Outline

To view content of layers as outlines, do this:

1. To display particular object as outline, click Outline column. To turn off outline display, click again Outline column (See Figure 4.8).

   To display all objects of layer as outline, click Outline Icon. To turn off outline display, click again Outline icon.

Guide Layer

Guide layer is a special kind of layer that does not export, when we export a Flash movie. This layer can be used to help registration of various elements of a Flash movie. For getting help when drawing, we can use Guide layers. We can make any layer as a Guide layer. Guide layers are indicated by a Guide icon to the left of the layer name (See Figure 4.9).

Guide layers are useful only for aligning objects on the Stage. These layers do not appear in a published Flash Player movie.

To assign a layer as a Guide layer, do this:

1. Select the layer which you want to assign a Guide layer.
2. Right click it and choose Guide option from the context menu. *Alternatively,* select Guide option from the Layer Properties dialog box as shown in Figure 4.5.
3. The layer icon is replaced by a T-square icon, indicating that this is now a Guide layer (See Figure 4.9).

To create a motion Guide layer, do this:

1. Drag a normal layer onto a Guide layer. This converts the Guide layer to a motion Guide layer and links the normal layer to the new motion Guide layer as shown in the Layer area of Timeline is shown in Figure 4.10.

Animation Basics

Animation can be an important part of any application or Website, whether we focus on e-commerce (where we can attract attention and provide product demonstration), or entertainment (where we can provide interactive games to the user).

How does Animation Work?

Animation is like a motion picture, which is made up of a series of still images. Animation can be as simple as moving a box across the Stage from one frame to the next. It can also be much more complex. The perception of motion in an animation is actually an illusion because our eye captures and holds an image for one tenth of a second before processing another image. By retaining each impression for one-tenth of a second, we perceive a series of rapidly displayed still images as a single, moving image. This is known as persistence of vision. It provides the basis for the frame rate in animation. Frame rates of 10–12 frames per second (fps) generally provide a smooth computer-based animation. Lower frame rates result in a jerky image, while frame rates over 30 fps may result in a blurred image. Flash uses a default frame rate of 24 fps or frames per second.

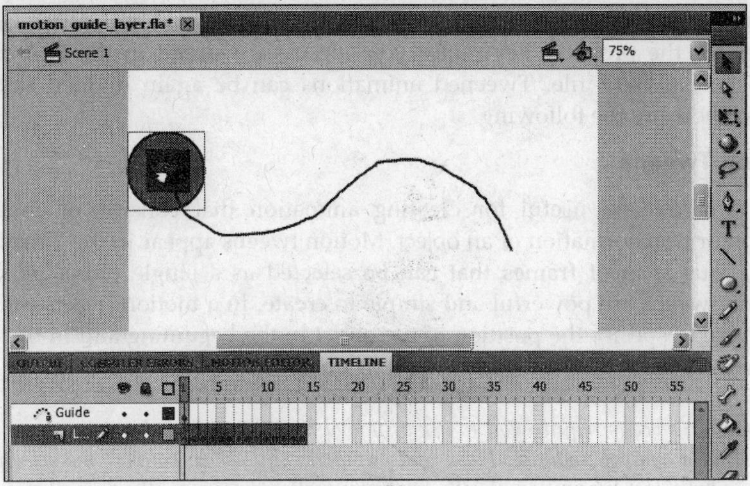

Figure 4.10 Motion Guide layer

Frame Rate is the playing speed of the animation. It is measured in number of frames per second (fps). The complexity of the animation and the speed of the computer playing the animation affect the smoothness of the playback. To determine optimum frame rates, test your animation on a variety of computers.

Creating Animation

Creating animation is one of the most powerful features of Flash. However, developing basic animations is a simple process. Flash allows you to animate many different aspects of a single object. You can change an object's position on the Stage, change its color or transparency, change its size or its rotation, and even animate the special filters. You also have control over an object's path of motion, and even its easing, which is the way an object accelerates or deaccelerates. Animations are created by changing the contents of successive frames.

Types of Animation

Flash Professional CS6 provides several ways to create animation and special effects. Each method provides different possibilities for creating and engaging animated contents. These methods are:

1. Tweened Animation

2. Frame-by-frame animation
3. Inverse Kinematic

Tweened Animation

Tweened animation is an effective and efficient way to create movement and changes over time while minimizing file size. In tweened animation, only the values for the property keyframes you specify are stored in the FLA file and published as SWF file. Tweened animations can be again divided into three types. These are the following.

Motion Tweens

Motion tweens are useful for creating animation that consists of continuous motion or transformation of an object. Motion tweens appear in the Timeline as a contiguous span of frames that can be selected as a single object by default. Motion tweens are powerful and simple to create. In a motion tween animation, you have to specify the position of the object in the beginning and in the ending frames and Flash fills in the in-between frames.

✍ *Motion tweens require you to use a symbol instance. If the object you have selected is not a symbol instance, Flash will automatically ask to convert the selection to a symbol. Flash also automatically separates motion tweens on their own layers, which are called Tween layers.*

Classic Tweens

Classic tweens are like motion tweens in which you can create animations that change the properties of an object over time. Motion tweens are easier to use and allow the greatest degree of control over tweened animation. But Classic tweens are a bit more complex to create, however, they provide certain capabilities that some developers desire.

Shape Tweens

Shape tweening is a technique for interpolating amorphous (shapeless) changes between shapes in different keyframes. For this, you have to draw a shape at one specific keyframe in the Timeline, and change that shape or draw another shape at another specific keyframe. Flash then interpolates the intermediate shapes for the keyframes in between and Shape tweens make it possible to smoothly morph one shape into another. For example, animation of clouds, water, or fire is perfect for shape tweening.

Frame-by-Frame Animation

Frame-by-frame animations are useful when you want to change individual parts of an image. Frame-by-frame animation changes the contents of the Stage in every frame and is best suited to complex animation in which an image changes in every frame instead of simply moving across the Stage. Frame-by-frame animation increases file size more rapidly than tweened animation.

Inverse Kinematics (IK) Poses

Inverse Kinematics (IK) allows you to easily create character animations. It allows you to stretch and bend shape objects and link groups of symbol instances to make them move together in a natural way. Once you have added bones to a shape or a group of symbols, you can change the position of the bones or symbols in different keyframes. Flash interpolates the positions in the in-between frames.

Classification of Animations in the Timeline

Flash distinguishes different types of animations in the Timeline by displaying different indicators. These indicators and their animation types are given in Table 4.2.

Table 4.2 Different Indicators of different Animations in Timeline

Indicators	**Types of Animation and Description**
	Motion Tween Animation A *black dot* in the first frame indicates that the tween span has a target object assigned to it. *Black diamond* indicates the last frame and any other property keyframes.
	Motion Tween Animation A *hollow dot* in the first frame indicates that the target object of the motion tween has been removed. The tween span still contains its property keyframes and can have a new target object applied to it.
	Inverse Kinematics (IK) Pose Pose layers contain IK armatures and poses. Each pose appears in the Timeline as a black diamond. Flash interpolates the positions of the armature in the frames in between poses.
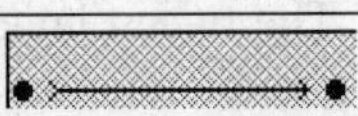	Classic Tween A *black dot* at the beginning keyframe with a *black arrow* and *blue background* indicates a *Classic tween.*

(Contd...)

Indicators	Types of Animation and Description
	Classic Tween A *dashed line* indicates that the Classic tween is broken or incomplete when the final keyframe is missing.
	Shape Tween A *black dot* at the beginning keyframe with a *black arrow* and a *light green background* indicates a *Shape tween*.
	Single Keyframe A *black dot* indicates a single keyframe. *Light gray frames* after a single keyframe contain the same content with no changes. These frames have a *vertical black line* and a *hollow rectangle* at the last frame of the span.
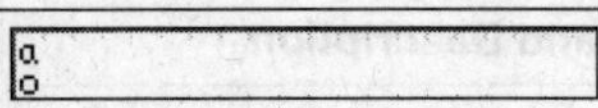	A *small a* indicates that the frame is assigned a frame action with the Actions panel.
	A *red flag* indicates that the frame contains a label.
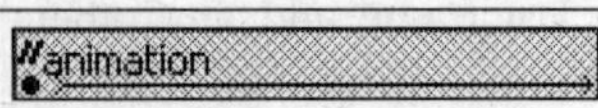	A *green double slash* indicates that the frame contains a comment.
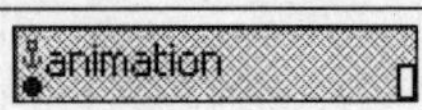	A *gold anchor* indicates that the frame is a named anchor.

Layers in Tweened Animation

Each scene in a Flash file can consist of any number of Timeline layers. To create an animation that includes tweened movement of more than one symbol or text field at once, place each object on a separate layer. You can use one layer as a background layer to contain static artwork and use additional layers to contain one separate animated object.

When you create a motion tween, Flash Professional CS6 converts the layer containing the object you selected to tween into a tween layer. The tween layer has a tween icon next to the layer name in the Timeline.

If other objects are present on the same layer as the tweened object, Flash Professional CS6 adds new layers above or below the original layer as needed. Any objects that existed below the tweened object on its original layer move to a new layer below the original layer. Any objects that were above the tweened object on its original layer move to a new layer above the original layer. Flash inserts these new layers between any pre-existing layers in the Timeline. In this way, Flash preserves the original stacking order of all the graphic objects on the Stage.

✍ *A tween layer can contain only tween spans (contiguous groups of frames containing a tween), static frames, blank keyframes, or empty frames.*

When a document has several layers, tracking and editing the objects on one or more of them can be difficult. This task is easier if you work with the contents of one layer at a time.

Understanding Motion Tweens

In a *Motion Tween* animation, you can specify the position of the object in the beginning and ending frames and Flash fills in the in-between frames, a process known as tweening. You can also change several properties with one Motion Tween. For example, you can place a symbol to the left of the Stage in frame 1, and move it to the right of the Stage in frame 20. At the same time, you can change the size of the symbol to give the impression that the symbol is moving away from the viewer. After that when you create a tween, Flash calculates all the positions and change the size of the movie-clip symbol in-between. The result is an animation of the symbol moving from left to right, from frame 1 to frame 20.

✍ *The Onion Skin feature is enabled so that outlines of the plane are displayed for each frame of the animation as shown in the Figure 4.11.*

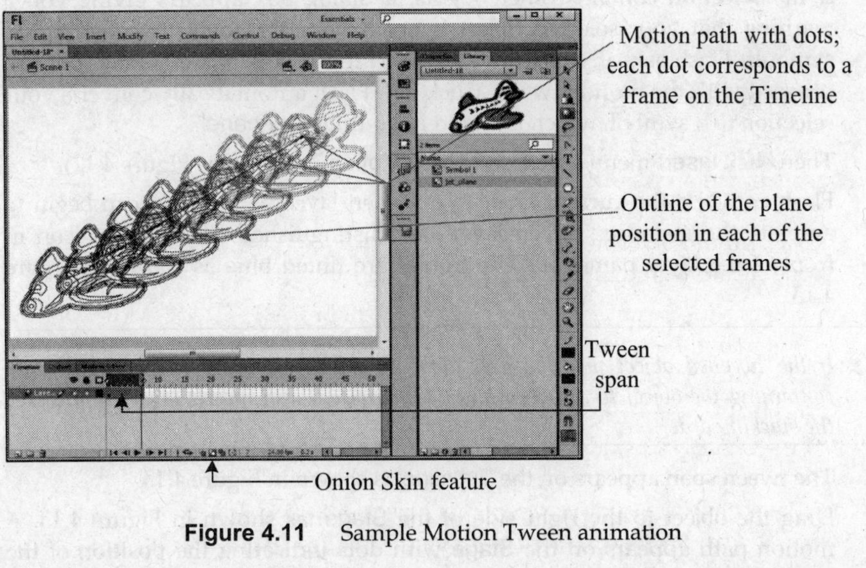

Figure 4.11 Sample Motion Tween animation

Tween Span

A *tween span* is a group of frames in the Timeline (See Figure 4.11). It appears in the Timeline in a single layer with a blue background. These tween spans can be selected as a single object. Only one object on the Stage can be animated in each tween span. This object is called the *target object* of the *tween span*.

Motion Path

A *motion path* is showing the path the tweened object taking during its movement on the Stage. Each dot on the path corresponds to a frame on the Timeline and indicates the location of the object when the frame is played (See Figure 4.11). A motion path can be altered by dragging a point on the path using the Selection tool or by using the Subselection tool.

Property Keyframe

Property Keyframe is a keyframe which indicates a change in a Flash movie, such as the start or ending of an animation.

✍ *Flash tweens only symbol, instances and text fields. All other object types are wrapped in a symbol when you apply a tween to them. The symbol instance can contain nested symbols,*

To create a motion tween animation, do this:

1. Select a symbol, instance or a text field to tween on the Stage.

   If the selection contains other objects, a dialog box appears giving you a warning that your selected object is not a symbol. Motion tweens require symbols. Flash asks if you want to convert the selection to a *symbol* so it can proceed with the motion tween. Click OK. Flash automatically converts your selection to a symbol, which is stored in your Library panel.
2. Then click Insert menu and then choose Motion Tween (See Figure 4.12).
3. Flash converts the current layer to a Tween layer so that you can begin to animate the instance. Tween layers are distinguished by a special icon in front of the layer name, and the frames are tinted blue as shown in Figure 4.13.

✍ *If the tweened object was the only item on the layer, Flash converts the layer containing the object to a Tween layer. Otherwise, Flash inserts layers to preserve the stacking order.*

---

4. The tween span appears on the Timeline as shown in Figure 4.13.
5. Drag the object to the right side of the Stage, as shown in Figure 4.13. A motion path appears on the Stage with dots indicating the position of the

object for each frame (See Figure 4.14). A diamond symbol appears in the last frame, which is the end of the tween span.

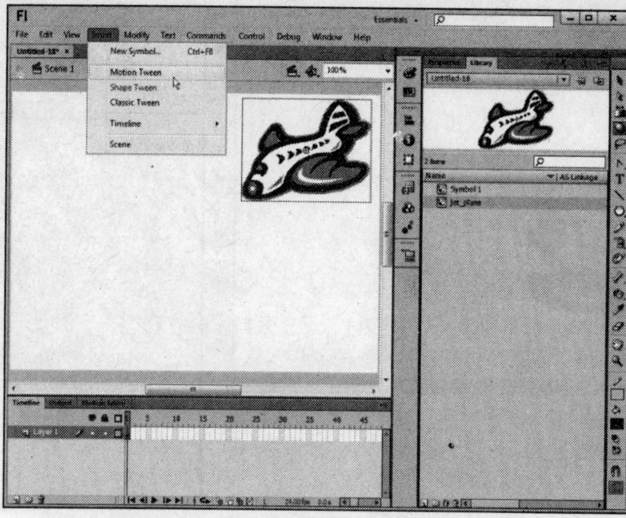

Figure 4.12 Creating Motion Tween

Tween layer icon

Figure 4.13 Tween layer

The diamond symbol is a position keyframe and it is automatically inserted at the end of the tween path.

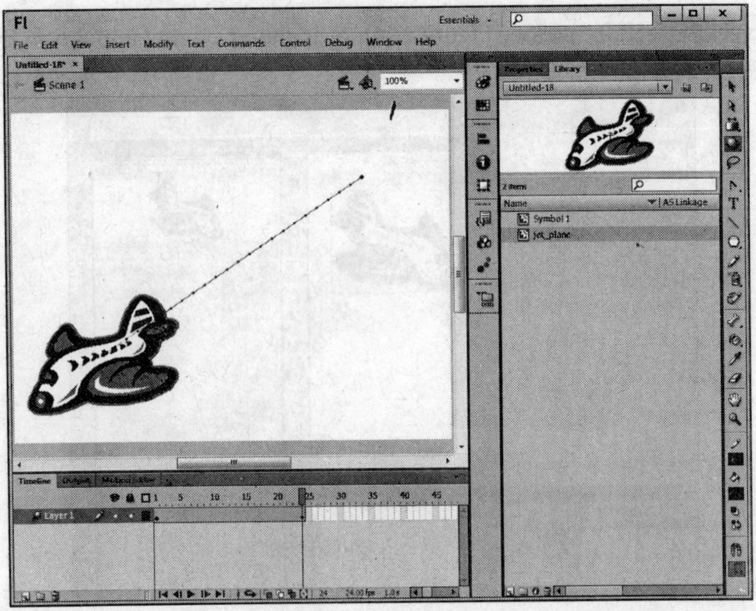

Figure 4.14 Motion path with dots indicating the position of the object

6. Point to the end of the tween span, when the pointer changes to a double arrow, drag the tween span in the **Timeline** to shorten or extend the span to the desired number of frames.
7. Click the frame 1 on the **Timeline**, then press the period (•) key to move the playhead one frame at a time and notice the position of the plane for each frame.
8. Click **Control** menu and then select **Play** or *alternatively*, press **Enter** key to play the movie (See Figure 4.15).

✍ *In Flash Professional CS6, you can also view your animation on the stage by clicking the Play button below the Timeline. In addition to the other (Digital Versatile Disk) DVD-like controls, you can use the Loop button to repeat a selected group of frames.*

To edit a motion path, do this:

1. Click the **Selection tool** on the **Tools panel**, and then click a blank area of the **Stage**.
2. Point to the middle of the motion path.
3. When the pointer changes to a pointer along with arc, then drag the pointer down, as shown in Figure 4.16.
4. Play the movie by pressing **Enter** key.

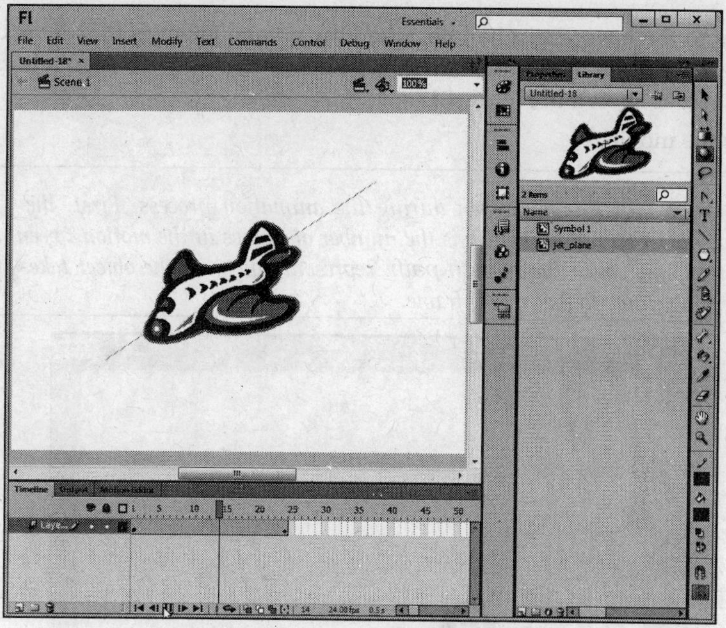

Figure 4.15 Playing the animation

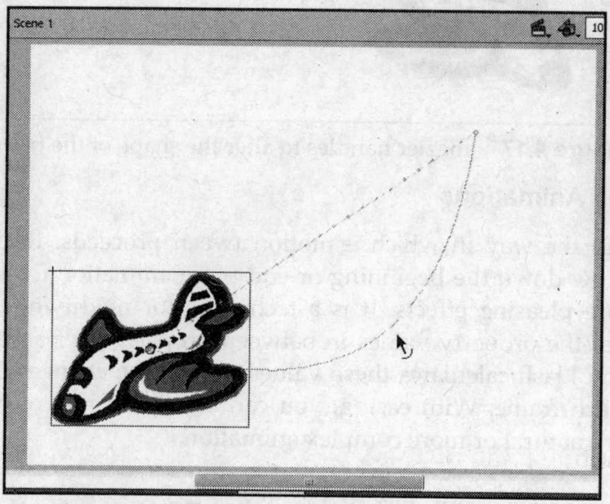

Figure 4.16 Dragging the motion path

5. Click the Subselection Tool on the Tools panel, point to the end of the motion path, when the pointer changes into an arrow with a small square.
6. Then click the end of path to display Bezier handles.

7. Point to the lower-right handle, when the pointer changes to a delta symbol, drag the handle up and towards the center of the **Stage** to form a horizontal **S** shape, as shown in Figure 4.17.
8. Play the movie.

Two important things happen during the animation process. First, the Timeline shows the **tween span**, *which is the number of frames in the motion tween. Second, a dotted line, called the* **motion path**, *represents the path the object takes from the beginning frame to the ending frame.*

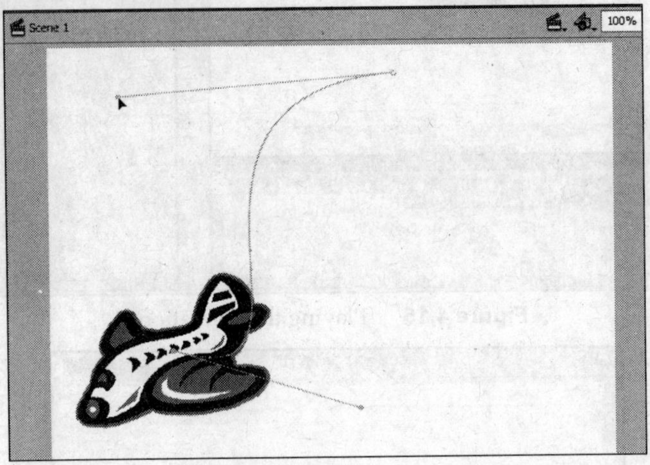

Figure 4.17 Bezier handles to alter the shape of the path

Easing Tween Animations

Easing refers to the way in which a motion tween proceeds. It allows you to speed up or slow down the beginning or end of an animation for more realistic motion or more pleasing effects. It is a technique for modifying the way that Flash calculates the property values in between property keyframes in a tween. Without easing, Flash calculates these values so that the change to the value is the same in each frame. With easing, you can adjust the rate of change to the values for more natural or more complex animation.

An ease is a mathematical curve that is applied to the property values of a tween. The final effect of the tween is the result of the combination of the range of property values in the tween and the ease curve.

You can apply easing in two different ways:

1. **Using Properties Inspector**: Eases applied in the **Properties Inspector** affect all of the properties that are included in a tween.

2. Using Motion Editor: Eases applied in the Motion Editor can affect a single property, a group of properties, or all properties of a tween.

Easing values applied via the Properties Inspector *will be applied globally to all the properties throughout the entire motion tween. With the* Motion Editor, *you have precise control over individual properties and eases between keyframes.*

To change ease value of an animation using Properties Inspector, do this:

1. Select the tween in the Timeline or the motion path on the Stage.
2. In the Properties Inspector, under the Ease section, enter a value for the strength of the ease in the Ease: field.
3. Now play the movie.

If the word "out" is displayed next to the Ease *value on the* Properties Inspector, *it indicates that the object will ease out, slow down at the end of the animation. But, if the word "in" is displayed next to the* Ease *value on the* Properties Inspector, *it indicates that the object does not move very far in that section of the path.*

To ease individual properties in the Motion Editor, do this:

1. Click on the motion tween in the Timeline and open the Motion Editor.
2. To add an ease to the list of eases available to the selected tween, click the Add (+) button in the Ease section of the Motion Editor and then select the ease to add as shown in Figure 4.18.

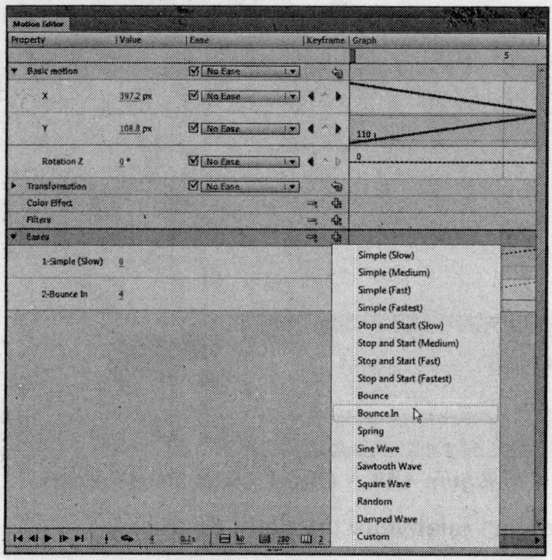

Figure 4.18 Motion Editor

3. To add an ease to a single property, select the ease from the Selected Ease menu for the property.

4. To add an ease to a whole category of properties, such as Basic motion, Transformation, Color Effect, or Filters, select an ease type from the Selected Ease menu for the property category.

5. To enable or disable the effect of the ease for a property or category of properties, click the Enable/Disable Ease checkbox for the property or category of properties. This allows you to quickly see the effect of an ease on property curves.

6. To remove an ease from the list of available tweens, click the Remove (–) Ease button in the Eases section of the Motion Editor and then select the ease from the pop-up menu.

Orienting Objects to the Path

Sometimes the orientation of the object traveling along the path is important. Suppose, you create a non-linear motion path, such as a circle and you want tweened object to rotate as it moves along the path (See Figure 4.19). The Orient to path option in the Properties Inspector gives you this facility.

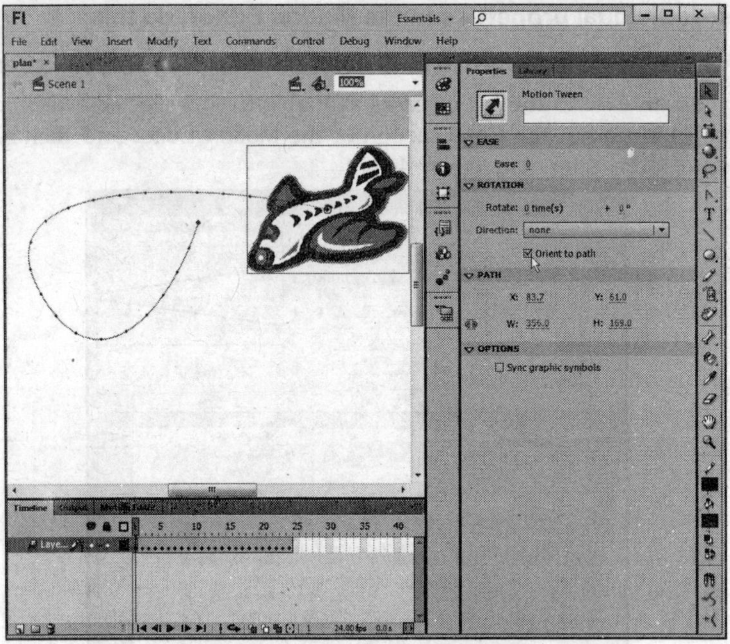

Figure 4.19 Object rotates along the path

To orient an object relative to the path, do this:

1. Select the Motion Tween on the Timeline.

2. In the **Properties Inspector**, select the **Orient to path** option from the **Rotation** Section as shown in Figure 4.19.
3. Flash inserts keyframes for rotation along the motion tween so that the plane is oriented to the path of the motion.

To direct the nose of the plane or any other object, along the path of its motion, you must orient its initial position so that it is facing in the direction that you want it to travel. Use the Free Transform tool to rotate its initial position so that it is oriented correct.

Swapping Tween Targets

In Flash Professional CS6, Motion Tween is based on object. This means that an object and its motion are independent of each other, and you can easily swap out the target of a Motion Tween.

To replace the target instance of a tween span, do this:

1. Select the Motion Tween.
2. From the **Library Panel**, drag the movie clip symbol of the different object (in our case it is helicopter) onto the plane as shown in Figure 4.20.

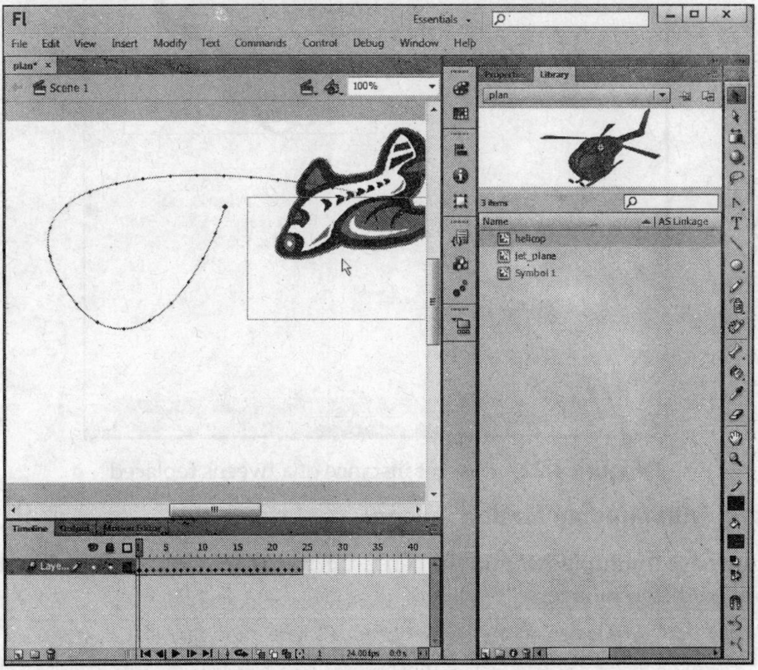

Figure 4.20 Dragging helicopter on to the plane

3. Flash asks you if you want to replace the existing object with a new object. Click **OK** (See Figure 4.21).

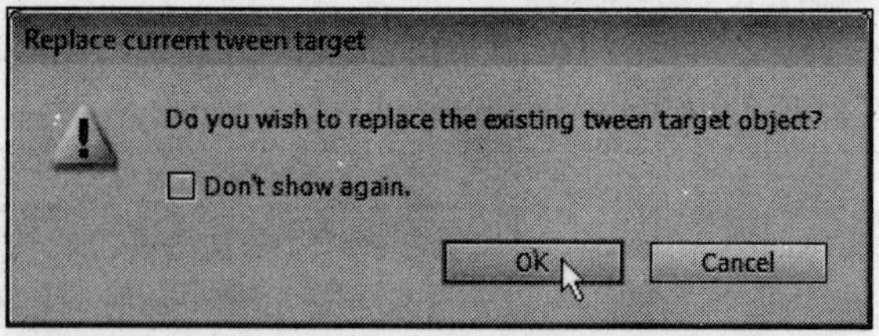

Figure 4.21 Replace current tween target dialog box

4. The helicopter is replaced with the plane. The motion remains the same, but the target of the Motion Tween has been swapped (See Figure 4.22).

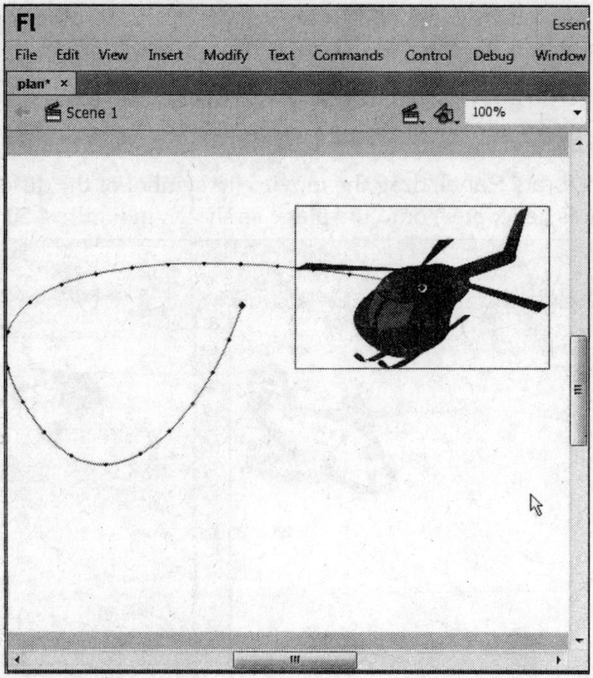

Figure 4.22 Target instance of a tweens replaced

Working with Multiple Motion Tweens

You can have multiple Motion Tween animations playing at the same time if they are on different layers.

Tween layer will not allow you to place or draw additional graphics on it once it has been created. You will get a warning dialog box if you attempt to add content to an existing tween layer.

To create multiple motion tweens, do this:

1. First of all create a Motion Tween animation in layer 1 as described earlier. (See Figures 4.12, 4.13 and 4.14).
2. Lock this layer and then insert a new layer above this layer and name it helico.
3. Click frame 11 on the helico.
4. Click Insert menu, select Timeline and then choose Keyframe.
5. Drag an instance of the helicop from the Library panel so it is on top of the layer1 on the Stage, as shown in Figure 4.23.
6. Then click Insert menu and then choose Motion Tween (See Figure 4.23).

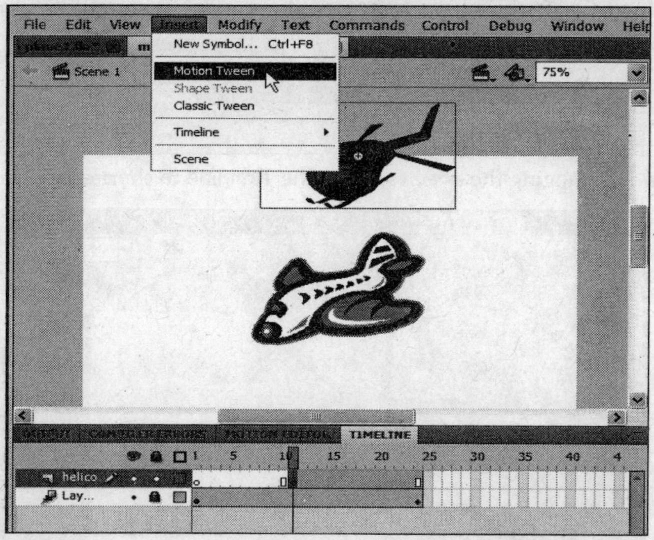

Figure 4.23 Insert menu with Motion Tween option selected

7. Point to the end of the tween span, when the pointer changes to a double arrow, drag the tween span in the Timeline to shorten or extend the span to the desired number of frames as shown in Figure 4.24.
8. Drag the object off the Stage, as shown in Figure 4.25.
9. Click the frame 1 on the Timeline, then press the period (•) key to move the playhead one frame at a time and notice the position of the plane for each frame.
10. Click Control menu and then select Play or *alternatively,* press Enter key to play the movie.

To remove a Motion Tween, do this:

1. Select the tween span on the Timeline.

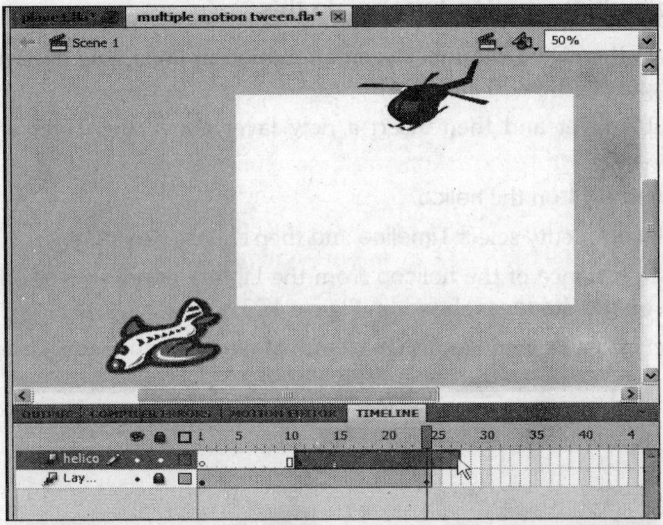

Figure 4.24 Dragging the tween span in the Timeline to shorten or extend the span

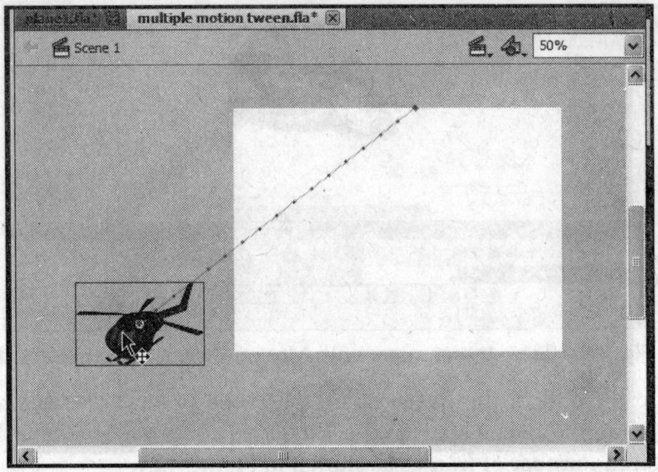

Figure 4.25 Dragging the object off the Stage

2. Click the **Insert** menu and then click **Remove Tween.**
3. Play the movie and see that the Object on the **Stage** is visible but it does not move.

You can convert a motion tween span to frame-by-frame animation by right-clicking the tween span and then choosing **Convert to Frame-by-Frame Animation.** *In* ***frame-by-frame animation****, each frame contains separate keyframes which each contains separate instances of the animated symbol.*

Motion Presets

If your project involves creating identical motion tweens repeatedly, Flash provides a panel called *Motion Presets* (several preconfigured motion tweens) that you can apply to an object on the **Stage**. Motion presets is a quick way to learn the basics of adding animation in Flash. You can create and save your own custom presets. These can be done from existing motion presets that you have modified, or from custom tweens that you have created on your own. The **Motion Presets panel** also allows you to import and export presets. You can share presets with other people.

Figure 4.26 shows the **Motion Presets panel** where you can choose a preset and apply it to an object. You can preview each preset before applying it and you can easily change to a different preset, if desired. Using presets can save significant production time during design and development of your projects, especially if you use similar kinds of tweens often.

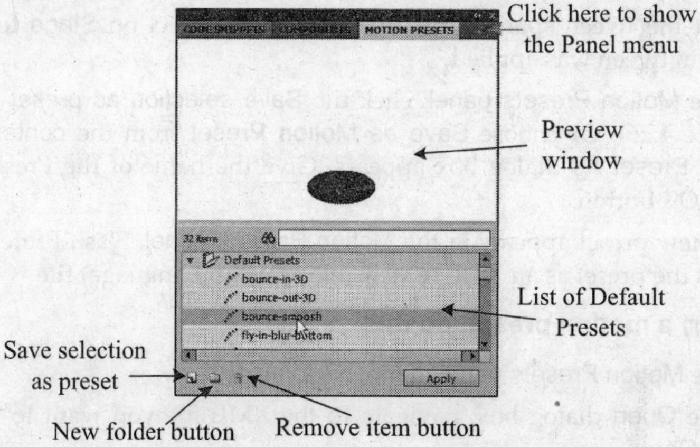

Figure 4.26 Motion Presets Panel

You can apply only one preset per object. If you apply the second preset to the same object, the second preset replaces with the first one.

To apply the motion preset, do this:

1. Select a tweenable object on the **Stage**.
2. Click the **Window** menu and then choose **Motion Presets**. A **Motion Presets panel** appears as shown in Figure 4.26.
3. In **Motion Presets panel**, click the **Expand icon** (i.e., arrow on the left side) for the **Default Presets**.
4. Select a preset from the **Default Presets list** and watch the animation in the preview window, as shown in Figure 4.26.

5. Click the Apply button in the panel or choose Apply at current location from the panel menu.
6. A dialog box opens asking if you want to replace the current motion object with the new selection.
7. You can only apply one Motion Tween or Motion Presets to an object at any one time. Here, click Yes.
8. The motion is applied so that the motion starts at the current position of the movie clip on the Stage.

Save a Tween as a Custom Motion Preset

If you create your own tween or modify a tween that you applied from the Motion Presets panel, you can save it as a new Motion Preset. The new preset appears in the Custom Presets folder in the Motion Presets panel.

To save a custom tween as a preset, do this:

1. Select the tween span in the Timeline or the object on Stage to which the custom tween was applied.
2. In the Motion Presets panel, click the Save selection as preset button (See Figure 4.26). Or choose Save as Motion Preset from the context menu. A Save Preset As dialog box appears. Give the name of the Preset and then click OK button.
3. The new preset appears in the Motion Presets panel. Flash Professional CS6 saves the preset as an XML (eXtensible Markup Language) file.

To Import a motion preset, do this:

1. In the Motion Presets panel menu, click Import.
2. In the Open dialog box, navigate to the XML file you want to import and click Open.
3. Flash Professional CS6 opens the XML file and adds the motion preset to the panel.

To Export a motion preset, do this:

1. Select the preset from the Motion Presets panel.
2. Click Export from the Motion Presets panel menu.
3. In the Save As dialog box, choose a name and location for the XML file.
4. Click Save.

To delete a motion preset, do this:

1. Select the preset, which you want to delete from the Motion Presets Panel.
2. In the Motion Presets Panel, click the Remove item button (See Figure 4.26). Or choose Remove from the Panel menu.

✍ *When you remove a preset, Flash Professional CS6 deletes its XML file from disk. So be careful while deleting any preset and have a backup of preset you might want to use again later by exporting copy of it first.*

About Classic Tween Animation

Classic tween animation is an older way of creating animation in Flash. Classic tweens are similar to the motion tweens except that they are more complicated to create and less flexible. However, classic tweens do provide some types of control over animation that motion tweens do not.

✍ *With a classic tween, you can alter the ease value so that an object starts out fast, slows down, and then speeds up again.*

In classic tweening, the object moves in a straight line from the beginning location to the ending location on the Stage. There is no path displayed. You can draw a path, called a Motion Guide. A motion Guide can be used to alter the path of a classic tween animation. A motion Guide is drawn on the Motion Guide layer with the Classic Tween animation placed on its own layer beneath a Motion Guide layer.

✍ *You can link multiple layers to a Motion Guide layer to have multiple objects follow the same path. A normal layer that is linked to a Motion Guide layer becomes a Guided layer.*

Transformation Point

Each symbol has a transformation point in the form of a circle (O) that is used to orient the object when it is being animated. The transformation point is also the point that snaps to a Motion Guide. When attaching an object to a path, you can drag the transformation point to the path. The default position for a transformation point is the center of the object. You can reposition the transformation point to a different location on the object.

Registration Point

Symbols also have a registration point. The registration point determines the X- and Y- coordinates of an object on the Stage. The transformation and registration points can overlap—this is displayed as a plus sign within a circle ⊕.

✍ *If you apply a classic tween and then change the number of frames between the two keyframes, or move the group or symbol in either keyframe, Flash Professional CS6 automatically tweens the frames again.*

To create a classic tween animation, do this:

1. Click an empty keyframe in the layer where you want the animation to start.

2. Drag an instance of a symbol (in our case it is helicop1) from the Library panel and name the layer heli.
3. Click on a frame where you want the animation to end.
4. Then click Insert menu, select Timeline and then choose Keyframe and leave this keyframe selected.
5. Drag the object to a new position and modify its size and color if you want as shown in Figure 4.27.
6. Click any frame in the tween's frame span.

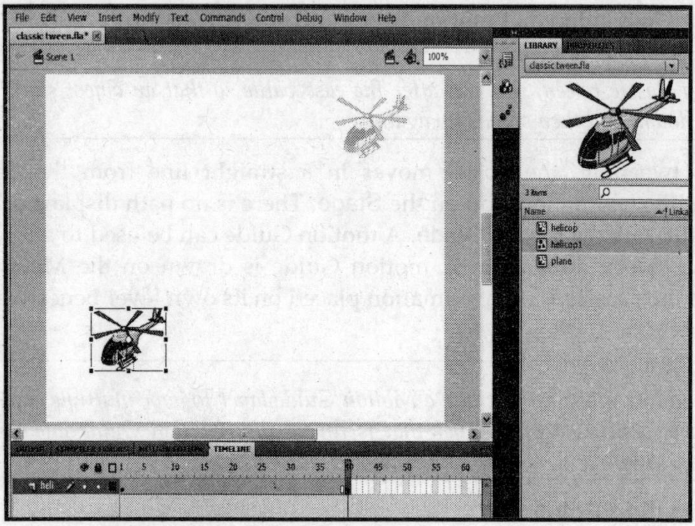

Figure 4.27 Dragging object into new location

7. Click Insert menu and then select Classic Tween. An arrow appears on the Timeline indicating that this is a classic tween as shown in Figure 4.28.
8. Play the movie.

To add a motion Guide and orient the object to the Guide in classic tweened animation, do this:

1. Create a classic-tweened animation sequence.
2. In the Properties Inspector, select Orient To Path check box, if you want that the tweened element orients to the motion path. Select Snap check box if you want that the tweened element snaps to the motion path.
3. Right click the layer name of that layer which contain classic tween and then choose Add Classic Motion Guide as shown in Figure 4.29. Flash Professional CS6 adds a Motion Guide layer above the Classic Tween layer and indents the name of Classic Tween layer below the Guide layer (See Figure 4.30).
4. Now click the frame 1 of the motion Guide layer.

Figure 4.28 Animation using Classic Tween

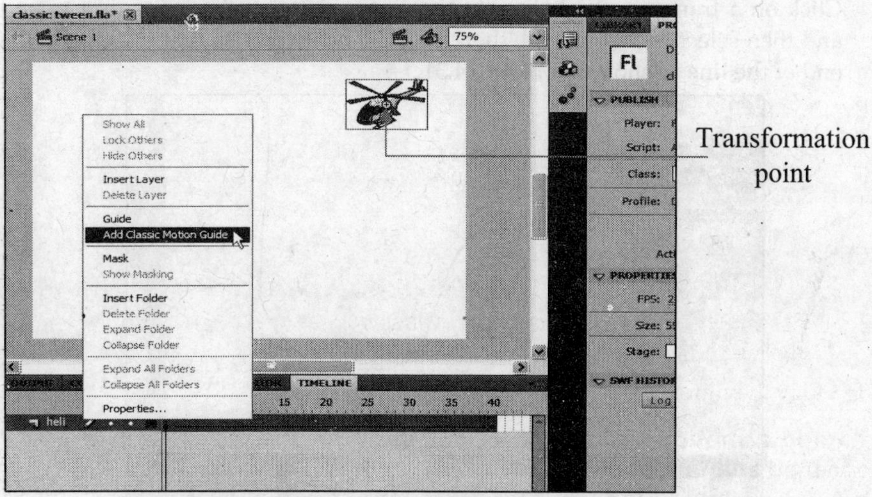

Figure 4.29 Add a motion Guide layer to the Classic Tween

If you already have a **Guide layer** *in the* **Timeline,** *you can drag a layer containing the* **Classic Tween** *below the* **Guide layer** *to convert the* **Guide layer** *to a* **motion Guide** *and bind the Classic Tween to it.*

---

5. Click **Pen, Pencil, Line, Circle, Rectangle** or **Brush Tool** to draw the desired path.
6. Point to the middle of the instance or object (in our case it is helicopter), then draw a line as shown in Figure 4.30.

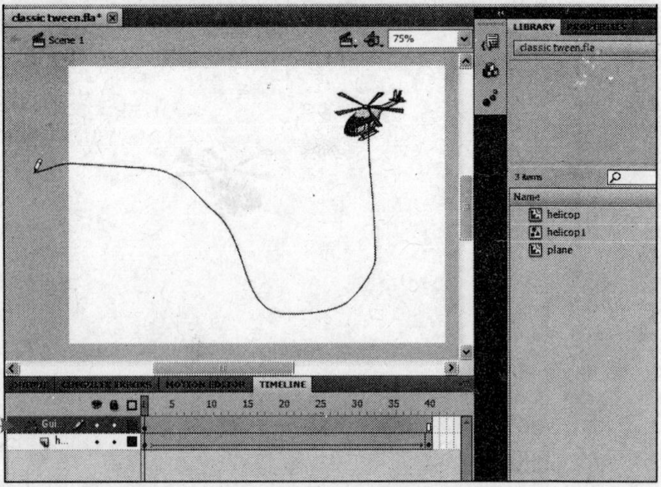

Motion Guide layer

Figure 4.30 Motion Guide layer above the layer containing the Classic Tween

7. Click on a frame on the helico layer where you want the animation to end and then select Selection tool, then drag the helicopter so that it snaps to the end of the line as shown in Figure 4.31.

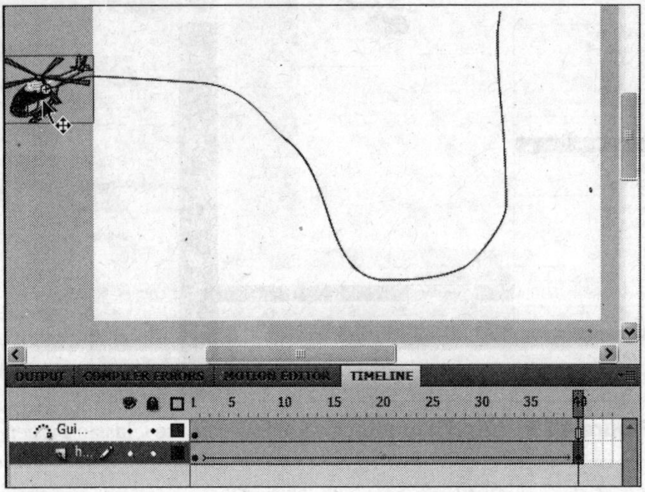

Figure 4.31 Object snapped to the end of the Guide stroke

8. To hide the motion Guide layer and the path so that only the object's movement is visible while you work, click in the Eye column on the motion Guide layer (See Figure 4.32).
9. The instance or object (helicopter) follows the motion path when you play the animation.

Figure 4.32 Playing Classic Tween along with path

Shape Tweening

Shape tweening is a technique for interpolating amorphous changes between shapes in different keyframes. Flash Professional CS6 can tween the location, size, color, and opacity of shapes. To apply Shape tweening to groups, instances, or bitmap images, you must first break these elements apart. For Shape tweening, you have to draw a shape at one point in time, and then change that shape or draw another shape at another point in time. Flash Professional CS6 interpolates the values or shapes for the frames in between, creating the animation.

With Shape tweening, you can create an effect similar to morphing, making one shape appears to change into another shape over time.

You can apply Shape tweening to more than one object at a time as long as all the objects are on the same layer. With the use of Shape tweening, you can move an object in a straight line, but other options, such as rotating an object, are not available in Shape tweening.

Creating a Shape Tween Animation

To create an animation using Shape tweening, we shall convert the shape of square into an Oval.

To create a Shape tweening animation, do this:

1. Open a new Flash document.
2. Draw a square at frame 1. (See Figure 4.33)
3. On the same layer, right-click on frame 30 and choose Insert Blank Keyframe from the context menu as shown in Figure 4.33.

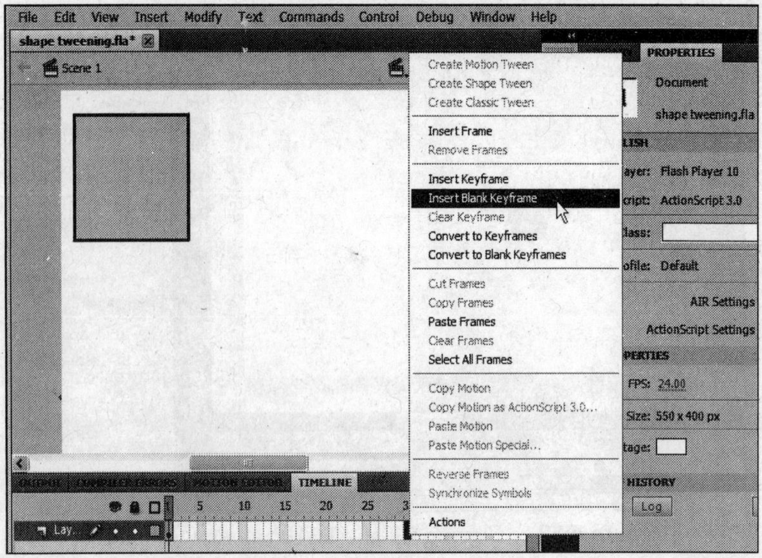

Figure 4.33 Inserting Blank Keyframe

4. In frame 30, draw an oval using Oval tool. Now you have a keyframe in frame 1 with a square and a keyframe in frame 30 with an Oval.
5. Click anywhere on the same layer between frames 1 and 30.
6. Click the Insert menu and then click Shape Tween.
7. Flash interpolates the shapes in all the frames between the two keyframes. The entire frame sequence between the starting and the ending frame will be turned green and an arrow will appear in the Timeline (See Figure 4.34).

Figure 4.34 Interpolating the shape

8. To add easing to the tween, select one of the frames between the two keyframes and enter a value in the Ease: field in the Properties Inspector (See Figure 4.34).
9. Enter a negative value to ease the beginning of the tween. Enter a positive value to ease the end of the tween.
10. Save and Test your movie to view your first shape tween animation. Press Enter key, you can see the view in the Stage.

Shape Hints

Shape hints are used to control more complex or improbable shape changes. It can change the shape's transition appearance during an animation. Shape hints allow you to specify a location on the beginning object that corresponds to a location on the ending object. Shape hints contain letters (a through z) for identifying which points correspond in the starting and ending shapes (See Figure 4.35). You can use up to 26 shape hints.

Shape hints are yellow in a starting keyframe as shown in Figure 4.35, green in an ending keyframe as shown in Figure 4.36, and red when not on a curve.

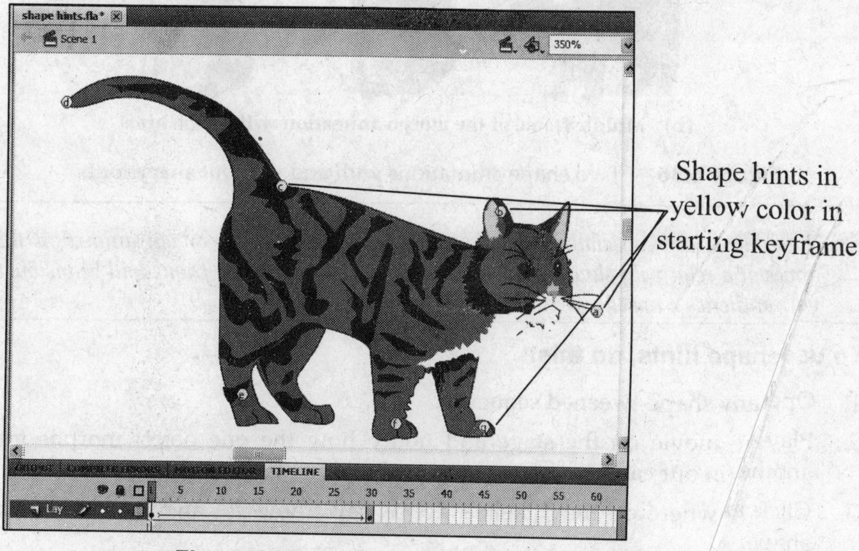

Figure 4.35 Shape hints in starting keyframe

Make sure that shape hints are logical. For example, if you are using three shape hints for a triangle, they must be in the same order on the original triangle and on the triangle to be tweened. The order cannot be *abc* in the first keyframe and *acb* in the second and Shape hints work best if you place them in counterclockwise order beginning at the top-left corner of the shape.

Figure 4.36 shows two shape animations of the same objects, one using shape hints and the other not using shape hints. Figure 4.36 also shows how the object being reshaped appears in one of the in-between frames. Notice that with the shape hints, the object in the in-between frame is more recognizable.

(a) Middle frame of the morph animation without shape hints

(b) Middle frame of the morph animation with shape hints

Figure 4.36 Two shape animations with and without shape hints

---

Shape hints are especially valuable when you are working on an animation that moves at a relatively slow frame rate, i.e., when each separate frame will be visible to your audience's naked eye.

To use shape hints, do this:

1. Open any shape-tweened sequence.
2. Play the movie on the stage and notice how the one object morphs into another (in our case first object is cat and another is the girl).
3. Click anywhere on the Timeline (let us say frame 25) and then notice the shape.
4. Now click the frame 1 on the same layer to display the first object.
5. Make sure the object is selected. Click the Modify menu, choose Shape and then select Add Shape Hint. Or *alternatively* press Ctrl + Shift + H keys together to add shape hint (See Figure 4.37). The beginning shape hint appears as circle with the letter a somewhere on the shape (See Figure 4.35).

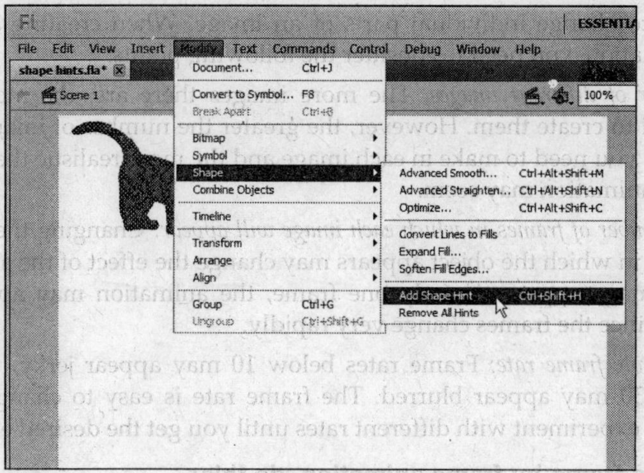

Figure 4.37 Modify menu with Add Shape Hint option selected

6. Drag the shape hint to a point to mark.
7. Repeat Steps 5 and 6 to add additional shape hints. New hints appear with the letters that follow (b, c, and so on).
8. Now click the last keyframe in the tweening sequence. The ending shape hints are stacked on top of each other.
9. Drag the shape hint to the point in the ending shape that should correspond to the first point you marked.
10. Now again click on the same frame, i.e., frame 25 of the Timeline then notice how the object is more recognizable now that the shape hints have been added.
11. To view how the shape hints change the shape tweening, play the animation again. To fine-tune the tweening, move the shape hints.

To view all shape hints, do this:

1. Click View menu then select Show Shape Hints. The Layer and Keyframe that contain shape hints will be active showing shape hints.

To remove a shape hint, do this:

1. Drag it off the Stage.

To remove all shape hints, do this:

1. Click Modify menu, choose Shape and then select Remove All Hints.

Understanding Frame-by-Frame Animation

A frame-by-frame animation is created by specifying the object that is to be appeared in each frame of a sequence of frames. This animation is useful when you want to change individual parts of an image. When creating a frame-by-frame animation, you need to consider the following points:

1. *Number of different images:* The more images there are, the more effort is needed to create them. However, the greater the number of images, the less change you need to make in each image and the more realistic the movement in the animation may seem.
2. *The number of frames in which each image will appear:* Changing the number of frames in which the object appears may change the effect of the animation. If each image appears in only one frame, the animation may appear rather jerky, since the frames change very rapidly.
3. *The movie frame rate:* Frame rates below 10 may appear jerky, while those above 30 may appear blurred. The frame rate is easy to change, and you should experiment with different rates until you get the desired effect.

To create a frame-by-frame animation, do this:

1. Click a layer name and then select the frame on the layer where you want the animation to begin.
2. Click Insert menu, select Timeline and then choose Keyframe to insert a keyframe, and then place the object on the Stage by using the drawing tools. Paste graphics from the Clipboard, or import a file (See Figure 4.38).
3. Next, select the frame where you want the change to be occurred. Insert a keyframe and then change the object. You can also add a new object in place of the original one (See Figure 4.39).
4. To complete your frame-by-frame animation sequence, repeat Step 3 until you have built the desired motion.

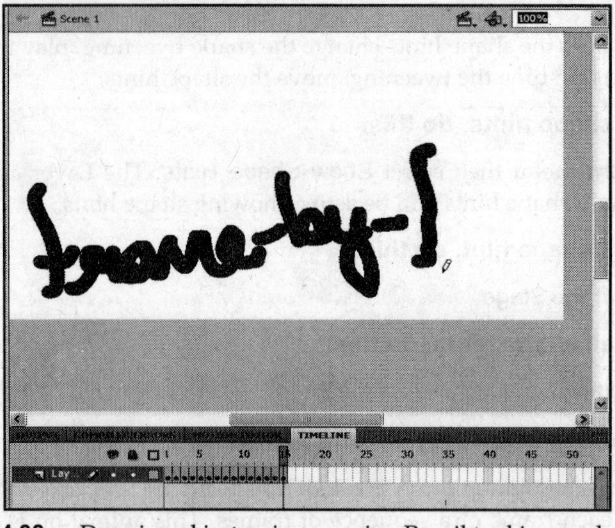

Figure 4.38 Drawing object or image using Pencil tool in new keyframe

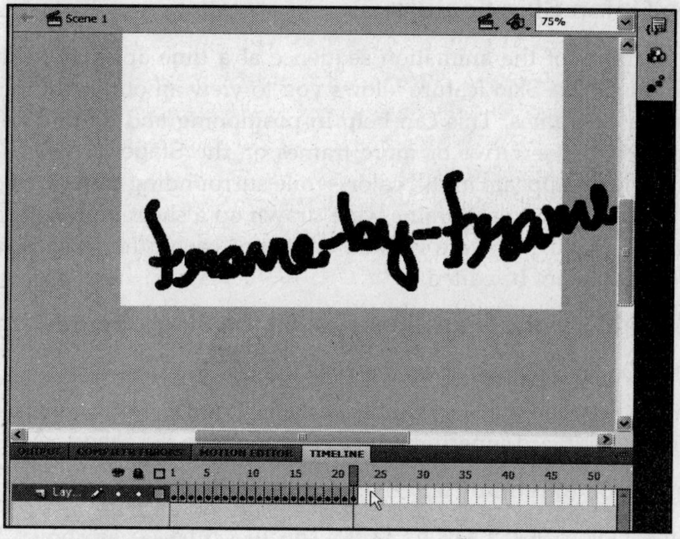

Figure 4.39 Completing frame-by-frame sequence

5. To test the animation sequence, click Control menu and then choose Play option as shown in Figure 4.40.

When you create frame-by-frame animation, every frame is a keyframe.

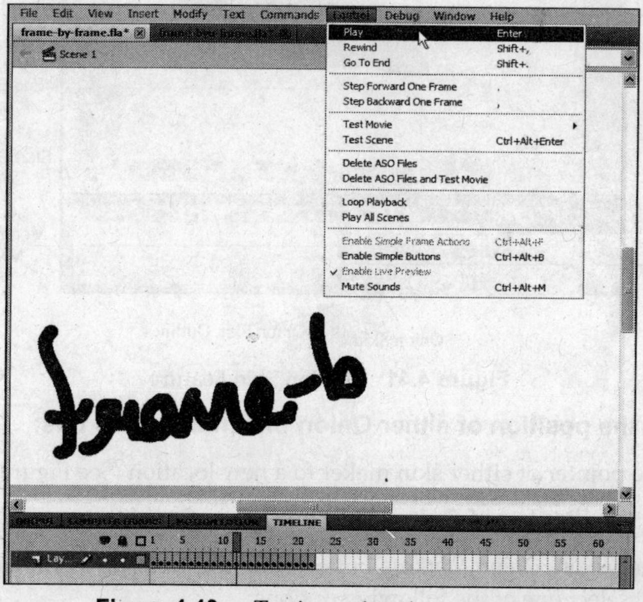

Figure 4.40 Testing animation sequence

Using the Onion Skin Feature

Usually, one frame of the animation sequence at a time appears on the Stage. Turning on the Onion Skin feature allows you to view an outline of the object(s) in any number of frames. This can help in positioning and editing a frame-by-frame animation or view two or more frames on the Stage at once. The frame under the playhead appears in full color, while surrounding frames are dimmed, making it to appear as if each frame were drawn on a sheet of translucent onion skin paper and the sheets were stacked on top of each other (See Figure 4.41). Dimmed frames cannot be edited.

To view several frames of an animation on the Stage, do this:

1. Click the Onion Skin button on the Timeline (See Figure 4.41).
2. All frames between the Start Onion Skin and End Onion Skin markers (in the Timeline header) are superimposed as one frame in the Stage.

To display onion skinned frames as outlines, do this:

1. Click the Onion Skin Outlines button on the Timeline as shown in Figure 4.41.

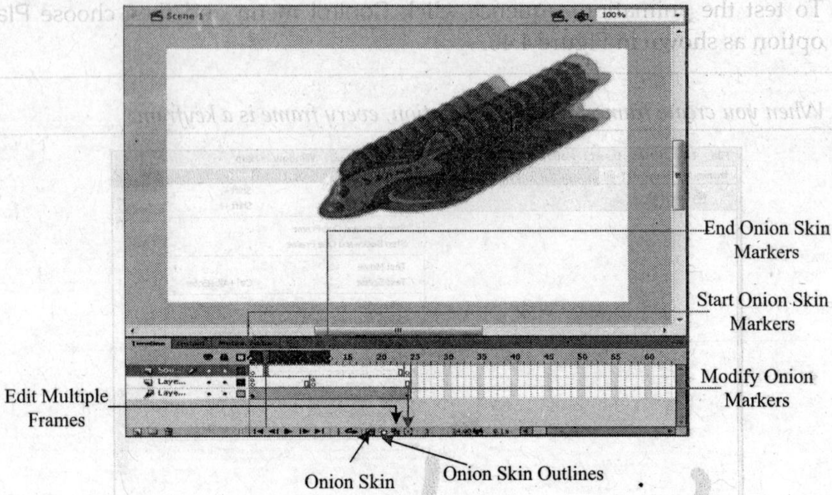

Figure 4.41 Onion Skin Feature

To change the position of either Onion Skin marker, do this:

1. Drag the pointer of either skin maker to a new location (See Figure 4.41).

To change the display of Onion Skin markers, do this:

1. Click the Modify Onion Markers button from the Timeline as shown in Figure 4.41 and select one of the following options:

Always Show Markers: To display the onion skin markers in the Timeline header whether or not onion skinning is on.

Anchor Markers: To lock the Onion Skin markers to their current position in the Timeline header.

Marker Range 2: To display two frames on either side of the current frame.

Marker Range 5: To display five frames on either side of the current frame.

Marker Range All: To display all frames on either side of the current frame.

Mask Layers to Creating a Mask Effect

Masking is a way of selectively hiding and revealing selected areas of artwork on your Stage using a Mask layer and a chosen shape.

For spotlight effects and transitions, we can use a mask layer to create a hole through which the contents of one or more underlying layers are visible. A mask item can be a filled shape, a type object, an instance of a graphic symbol, or a movie clip.

We can think mask as a stencil. For concise letters, we lay the stencil on top of a piece of paper and paint in the holes. The stencil protects the underlying paper except where the holes are. When we peel off the stencil, we can see nice neat painted letter. This same work is done by mask in Flash. It screens off the underlying layer so that we can see only the part where the holes are.

A mask layer allows you to cover up the objects on one or more layers and, at the same time, it creates a window through which you can view objects on those layer(s).

You need at least two layers on the Timeline when you are working with a Mask layer. One layer, called the Mask layer, contains the window object through which you view the objects, which are on a second layer below the Mask layer. The second layer, called the Masked layer, contains the object(s) that are viewed through the window.

To enable a masking effect, both the Mask layer and the layer being masked must be locked.

To create Mask layer, do this:

1. Create a layer that will be visible through the holes in the mask. (In this case, we types text "**Spotlight Effects and Transitions**") and name this layer as Masked.
2. Then click the Insert menu, select Timeline and then choose Layer to create a new layer above it and name this layer as **Mask**.
3. Draw any filled shape (In this case, we draw a circle) as shown in Figure 4.42. Because any filled shape will be completely transparent in the mask. But if you draw any non-filled area, it will be opaque.

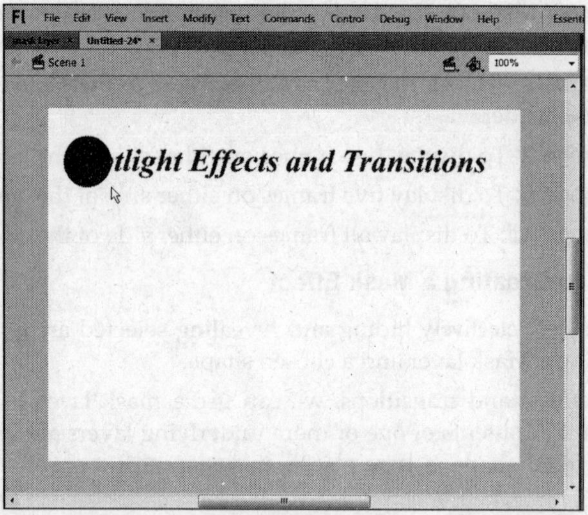

Figure 4.42 Drawing Circle to be used as the window on a Mask layer

4. Then select the circle with Selection tool.
5. Then right click the first frame of the **Mask** layer on the Timeline and then choose Create Motion Tween (See Figure 4.43). Click OK to convert the circle into a symbol so that it can be tweened.

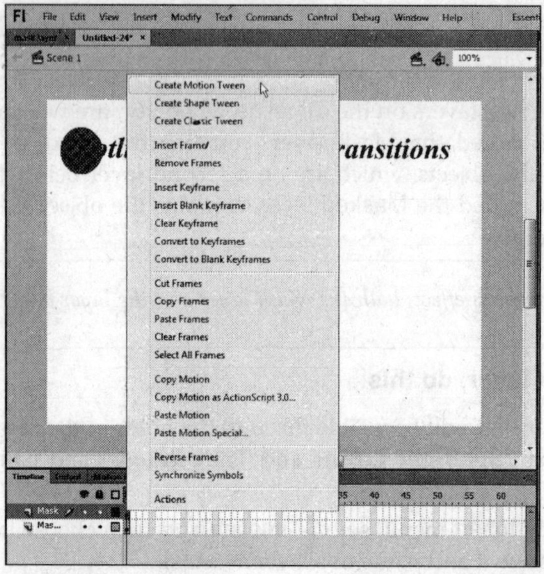

Figure 4.43 Displaying Create Motion tween option

6. Drag the tween span in the Timeline to extend the span to frame 50 on the **Mask** layer, and then drag the circle to the right side of the Stage as shown

in Figure 4.44. A motion path appears on the Stage with dots indicating the position of the circle for each frame (See Figure 4.44).

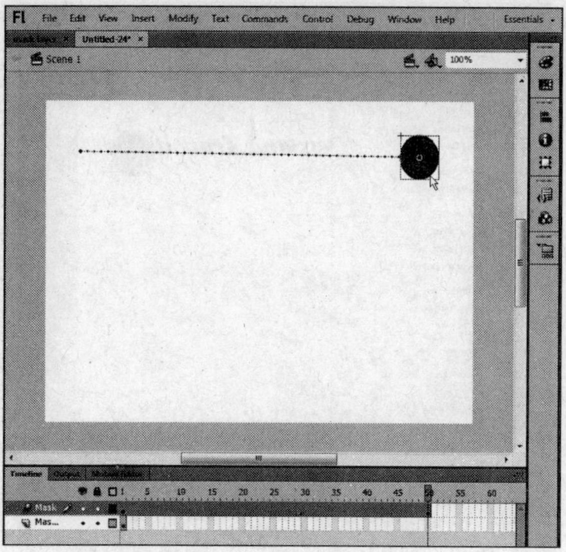

Figure 4.44 Repositioning the Circle

7. Right click the first frame of the **Masked** layer on the Timeline and then choose Create Motion Tween as shown in Figure 4.45, and drag the tween span in the Timeline to extend the span to frame 50.

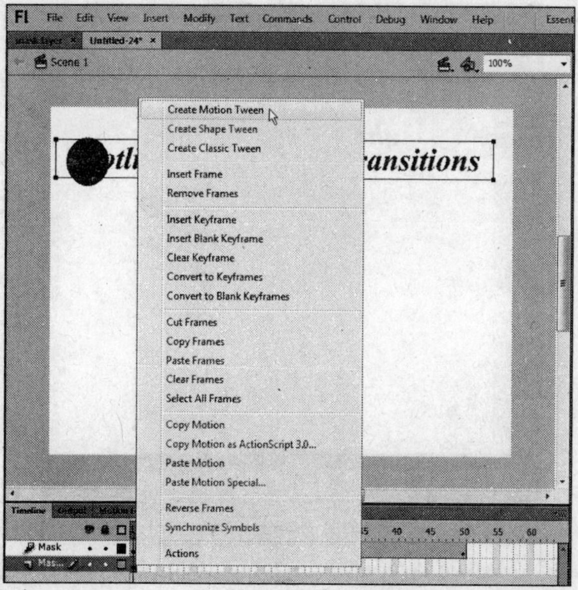

Figure 4.45 Creating Motion Tween in Masked layer

8. Then Right-click on the **Mask** layer and then choose Mask from the context menu (See Figure 4.46).

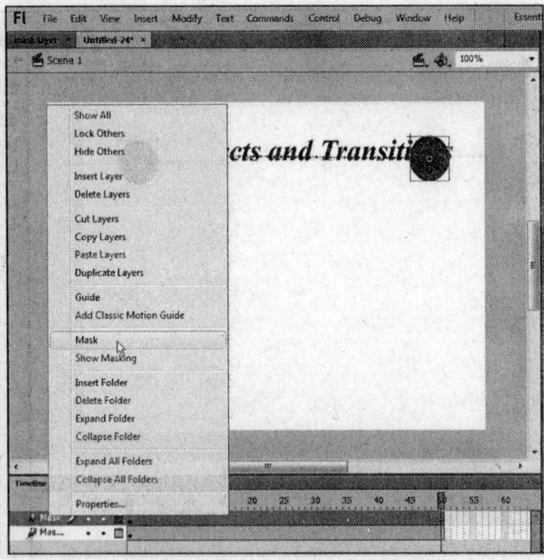

Figure 4.46 Creating Mask layer

9. The selected layer is converted to a mask layer, indicated by a down arrow icon as shown in Figure 4.47. The layer immediately below it, is linked to the mask layer. The Masked layer's icon changes to a right-pointing arrow.

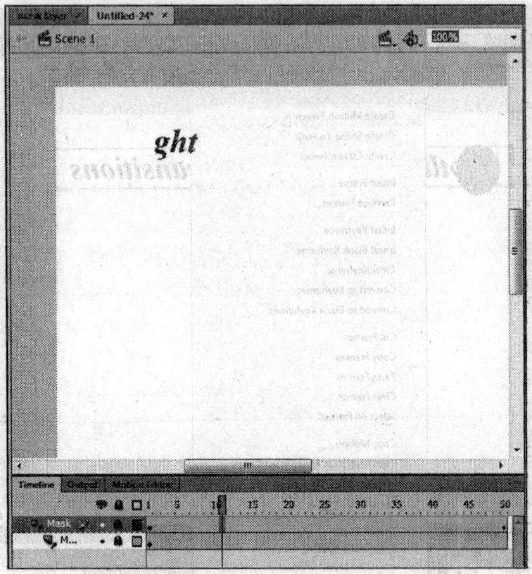

Figure 4.47 Masked layer after applying Mask; you only see what appears through the window

10. To display the Mask effect in Flash, lock the Mask layer and the Masked layer (if this will not automatically lock) then test it. Screen with locked mask and masked layer is shown in Figure 4.47.

A mask layer always masks the layer immediately below it, so be sure to create the mask layer in the proper place.

To mask additional layers after creating a mask layer, do this:

1. Create a new layer.
2. Drag layer directly below the mask layer.
3. Then right-click on the newly created layer, select Properties and then choose Masked option from the Layer Properties dialog box.

About Inverse Kinematics

When you want to animate an articulated object (one that has multiple joints), such as a walking person, Flash Professional CS6 makes it easy with inverse kinematics.

Inverse Kinematics (IK) is an easy way to animate objects using bones chained into linear or branched armatures in parent-child relationships. When one bone moves, connected bones move in relation to it. For example, if you draw an image of a person, create the bone structure, and then move the person's right foot, then all parts of the leg (lower leg, knee, upper leg) respond. This makes it easy to animate various movements.

Inverse kinematics lets you easily create natural motion. To animate using inverse kinematics, you simply specify the start and end positions of bones on the Timeline. Flash automatically interpolates the positions of the bones in the armature between the starting and ending frames.

Inverse kinematics makes animating easy because you do not have to worry about animating each segment of an object or limb of a character. You just focus on the overall poses.

You can use Flash's Inverse Kinematics (IK) bones in two ways:

1. **By using a shape as a container for multiple bones:** You can use bones with shapes. In the past, to squirm and slither snake, you would have had to reposition, distort, or even redraw several versions of the snake to make a good animation. But, now you can add bones to a drawing of a snake so that it slithers realistically.
2. **By chaining symbol instances:** When you use bones with symbols, you link one symbol to another. For example, you can link movie clips showing a torso, arm, lower arm, and hand so that they move realistically in relation to each other. Each instance has only one bone.

Bone Styles

There are three styles that Flash can draw bones on the Stage.

To set the Bone Style, do this:

1. Select the IK span in the Timeline (See Figure 4.48).
2. In Properties panel, select one of the following styles from the Style menu in the Options section:

   Solid: This is the default style.

   Wired: It is useful when the solid style hides too much of the artwork beneath the bone.

   Line: It is basically useful for smaller armatures.

   None: No style for bone.

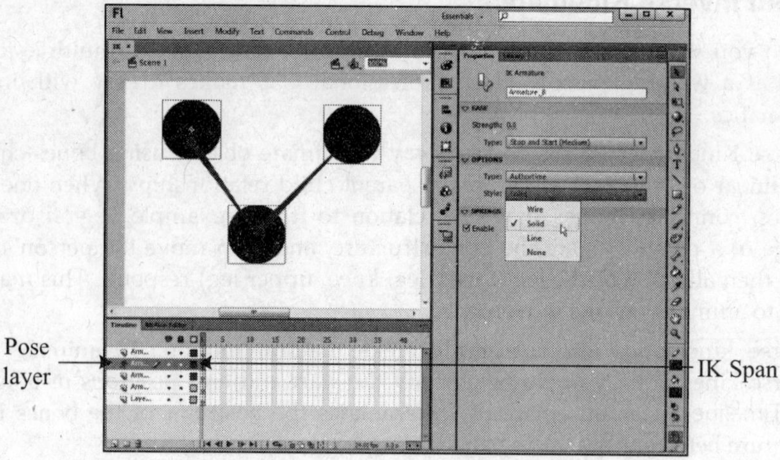

Figure 4.48 Different Bone Styles in Properties panel

Pose Layers

When you add bones to symbol instances or shapes, Flash creates a new layer for them in the Timeline. This new layer is called the *pose layer*. It is similar to a Motion Tween Layer, but with a couple of twists to make it work with bones. Flash adds the pose layer to the Timeline between existing layers to maintain the previous stacking order of objects on the Stage.

Each pose layer can contain only one armature and its associated instances or shape.

Add Bones to Symbols

You can add IK bones to movie clip, graphic, and button instances. To use text, convert it to a symbol first. The symbol instances can be on different layers before you add bones. Flash adds them to the Pose layer.

To create an IK armature linking a series of symbols instances, do this:

1. Place a series of symbol instances on the Stage as you want (See Figure 4.49).

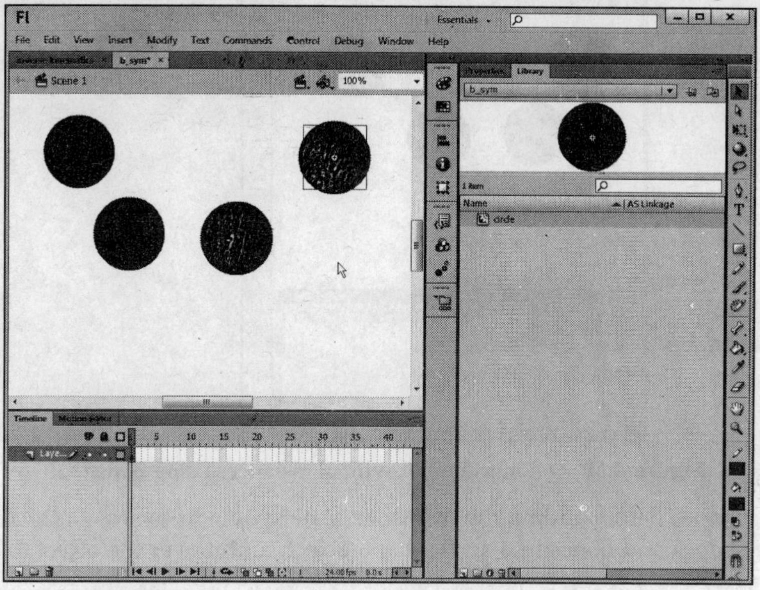

Figure 4.49 Placing series of symbols on the Stage

2. Click the Bone tool from the Tools panel.
3. Then click on the symbol instance that you want to start your bone chain.
4. Drag to another symbol instance and release the mouse button at the point where you want to attach it.
5. To add another bone to the armature, drag from the tail of the first bone to the next symbol instance.
6. To create a branched armature, click the head of an existing bone where you want the branch to begin. Then drag to create the first bone of the new branch. Continue clicking and adding sequential bones to create a series of joined symbol instances. Figure 4.50 shows a bone chain created to connect the symbol instances into an IK armature.
7. After you create an armature, you can still add new instances from different layers to the armature. Drag a new bone to the new instance and Flash moves the instance to the Pose layer of the armature.

Add Bones to Shapes

You can also add bones to a single shape or to a group of shapes that are on the same layer. This is very useful for animating objects without obvious joints and segments but can still have an articulated motion. In either case, you must select

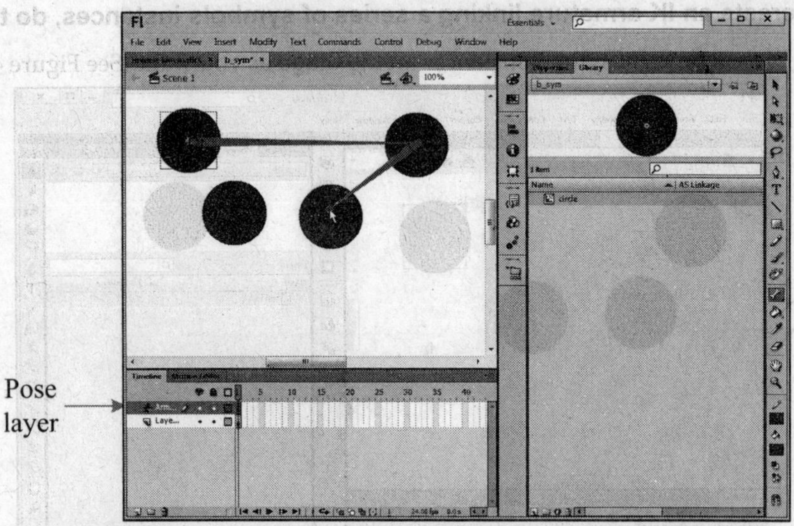

Figure 4.50 Connection of symbol instances using Bone tool

all the shapes before adding the first bone. After you add bones, Flash converts all the shapes and bones into an IK shape object, and moves the object to a new pose layer.

To add bones to shapes, do this:

1. Create a filled shape or shapes on the Stage.
2. Select the entire shape on the Stage (See Figure 4.51).
3. Select the Bone tool from the Tools panel.

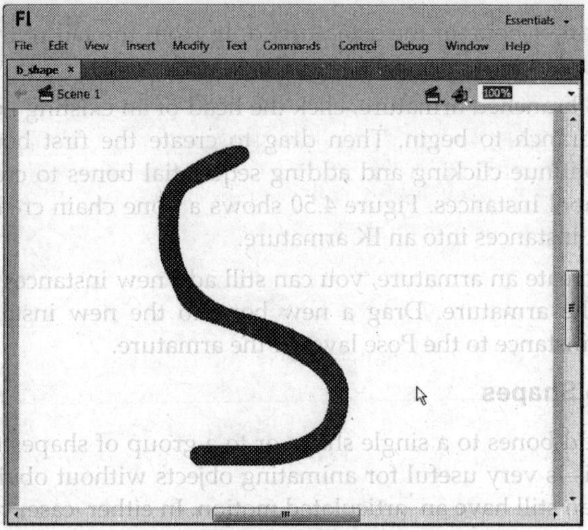

Figure 4.51 Selecting the shape

4. With the **Bone tool**, click inside the shape and drag to another location within the shape (See Figure 4.52).

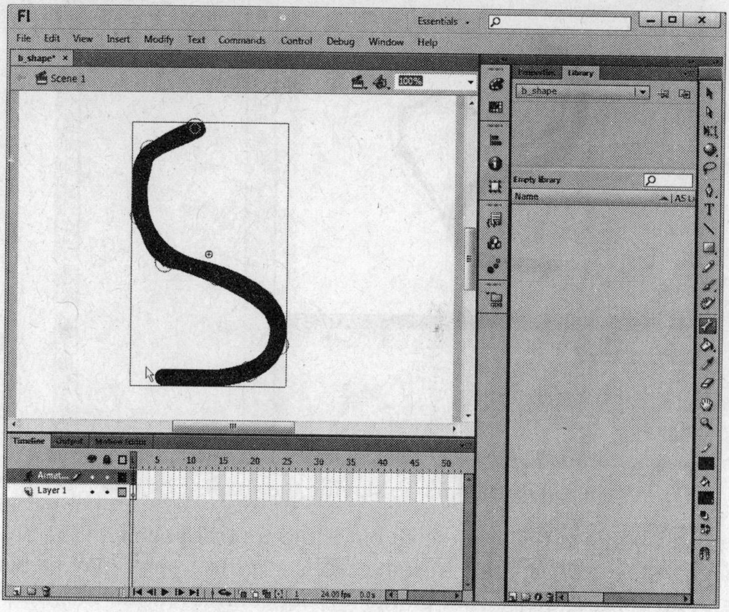

Figure 4.52 Defining bones inside the shape

5. To add another bone, drag from the tail of the first bone to another location in within the shape.
6. To create a branched armature, click the head of an existing bone where you want the branch to begin. Then drag to create the first bone of the new branch.
7. To move the armature, select the IK shape object with the **Selection tool** and then drag any of the bones to move them (See Figure 4.53).

You can easily remove bones or add more bones to your armature. Choose the Selection tool and click on the bone you want to delete. Press the Delete key to remove the selected bone; all the child bones will be removed as well.

Refining Shape Behavior with the Bind Tool

When you place bones inside shapes, Flash automatically creates control points around the outline of the shape as shown in Figure 4.52. The control points establish the perimeter of the shape as you create different poses. Some shapes, especially more complex and branched shapes, can get twisted in unexpected ways. You can solve the problem by repositioning the control points. With the **Subselection tool**, click the boundary of the shape. The control points and the edge of the shape appear highlighted. Then just drag the control points to adjust the shape.

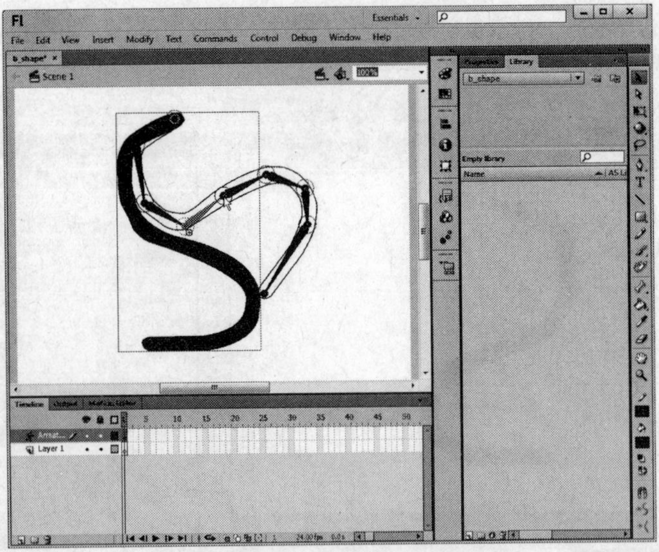

Figure 4.53 Moving the shape

When you add bones to a shape, Flash binds the control points on the perimeter of the shape to the nearest bone. In some cases, a control point may be bound to more than one bone. If the control points are not configured the way you would like, you can edit the connections between the bones and their control points with the Bind tool. This tool is hidden under the Bone tool. The Bind tool displays which control points are connected to which bones and let you break those connections and make new ones (See Figure 4.54).

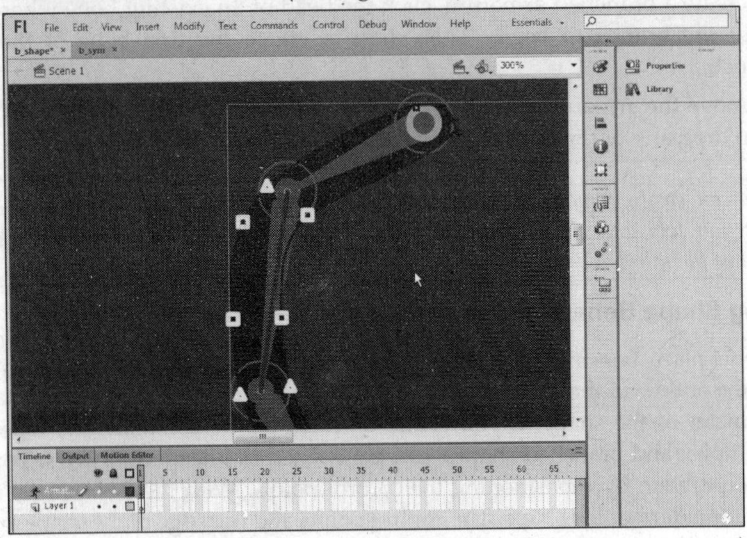

Figure 4.54 Various Control Points

To redefine which control points are connected to the selected bone, do the following:

- View control points bound to a bone: Choose the Bind tool and click on any bone in the shape. The selected bone is highlighted in red, and all the connected control points on the shape are highlighted in yellow.
- View bones bound to a control point: Choose the Bind tool in the Tools panel, and Flash displays the bones and control points in the armature. *Square control points* are bound to a single bone. *Triangular control points* are bound to more than one bone. Click a control point, and it shows a red highlight. Bones bound to the control point are highlighted in yellow.
- Bind a control point to a bone: Click a bone with the Bind tool. The control points bound to the bone appear highlighted in yellow. With the Bind tool, Shift + click a control point that does not show a yellow highlight, and Flash binds it to the selected bone.
- Remove (unbind) control points from a bone: Click a bone with the Bind tool. Ctrl + click a control point that is highlighted in yellow. The control point changes from yellow to blue, indicating that it is no longer bound to the selected bone.
- Bind a bone to a control point: Select a control point with the Bind tool, and then drag to the bone you want to bind to.
- Remove (unbind) a bone from a control point: Select a control point with the Bind tool, and then drag away from the shape to unbind the control point.

Pinning IK Bones

Flash Professional CS6 has introduced new time-saving feature for IK Bones called *pinning*. This feature lets you control the rotation or position of your armature more precisely, leaving the child nodes free to move in a different pose.

Pinning fixes the tail of any bone in place but lets the bone rotate around the spot. The pin feature works like a toggle, so you can turn it off with the same steps. Tail joints that are pinned show a big X over the joint as shown in Figure 4.55. You can pin more than one tail joint in the armature.

To pin the tail of a bone to the stage, do this:

1. With the Selection tool click the bone whose tail you want to fix or lock.
2. In the Properties Inspector, check the Pin option (See Figure 4.55).
3. The tail, or end of the selected node, is fixed to the Stage in the current reposition. An "X" appears on the joint to indicate that it is pinned (See Figure 4.56).
4. When you pin a node, the pinned node remains fixed, but you are free to move all the child nodes.

You can also select a node and click on its tail when the icon of a pushpin appears as your cursor. That selected node will be pinned. Click again to unpin the node.

Figure 4.55 Selecting Pin option

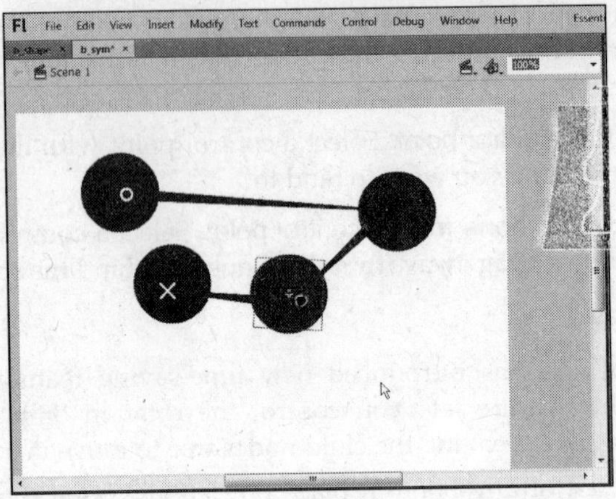

Figure 4.56 'X' mark is visible on the tail of the selected node

Animating an IK Armature

After creating the bone structure, a layer named Armature is added to the Timeline, and the image with the bone structure is placed in frame 1 on that layer (See Figure 4.50). This new layer is called a *Pose layer*. Each Pose layer can contain only one armature and its associated image.

You can animate IK armatures differently from other objects in Flash. With armatures, you simply add frames to the Pose layer and reposition the armature on the Stage to create a keyframe. Keyframes in Pose layers are called *poses*. Because IK armatures are typically used for animation purposes, each Pose layer acts as a Tween layer automatically.

Once you specify the start and end positions of the image, Flash interpolates the position of the parts of the image for the in-between frames. So, when one bone moves, the other connected bones move in relation to it.

To animate an IK armature in the Timeline, do this:

1. In the Timeline, if needed, add frames to the Pose layer of the armature to make room for the animation you want to create.

   To add a pose to a frame in the pose layer, right-click the Pose layer and then choose Insert Pose (See Figure 4.57). Or *alternatively*, place the playhead in the frame where you want to add the pose and then press F6 key. Flash inserts a pose into the pose layer in the current frame. A diamond-shaped pose marker in the frame indicates the new pose (See Figure 4.57).
2. With the help of the Selection tool, make the changes (by dragging) to the position of the armature (See Figure 4.58).
3. Add additional poses as described in Step 2 in separate frames to complete the animation according to your need.
4. Preview your animation.

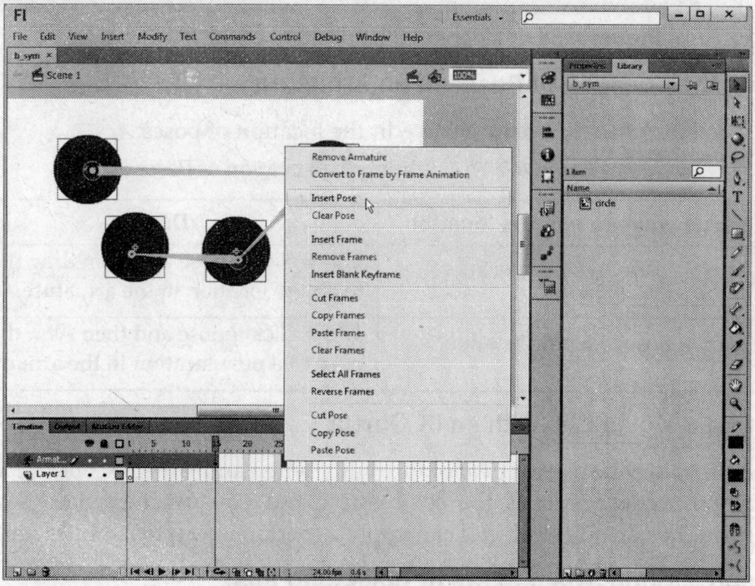

Figure 4.57 Inserting Pose

You can also change the length of the animation in the Timeline. To do this, hover the mouse cursor over the last frame of the armature until the Resize cursor appears. Then drag the last frame of the Pose layer to the right or left to add or remove frames.

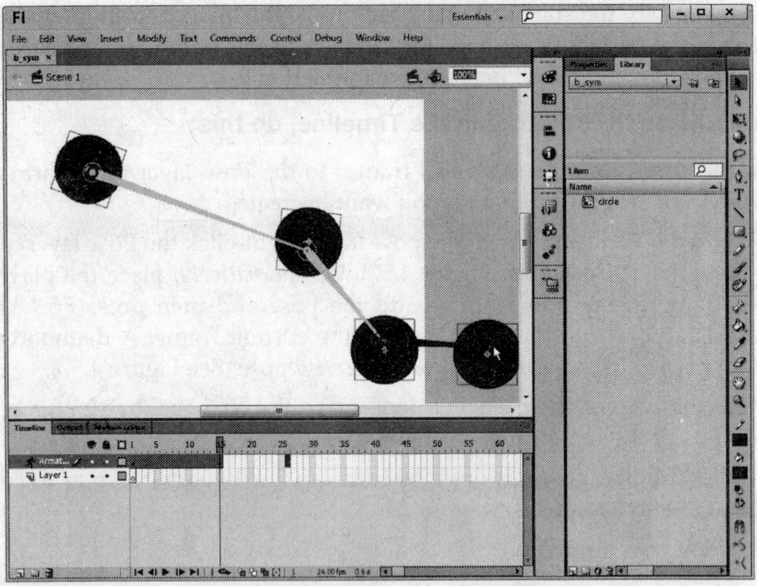

Figure 4.58 Changing the position of the IK armature

Editing the Location of Poses in an Armature

Table 4.3 shows the various ways to edit the location of poses.

Table 4.3 Editing the Location of Poses

Various ways to edit the location	Do this
To move a pose to a new location	Ctrl + click a pose and then drag the pose to a new location in the armature.
To copy a pose to a new location	Ctrl + click a pose and then Alt + drag the pose to a new location in the armature.

Creating a Movie Clip with an IK Object

Movie clips provide a great deal of flexibility when animating IK objects. You can change properties, such as the color effect and you can nest one movie clip within another. In addition, you can apply a motion tween to a movie clip.

To apply motion tween to the IK object, do this:

1. Select the IK armature and all of its associated objects by clicking on the pose layer in the Timeline or drag a selection marquee around all of the linked symbols on the Stage.
2. Right-click the selection and choose Convert to Symbol... from the context menu (See Figure 4.59).

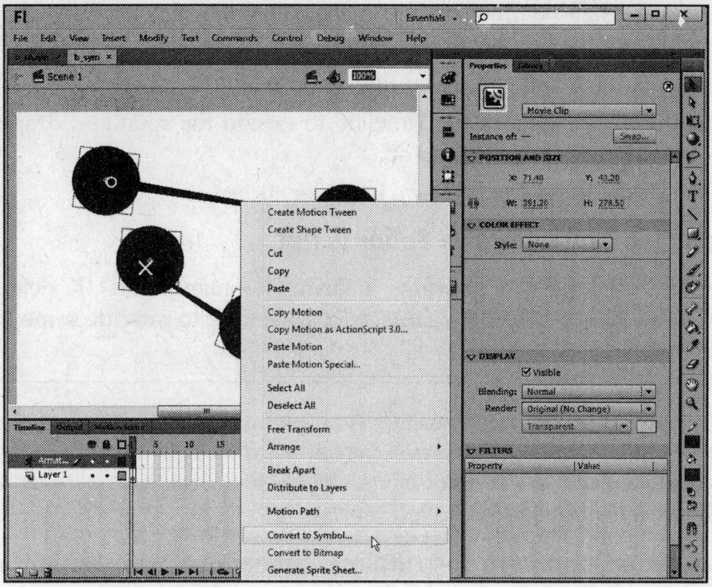

Figure 4.59 Convert an IK armature to symbol

3. In the Convert to Symbol dialog box, enter a name for the symbol and choose either Movie Clip or Graphic from the Type menu. Click OK.
4. Flash creates a symbol with its own Timeline containing the Pose layer for the armature (See Figure 4.60).

Pose layer for armature

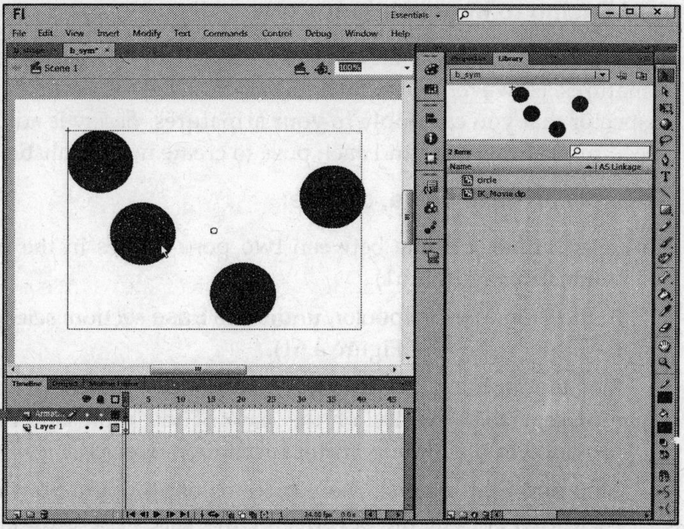

Figure 4.60 Symbol containing the Pose layer for an armature

5. To use the new symbol on the main Timeline of your FLA file, drag the symbol from the Library to the Stage.
6. Now click the Insert menu and then choose Motion Tween.
7. Drag the tween span in the Timeline to extend the span and drag the object down or up wherever you want.
8. Then test the movie by pressing Enter key.

Animating an Armature with ActionScript

Runtime feature of Flash provides a facility to manipulate IK object. This is useful when you are creating a game or just wanting to provide some interaction on a Website.

Runtime feature only works with IK structures connected to drawn shapes or movie clip symbols. It will not work with graphic or button symbols. Only armatures with a single pose can be controlled with ActionScript. Armatures with more than one pose can only be controlled in the Timeline.

To prepare an armature for runtime animations with ActionScript, do this:

1. With the Selection tool, select a frame in a Pose layer containing an armature.
2. In the Properties Inspector, under the Options section, choose Runtime from the Type menu.

Add Easing to IK animation

The Motion Editor and its sophisticated controls for easing cannot be used with armatures. However, there are a few standard eases available from the Properties Inspector that you can apply to your armatures. *Easing* is adjusting the animation speed in the frames around each pose to create more realistic motion.

To apply an ease value, do this:

1. Select either a frame between two pose frames in the pose layer or a pose frame (See Figure 4.61).
2. In the Properties Inspector, under the Ease section, select a type of ease from the Type menu (See Figure 4.61).

   Simple eases: The variations of Simple eases (from Slow to Fastest) represent the severity of the ease. They represent the same curvatures provided in the Motion Editor for motion tweens.

   Stop and Start eases: The variations of Stop and Start eases (from Slow to Fastest) represent the severity of the ease. The Stop and Start eases have curves on both ends of the motion, so the easing values affect the start of the motion and the end of the motion.

3. Enter a value for the Strength of the ease in **Strength:** box or move the slider (See Figure 4.61). The **Strength:** represents the direction of the ease. A negative value is an ease-in and a positive value is an ease-out.

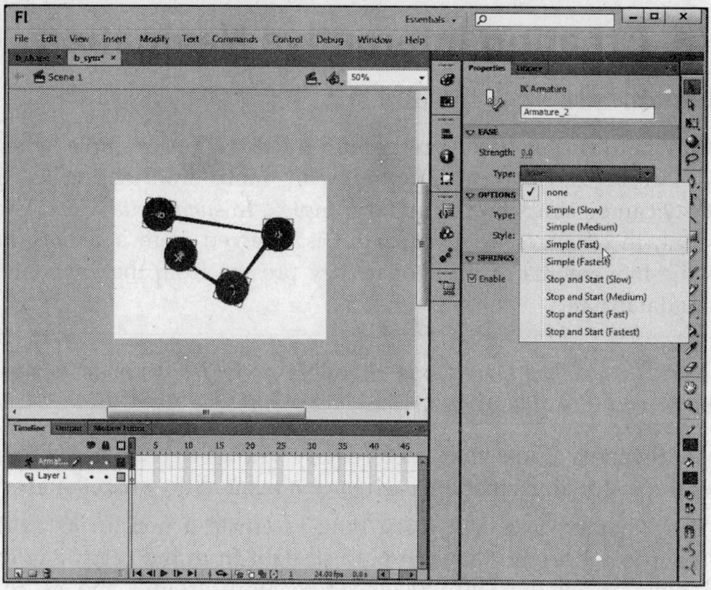

Figure 4.61 Ease Section in the Properties Inspector

4. When you finish, preview the eased motion on the **Stage**. Scrub the playhead in the **Timeline** between the two pose frames where you applied the ease.

CHAPTER 5

Creating Interactive Navigation

Introduction

Interactivity in movies is based on the user's actions. For example, when the user clicks a button, a different graphic with more information is displayed. Interactivity can be simple or it can be complex. In *simple interactive*, user clicks a button. But, in *complex interactive*, input is received from a variety of sources, such as the movements of the mouse, key presses from the keyboard, or even data from databases.

In Flash Professional CS6, Code Snippets panel *lets you add* ActionScript 3.0 code *to your* FLA *(Flash) file to enable interactivity.*

Code Snippets panel does not require knowledge of ActionScript 3.0. It provides the instructions that tell each button what to do when the user clicks.

In this Chapter, you will learn how to create a non-linear navigation in which the movie does not have to play straight from the beginning to the end. ActionScript can tell the Flash playhead to jump around and go to different frames of the Timeline based on which button the user clicks. Different frames on the Timeline contain different contents. The user does not actually know that the playhead is jumping around the Timeline. The user just sees (or hears) different contents appear as the buttons are clicked on the Stage.

With the Code Snippets panel, *you can add code that affects the behavior of an object on the* Stage, *controls the movement of the playhead in the* Timeline.

Understanding Button Symbols

Button symbols are used to provide interactivity. When you click a button, an action occurs, such as starting an animation or jumping to another frame on the Timeline. Any object, including Flash drawings, text blocks, and imported graphic images, can be made into buttons. When you create a button symbol, Flash automatically creates a new Timeline. The Timeline has only four frames or states. These states correspond to the use of the mouse and recognize that the user requires feedback when the mouse is pointing to a button and when the button has been clicked. This is shown by a change in the button (such as a different color or different shape). These four states are as follows:

(a) Up State – It represents how the button appears when the mouse pointer is not over it.

(b) Over State – It represents how the button appears when the mouse pointer is over it.

(c) Down State – It represents how the button appears after the user clicks the mouse.

(d) Hit State – It defines the area of the screen that will respond to the pointer. This area is invisible whenever a SWF (a file extension for a Shockwave Flash file format and stands for Small Web Format) file plays in Flash Player. In most cases, you will want the Hit state to be the same or similar to the Up state in location and size.

Creating Button Symbols

Button symbols are actually a special type of four-frame interactive movie clip. When you select the button type for creating a symbol, Flash Professional CS6 creates a Timeline with four frames. The first three frames display the button's three possible states, Up, Over, and Down and the fourth frame defines the active area of the button.

Flash also gives you a handful of built-in graphic effects, called *filters*, which you can apply to buttons to get professional looking results. Button symbols are not the only way to provide clickable interactivity to your projects. ActionScript coders often create their own buttons or use button components.

✍ *The Button Symbol Timeline does not actually play linearly like a normal Timeline.*

The button symbol timeline reacts to pointer movement and actions by jumping to the appropriate frame. To make a button interactive, you have to place an instance of the button symbol on the Stage and assign actions to the instance. You assign the actions to the root timeline of the FLA file. If the button is inside a movie clip, you can add the actions to the Movie Clip Timeline. You should not add actions to the Timeline of the button symbol.

To create a button symbol, do this:

1. Click the Insert menu and choose New Symbol… . Or *alternatively*, press Ctrl+F8 keys together. The Create New Symbol dialog box appears as shown in Figure 5.1.

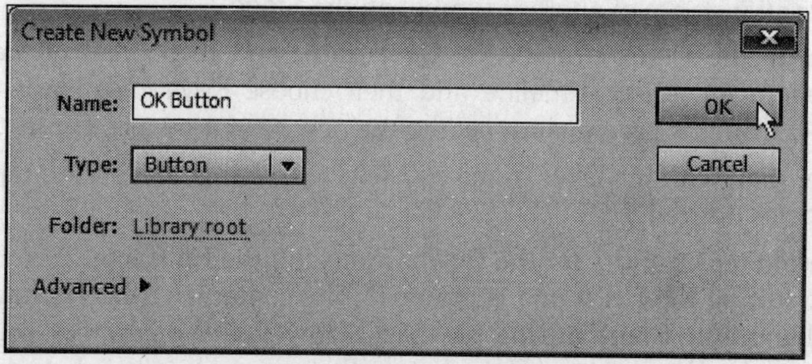

Figure 5.1 Create New Symbol Dialog box

2. Enter a symbol name in the **Name**: text box. For example, type **OK Button** to give the symbol name.
3. Select a behavior type for the symbol in the **Type**: drop-down list box. For example, select **Button** as a type of symbol (See Figure 5.1).
4. Click **OK** button to close the dialog box. The dialog box will get closed, symbol adds to the library and you will be moved to the **Symbol Editing mode** and the **Timeline** changes to display four consecutive frames labeled **Up**, **Over**, **Down**, and **Hit** (See Figure 5.2). The first frame, **Up**, is a blank keyframe.

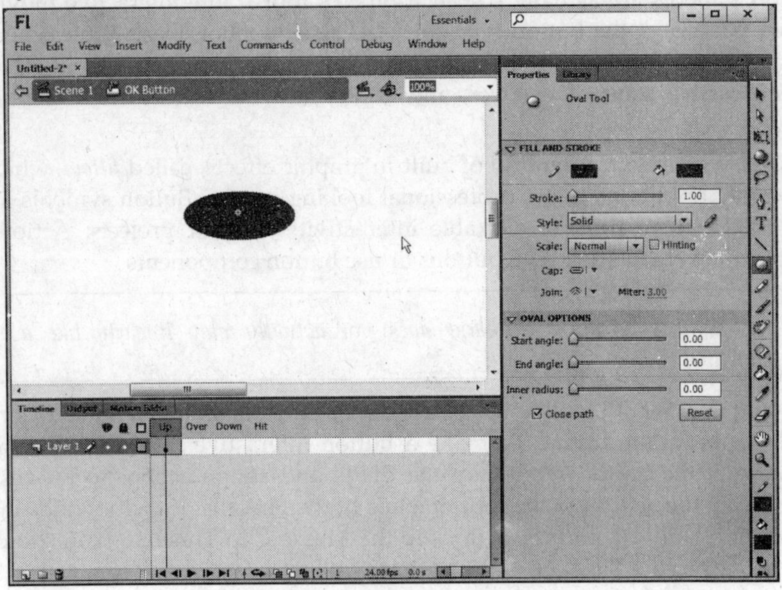

Figure 5.2 Symbol Editing mode

5. After that to create the **Up** state button image, select the **Up** frame in the **Timeline** and then use the drawing tools to create an image. Here, we select **Oval tool** to create an oval image as shown in Figure 5.2, import a graphic, or place an instance of another symbol on the **Stage**.
6. Then in the **Timeline**, click the **Over** frame and then press **F6** key or click **Insert** menu, select **Timeline** and then choose **Keyframe**. Flash copies the object from the previous frame into the new **Keyframe** (See Figure 5.3).
7. After that, with the **Over** frame still selected, change the button image on the **Stage** as desired.
8. Repeat Steps 6 and 7 for the **Down** frame and the **Hit** frames (See Figure 5.3). But, editing the Hit frame is optional. The contents of the **Hit** frame are not visible on the **Stage** during playback. However, the graphics you add to it defines the physical area of the button that responds when clicked.

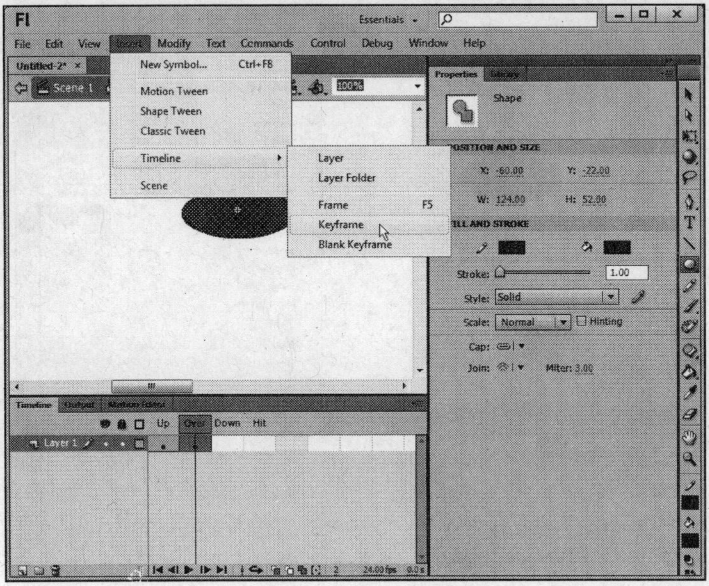

Figure 5.3 Inserting Keyframe

The graphics for the **Hit** *frame must be a solid area large enough to encompass all the graphic elements of the* **Up**, **Down**, *and* **Over** *frames. It can also be larger than the visible button. If you do not specify a* **Hit** *frame, the image for the* **Up** *state is used as the* **Hit** *frame.*

---

9. To add a sound file, select that state of the frame in the Timeline then click **Window** menu, select **Common Libraries** and then choose **Sounds** (See Figure 5.4). It will display **Sound Library** as shown in Figure 5.5.
10. To assign a sound to a state of the button, drag the sound file from the **Sounds library** to the **Library panel** of your **FLA file** (See Figure 5.5).
11. Now, select the frame on the Timeline and then select a sound from the **Sound menu** in the **Properties Inspector** as shown in Figure 5.6. Only sounds you have already imported appear in the **Sound menu**.
12. When you finish, click **Edit** menu, select **Edit Document** as shown in Figure 5.7. Flash Professional CS6 returns you to the main Timeline of your **FLA file**.
13. To create an instance of the button you created on the **Stage**, drag the **button symbol** from the **Library panel** to the **Stage**.
14. Then save the file.
15. After that, click **Control** menu, select **Test Movie** and then choose **in Flash Professional** or press **Ctrl + Enter** keys together as shown in Figure 5.8.
16. It will show a window called **Exporting SWF Movie** as shown in Figure 5.9. This shows exporting of SWF movie in Flash Player.

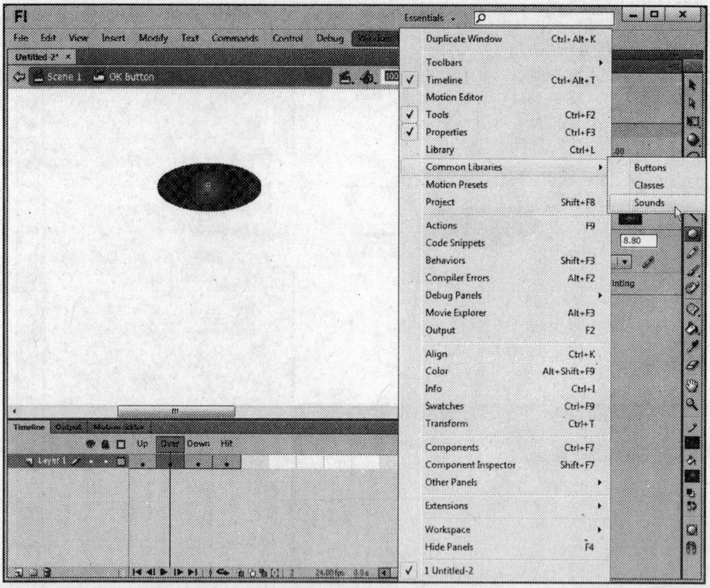

Figure 5.4 Window menu with Common Libraries option selected

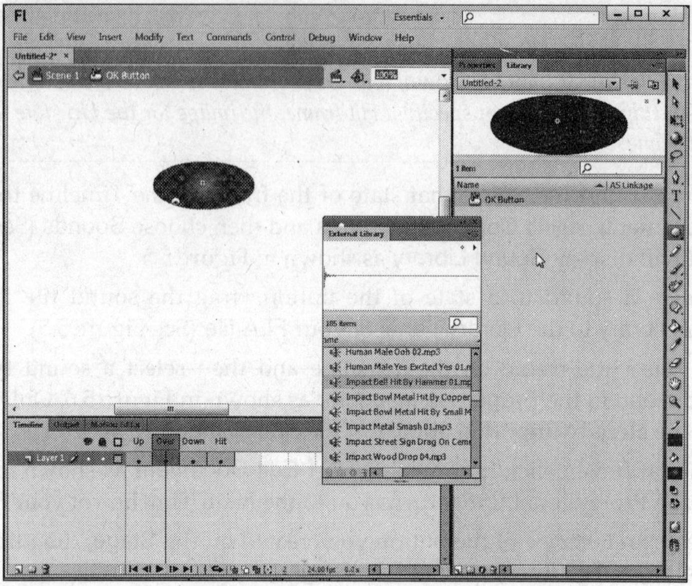

Figure 5.5 Sound Library

17. After that, the button image will automatically open in Flash Player window as shown in Figure 5.10.

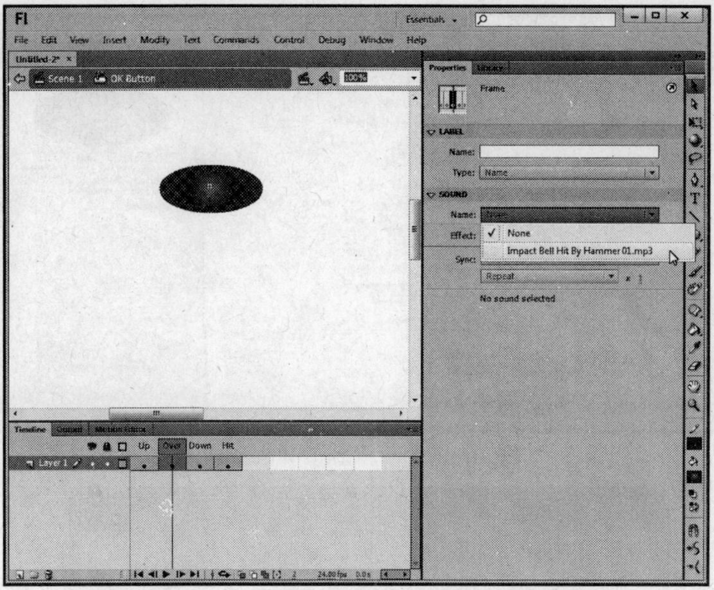

Figure 5.6 Sound menu of Properties Inspector

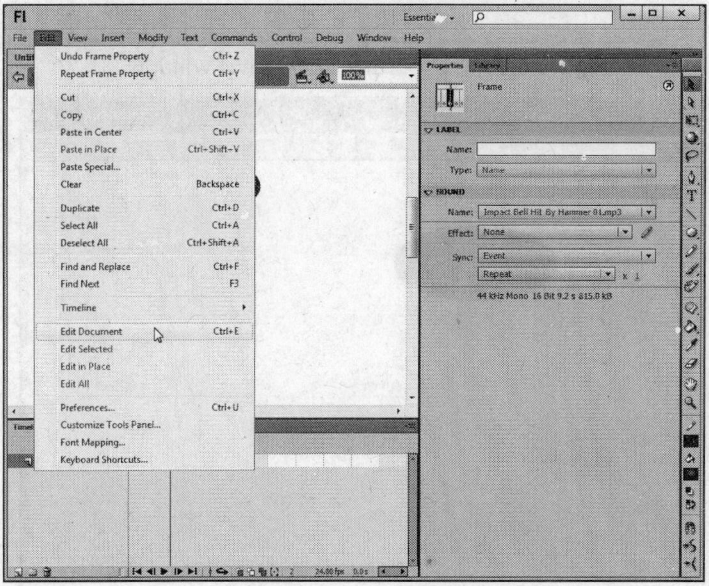

Figure 5.7 Edit menu

You can also use the **Library panel** *to test a button. To do this, select the button in the* **Library panel** *and then click the* **Play** *button in the* **Library Preview window.**

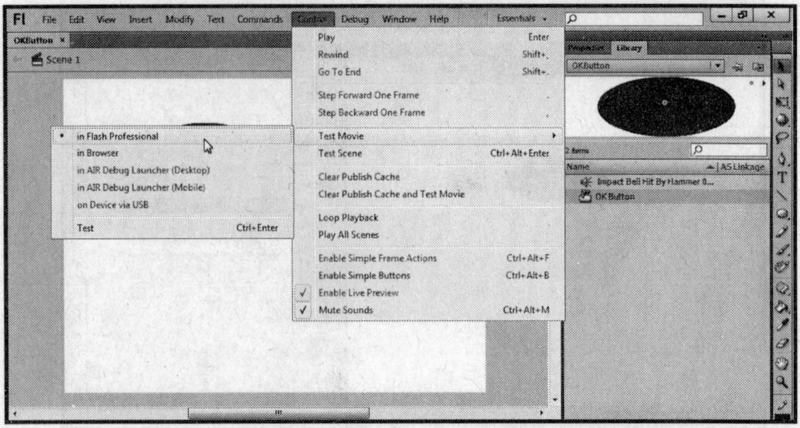

Figure 5.8 Control menu

Figure 5.9 Exporting SWF Movie window

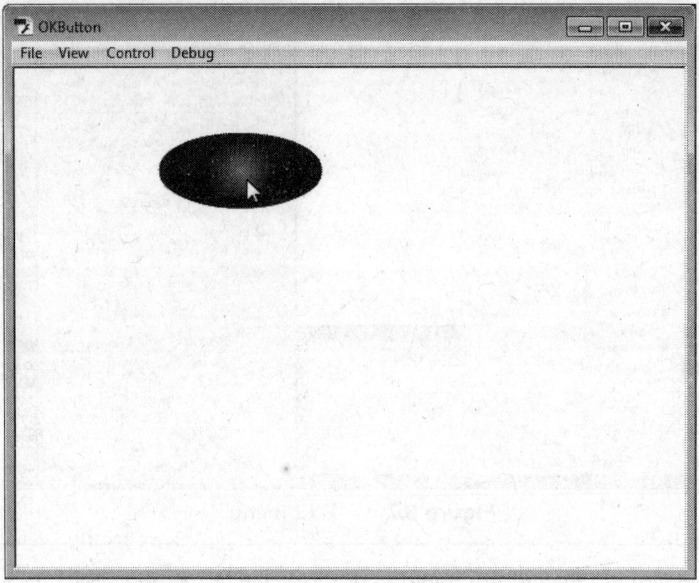

Figure 5.10 Testing movie in Flash Player window

By default, Flash Professional CS6 keeps button symbols disabled as you create them. When a button is disabled, clicking the button selects it. But, when a button is enabled, it responds to the mouse events that you have specified as if the SWF file were playing. You can still select enabled buttons. Disable buttons as you work, and enable buttons to quickly test their graphical behavior when rolled over or clicked.

To enable button on the Stage, do this:

1. Click Control menu, select Enable Simple Buttons (See Figure 5.8). A check mark appears next to the command to indicate buttons are enabled.
2. Any buttons on the Stage now respond with state changes as if it is tested in Flash Player. As you move the pointer over a button, Flash Professional CS6 displays the Over frame. When you click within the button's active area, Flash Professional CS6 displays the Down frame.

To disable button on the Stage, do this:

1. Select Enable Simple Buttons command from the Control menu again to disable buttons.

Editing a Button Symbol

You can edit a button symbol, the same way you edit a single-frame graphic symbol: by switching to symbol editing mode. In both cases, Flash immediately applies the changes you make to the button symbol itself, as well as all the instances of that button symbol.

To edit the button symbol, do this:

1. Select the button.
2. Click Edit menu, select Edit Symbols. Or *alternatively*, double-click the button symbol in the Library panel.
3. This displays button in the edit window, which includes the button Timeline as shown in Figure 5.11.
4. Change the button's state on the Stage as desired.
5. Once you have finished editing a button, click Edit menu, select Edit Document (See Figure 5.7). Or click Scene 1 above the Edit window. Flash returns you to the main timeline of your FLA file.

Understanding Actions

In a simple movie, Flash plays the frames sequentially without stopping for user input. However, if you want to provide the ability to the user to interact with the movie by allowing them to perform actions, such as starting and stopping the movie or jumping to a specific frame in the movie. One way to provide user interaction is to assign an action to the Down state of a button. Then, whenever the user clicks the button, the action occurs. Flash Professional CS6 provides a

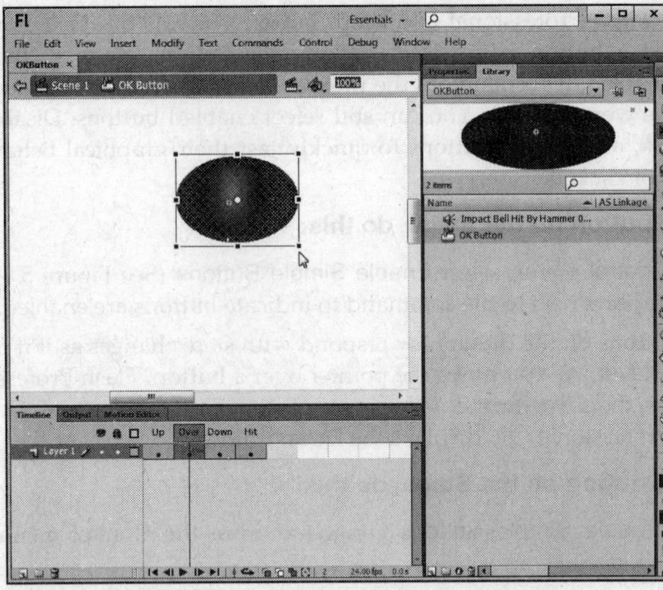

Figure 5.11 Button symbol in Edit window

scripting language, called ActionScript 3.0, that allows you to add actions to buttons and frames within a movie. For example, you can place a stop action in a frame that pauses the movie and then you can assign a play action to a button that starts the movie when the user clicks the button.

Understanding ActionScript 3.0

ActionScript is a powerful scripting language. It allows those users with limited programming experience to add complex interactivity, playback control, and data display in Flash animations. With ActionScript, you can control symbols at runtime. Using ActionScript, you can create interaction and other capabilities in your FLA files that are not possible with the Timeline alone.

A basic ActionScript involves an event (such as a mouse click) that causes some action to occur by triggering the script. For example:

```
on (release) {
gotoAndPlay(10);
}
```

In this example, the event is a mouse click (indicated by the word release) that causes the movie's playback head to go to frame 10 and play the frame. This is a simple example of ActionScript code and it is very easy to follow.

Flash Professional CS6 uses ActionScript 3.0 to extend the functionality.

Navigating the Actions Panel

You can add ActionScript code in the authoring environment by using the Actions panel, Script window, or an external editor. This code is interpreted and carried out by the Flash Player during playback.

To open the Actions Panel, do this:

1. Click the Window menu and choose Actions. Or *alternatively*, press F9 key. The Actions Panel window appears as shown in Figure 5.12.

✍ *The Titlebar of the Action panel will depend on what you have selected. If you have selected a keyframe in the Timeline window, it will be titled as Actions-Frame. If you have a button symbol instance selected on the Stage, the Actions panel will be titled as Actions Button.*

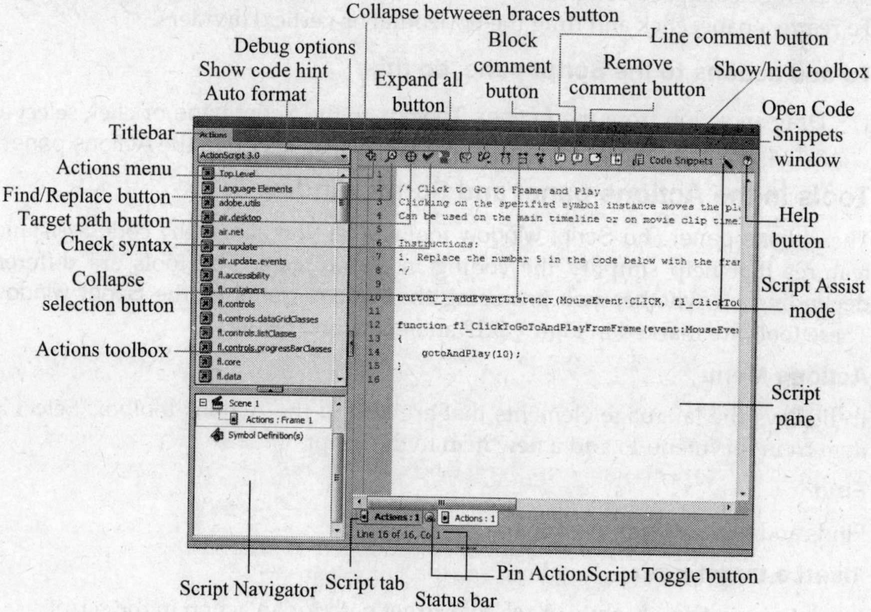

Figure 5.12 Actions Panel

The Actions panel gives you quick access to the core elements of ActionScript as well as it provides you with different options to help you write, debug, format, edit, and find code. Basically, Actions panel is divided into three panes. These are as follows:

(a) At the top-left corner is the Actions toolbox, which contains categories that organize all the ActionScript code (See Figure 5.12). At the top of the Actions toolbox is a pull-down menu that displays only the code for the version of ActionScript you select. You should select ActionScript 3.0, the latest version.

At the very bottom of the Actions toolbox categories is a yellow Index category that lists, in alphabetical order, all the language elements. You need not use the toolbox to add code to your script, but it can help to ensure that you are using the code correctly.

(b) At the top right of the Actions panel is the Script pane—the blank slate in which all your code appears. You enter ActionScript in the Script pane just as you would in a text-editing application (See Figure 5.12).

(c) At the bottom left of the Actions panel is the Script navigator, which can help you find a particular piece of code (See Figure 5.12). ActionScript is placed on keyframes on the Timeline, so the Script navigator can be particularly useful if you have lots of code scattered in different keyframes and on different Timelines.

All the panes in the Actions panel can be resized to suit your working style. They can even be collapsed completely to maximize the pane that you are working in. To resize a pane, click and drag the horizontal or vertical dividers.

To add actions to the Script pane, do this:

1. Drag an action from the Actions Toolbox to the Script pane or click select an action from the Actions menu or double-click an action in the Actions pane.

Tools in the Actions panel and Script window

The Actions panel and Script window toolbars let you access the code-assistance features that help simplify the coding in ActionScript. The tools are different depending on whether you are using the Actions panel or the Script window. These tools are marked in Figure 5.12 and explained below.

Actions Menu

It displays the language elements that are also in the Actions toolbox. Select an item from this menu to add a new item to the script.

Find

Finds and replaces text in your script.

Insert a target path

It helps you set an absolute or relative target path for an action in the script.

Check Syntax

It checks for syntax errors in the current script. Output panel displays some information related to error.

Auto Format

It formats your script for proper coding syntax and improved readability.

Show Code Hint

Show Code Hint button is used to display a code hint for the line of code.

Debug Options

It is used to set and remove breakpoints so that you can proceed line-by-line through the script when debugging.

Collapse between Braces

It collapses code that appears between the curly braces or parentheses.

Collapse Selection

It is used to collapse the currently selected code block.

Expand All

It is used to expand all collapsed code in the current script.

Apply Block Comment

It is used to add comment to the beginning and the end of the selected code block.

Apply Line Comment

It is used to add a single-line comment marker at the insertion point, or at the beginning of each line of code in a multiline selection.

Remove Comment

It removes comment markers from the current line or all lines of the current selection.

Show/Hide Toolbox

It displays or hides the Actions Toolbox.

Script Assist

Script Assist mode provides a user interface for entering the elements needed to create scripts.

Help

It displays reference information for the ActionScript element that is selected in the Script pane.

Options Menu

It contains the commands and preferences that apply to the Actions panel.

Add interactivity with Code Snippets Panel

The Code Snippets panel (new in Flash Professional CS5) contains many useful prewritten blocks of code that make it easy for non-programmers to start using simple ActionScript 3.0 quickly. It lets you add ActionScript 3.0 code to FLA file to easily add simple interactivity to your Flash project. The Code Snippets panel gives you a preview of the actual code, allow you to modify the critical parameters of the code, and use a visual pointer, called the *pick whip*, to point to objects on the Stage. Using the Code Snippets panel does not require knowledge of ActionScript 3.0. You can also save, import, and share code between a team of developers to make the development and production process more efficient.

✍ *Code Snippets panel not only makes adding interactivity quick and learning code easy, but it can help organize frequently used code for yourself and for a team working on the same project. There are additional options in the Code Snippets panel for saving your own code and sharing your code with others.*

With the Code Snippets panel, you can:

(a) Add code that affects the behavior of an object on the Stage.

(b) Add code that controls the movement of the playhead in the Timeline.

(c) Add new code snippets that you create to the panel.

✍ *When you apply a code snippet, the code is added to the current frame of the Actions layer in the Timeline. If you have not created an Actions layer yourself, Flash adds one above all other layers in the Timeline.*

Suppose that you have a short, endlessly movie and suppose that you want to add a Stop button to your movie that, when clicked, stops the playback of the looping movie and Play button that, when clicks, again play movie. Let us discuss the steps required to add a code snippet to an object or Timeline frame.

To add a code snippet to an object or Timeline frame, do this:

1. Open a movie in which you want to add code snippet.
2. Click Insert menu, select Timeline and then choose Layer or click the New Layer button at the bottom of the Timeline to create a new layer and name it as Button.
3. Then click Window menu, select Common Libraries and then choose Buttons. It will display an External Library for buttons as shown in Figure 5.13.
4. Then in Library, click the Classic buttons folder, click Circle Buttons and then choose **Stop button**.
5. Now drag a **Stop button** from the Library and place it on the Button layer on the Stage.
6. Select the button instance, and open the Properties panel and change the name of the button as **Stop_Button**.
7. With the Stop button instance selected, click the Window menu and then choose Code Snippets. It will display Code Snippets panel as shown in Figure 5.14.
8. In the Code Snippets panel, from the Timeline Navigation section, double-click the snippet called **Click to Go to Frame and Stop**.
9. Now, it will add a block of code to the Tineline and open the Actions panel as shown in Figure 5.15.

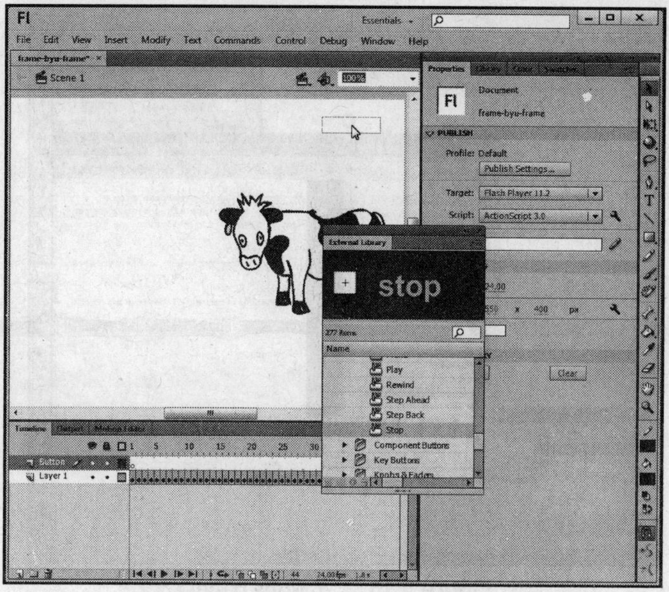

Figure 5.13 Dragging Stop button from the Buttons Library to the Stage

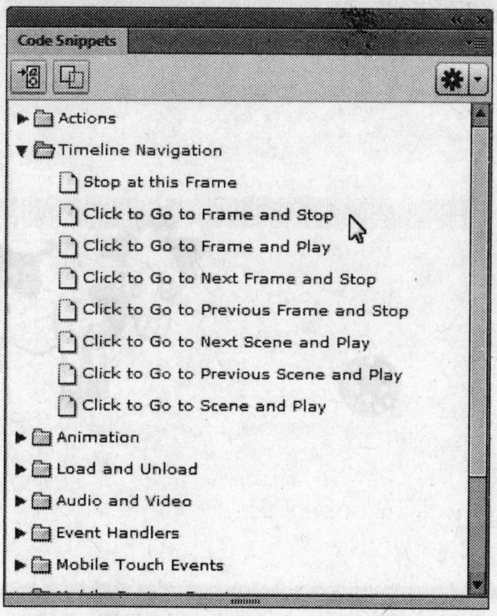

Figure 5.14 Code Snippets panel

10. In the Actions panel, view the newly added code and replace the line code gotoAndStop(5) with stop().
11. Now we have **stop** button in Flash movie that stops movie's playback when button, clicked.
12. Then save Flash document.

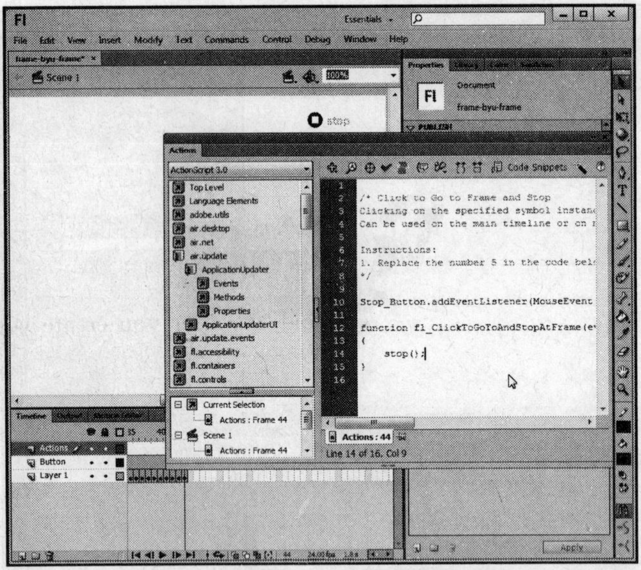

Figure 5.15 Actions panel

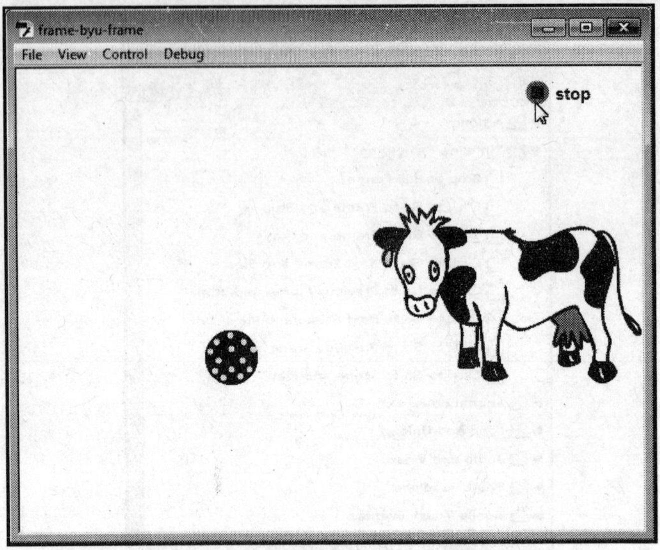

Figure 5.16 Testing movie in Flash Player window

13. After that click Control menu, select Test Movie and then choose in Flash Professional.
14. It will automatically open in Flash Player window as shown in Figure 5.16.
15. In this window, when you click the **stop** button, the movie will stop.

CHAPTER 6

Working with Text

Introduction

Flash Professional CS6 provides a great deal of flexibility when working with the text. Among other settings for text, you can specify the typeface (font), size, style (bold, italic), and color (including gradients). You can also transform the text by rotating, scaling, skewing and flipping it. You can even break apart a letter and reshape its segments. There are two different text engines for working with text. These are as follows:

(a) Classic Text: This mode is appropriate for many text applications and is easy to work with (This has already been discussed in Chapter 2).

(b) Text Layout Framework (TLF): This mode provides advanced features and is appropriate for more text intensive applications.

Choose Classic Text when you do not need layout control or if you need to target an older version of the Flash Player. Choose TLF Text when you want to use more sophisticated controls for text formatting such as multiple columns or wrap-around text.

In this Chapter, you will learn many of the features and fine control of text attributes that are unique to TLF Text.

Understanding Text Layout Framework (TLF) Text

Text Layout Framework (TLF) provides several advanced text features such as *character color highlighting*, *underlining*, and *strikethrough*. It also provides better *print-quality typography* over Classic text. Text in the TLF format is displayed in a container. These containers are called *threaded* or *linked text containers*. These containers can be resized and linked using a Container icon. This allows you to flow the text between them. The containers can have a border and background color, and the text in containers can be formatted into columns. You can also apply attributes such as *3D Rotation, Color Effects*, and *Blend Modes* to TLF text without placing it in a movie clip symbol.

TLF format has support for bi-directional text, where right-to-left text can contain elements of left-to-right text. This is important for embedding English words or Arabic numerals within Arabic/Hebrew text.

TLF Text depends on a specific external ActionScript library to function properly. When you test a movie or publish a movie that contains TLF Text, an additional Text Layout SWZ file is created next to your SWF (a file extension for a Shockwave Flash file format) file.

SWZ file is the external ActionScript library that supports TLF Text.

You should always keep the SWZ file with your SWF file so the TLF Text features work properly when you test your movies locally or when you upload it to your Web server.

If you do not want to maintain the separate SWZ file, you can merge the required ActionScript library with your SWF file. However, doing so adds substantially to the size of your published SWF file and is generally not recommended.

Adding Simple Text

When you add text, whether TLF Text or Classic Text, the text remains fully editable. So, after you create your text at any point, you can return to it and change it or also set any of its properties, such as its color, font, size, or alignment.

To add TLF text on the Stage, do this:

1. Select the Text tool from the Tools panel.
2. In the Properties Inspector, Select TLF Text from the Text Engine drop-down list (See Figure 6.1).

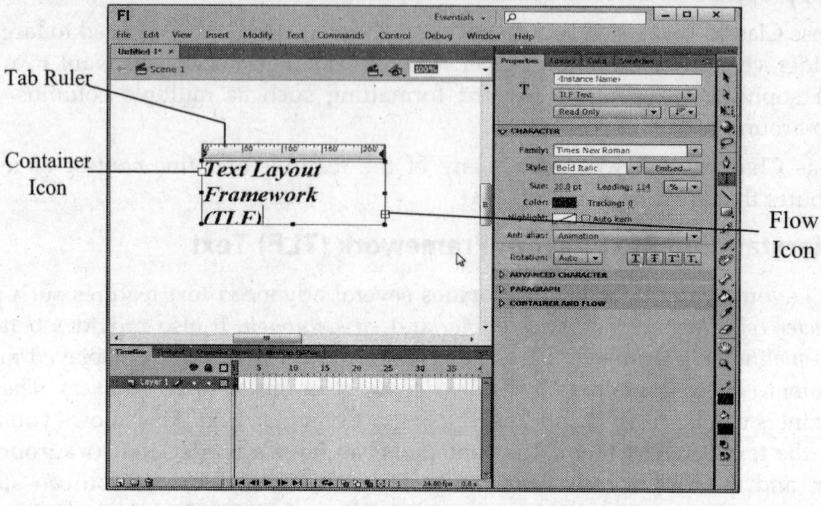

Figure 6.1 Entering text using Text tool

3. In Text Type: field, select one of the following text types:

   Read Only: It displays the text that cannot be selected or edited, when published as SWF file. This setting is the *default* for TLF text.

   Selectable: It displays the text that is selectable and can be copied to the clipboard, but is not editable, when published as SWF file.

   Editable: It displays the text that is selectable and can be edited, when published as SWF file. Use the **Editable** option for text input fields, such as login and passwords.

4. Select a direction for text orientation and flow from the Change orientation of text button. (*Horizontal* is the default setting.)

Although, vertical text is not common, it can be useful for unusual displays. For many Asian languages, vertical text is essential to display them correctly.

---

5. Under the Character section, select one of the following options:

   Family: Choose the name of the font.

TLF text only supports OpenType and TrueType fonts.

   Style: Choose the style for the text such as Regular, Bold, or Italic.

   Size: Choose the size of the text. The size of the character is measured in pixels.

6. Click the stage and drag to create a text field.
7. Begin entering the text and exit the Text tool by choosing the Selection tool.

In the Character section of the Properties Inspector, you can also choose 270° from the Rotation: drop-down list to change the orientation of the individual characters as well as the lines of text.

Formatting Text

Character and Paragraph section of Properties Inspector gives you an easy access to commonly used text formatting options. In addition to this, options in the Advance Character section let you easily change *case, add links, control baseline shifts*, etc.

To select text, do this:

1. To *select an entire text object*, click the object using Selection tool.
2. To *select specific characters*, drag across the text using the Text tool.

Character Formatting

Character formatting applied to a single character or a set of characters, rather than to whole paragraphs or text containers. To apply the character formatting, you have to work with the Character and Advanced Character sections of the Properties Inspector.

To format characters, do this:

1. Select the Characters you want to modify.
2. The Character section of the Properties Inspector includes the following text properties as shown in Figure 6.1, select the options as per your choice:

   Embed: When we published SWF files on the Internet, there is no guarantee that the fonts we used are available on all the machines. To ensure that text maintains the appearance as we want, we can embed entire fonts or specific subsets of characters from a font. By embedding the characters in published SWF file, we make the font available for all computers that play the file. Once a font is embedded, we can use it anywhere in your published SWF file.

Embedding fonts dramatically increases the size of your final SWF, so be cautious while doing so, and limit the number of fonts and characters wherever possible.

To embed font in a SWF file:

- Click on the Embed button from the Properties Inspector.
- It will display Font Embedding dialog box as shown in Figure 6.2 and a font item appears automatically in the dialog box.
- In the Font Embedding dialog box, under the Options tab, select the Family and Style from the Family: and Style: drop-down list, respectively which you want to embed.
- In the Character ranges: section, select the character ranges you want to embed. The more characters you embed, the larger your published SWF file will be.
- If you want to embed any additional specific characters, enter them in the Also include these characters: field.
- Then click OK button.

Leading: It specifies the vertical space between lines of text. By default, Leading is expressed as percentage (%) but you can also express it in points.

Tracking: It specifies the amount of space between the selected characters.

Highlight: It is used to set the color to highlight the text.

Kerning: It is used to add or subtract space between specific pairs of characters. TLF text automatically kerns characters using the kerning information built into most fonts.

Anti-alias: Anti-aliasing lets you smoothen the edges of on-screen text. The anti-aliasing options are particularly effective for rendering smaller font sizes. Anti-alias: drop-down list can have the following three modes:

- Use Device Fonts: It specifies that the SWF file use only those fonts which are installed on the local computer. While using this option, choose only commonly installed font families.
- Readability: It allows for improved legibility of fonts. If you want to use this option, first of all embed the font used by the text object.
- Animation: It creates a smoother animation. Embedding is also necessary for this option.

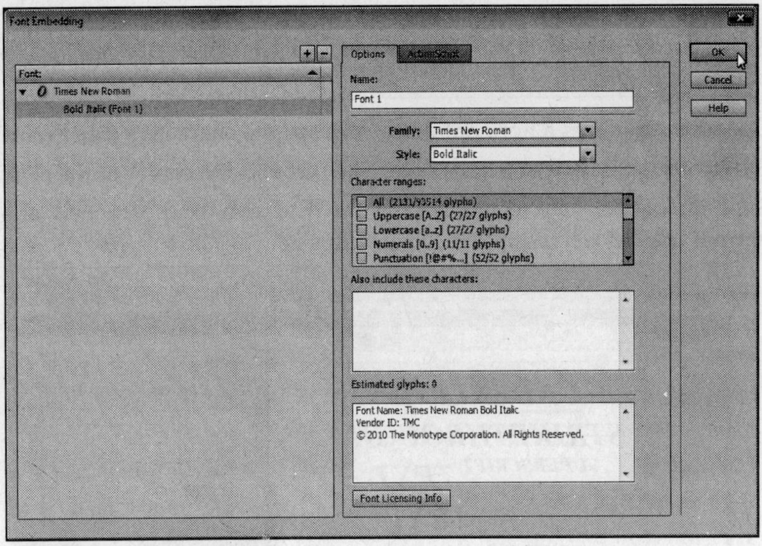

Figure 6.2 Font Embedding dialog box

Rotation: Select this option, if you want to rotate individual characters. Rotation: drop-down list can have the following options (See Figure 6.3):

- Auto–It specifies a 90 degree counter-clockwise rotation for full width and wide characters only. This rotation is applied only in vertical text to return full width without affecting other characters.

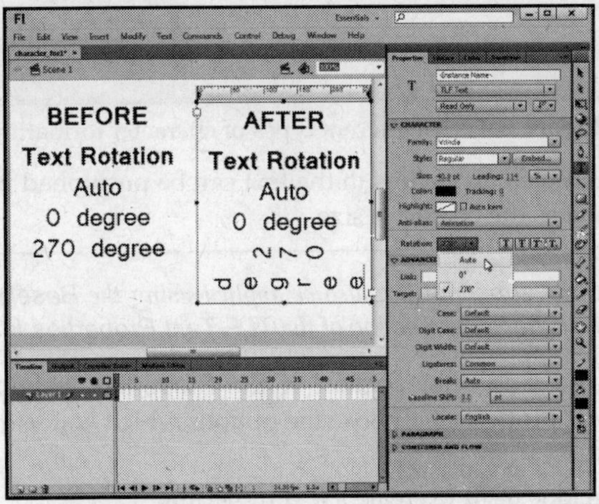

Figure 6.3 Different types of Rotations

- 0° - It forces all characters to have no rotation.
- 270° - It rotates text by 270° and make it appear as it is written in vertical style.

If you specify rotation for those fonts that do not contain vertical layout information can give undesirable results.

Underline: It places a horizontal line beneath the characters (See Figure 6.4).

Strikethrough: It places a horizontal line through the center of the characters.

Superscript: Selected characters in the text can be positioned above the normal line, which reduces the character size.

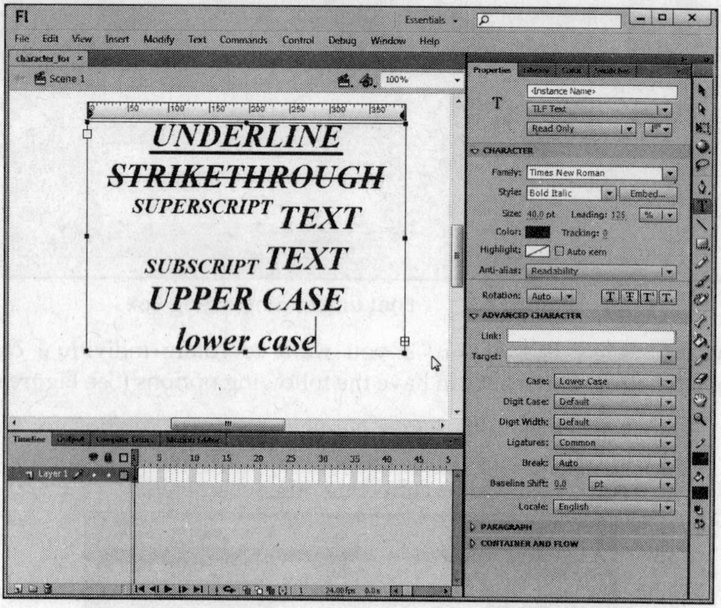

Figure 6.4 Different types of character formatting

Subscript: Selected characters in the text can be positioned below the normal line and reduces the character size.

Superscript and subscript can also be applied using the Baseline Shift menu in the Advanced Character section of the TLF Text Properties Inspector.

3. The Advanced Character section of the Properties Inspector includes the following text properties. Choose the options which you want to apply in the selected text.

   Link: This field is used to create a text hyperlink.

   To add a hyperlink, do this:

   - Select the word or characters.
   - Then in Advanced Character section of the Properties Inspector, click on the Link: field; to enter the name of the URL (Uniform Resource Locator)

to load when the selected characters or word are clicked in the published SWF file at runtime.

- Then select the Target: pull-down menu to specify the window in which the URL loads. Target: can have the following values (See Figure 6.5):

  _self – It loads the URL in the same browser window.

  _blank – It loads the URL in a blank browser window.

  _parent – It loads the URL in the parent of the current frame.

  _top – It loads the URL in the top-level frame in the current window.

- The selected word or characters become underlined, indicating that it hyperlinked.

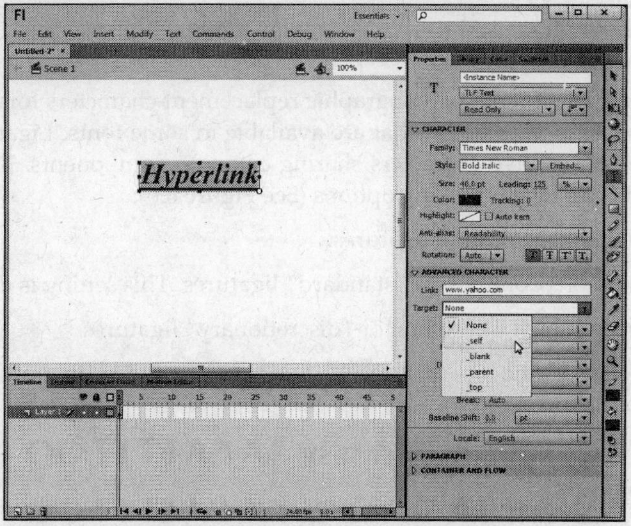

Figure 6.5 Text hyperlink

Case: This field is used to specify how capital and lower-case characters are used. Case: field can have the following values:

- Default: It uses each character's default typographic case.
- Upper Case: It changes all characters in upper case (See Figure 6.4).
- Lower Case: It changes all characters in lower case (See Figure 6.4).
- Caps to Small Caps: It changes all capitalized characters in small upper case.
- Lower Case to Small Caps: It changes all lower case characters into small uppercase.

Digit Case: It controls the presentation of numbers. Digit Case can have the following options:

- **Default:** It specifies default digit case.
- **Lining:** It is used to keep numbers aligned.
- **Old Style:** It is used to keep the original style of the font. It is only available for certain typefaces.

Digit Width: It lets you control the spaces between the numbers. **Digit Width:** can have the following values:

- **Default:** It specifies default digit width.
- **Proportional:** In this setting, the total character width of the figures is based on the width of the numeral itself plus a small amount of white space around it. For example, an 8 takes up more width than a 1.
- **Tabular:** It is used to specify tabular figures. It gives each digit an equal amount of space.

Ligatures: Ligatures are typographic replacement characters for certain letter pairs, such as "fi" and "fl" that are available in some fonts. Ligatures usually replace consecutive characters sharing common components. The Ligatures property can take following options (See Figure 6.6):

- **Minimum:** Minimum ligatures.
- **Common:** Common or "standard" ligatures. This setting is the default.
- **Uncommon:** Uncommon or "discretionary" ligatures.
- **Exotic:** Exotic or "historical" ligatures. Included in only a few font families.

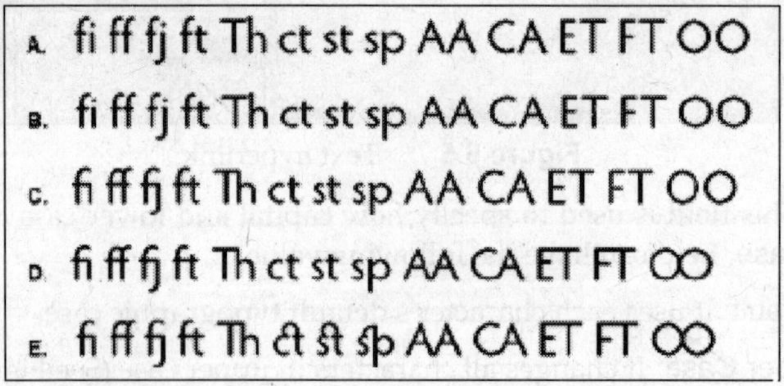

A. No ligatures applied B. Minimum ligatures C. Common ligatures D. Uncommon ligatures E. Exotic ligatures

Figure 6.6 Options in Ligatures property

Break: It is used to prevent words from breaking at the end of lines, such as proper names or words that could be misread when hyphenated. It is also used to keep multiple characters or groups of words together. It can take the following options:

- Auto: This is the default setting. It creates line breaks using word wrap, so full words are not broken between lines.
- All: It creates a new line for each character in the text box.
- Any: It creates line breaks when the text reaches at the end of the text field's width, even if it breaks a word in multiple parts.
- No Break: This option does not automatically add line breaks.

Baseline Shift: It sets the Baseline Shift in percent or pixels. Positive values move the characters below the baseline and the negative values move it above the baseline. The Superscript or Subscript attribute can also be applied from this menu.

Locale: It sets the character locale of for the language you are using.

Paragraph Formatting

Paragraph formatting applied to whole paragraph. To apply the paragraph formatting, you have to work with the Paragraph and Advanced Paragraph sections of the Text Properties Inspector.

To format paragraphs, do this:

1. Select the paragraph text you want to modify.
2. The Paragraph section of the Properties Inspector includes the various text properties. You can select the following options as per your choice:

   Align: This property is used to modify the alignment of the text (See Figure 6.7). It can be used with horizontal or vertical text. This property has three buttons for alignment of text, i.e., Left, Center or Right and four buttons for Justification, i.e., justification to the start of a line, center of the line, end of the line or fully justified.

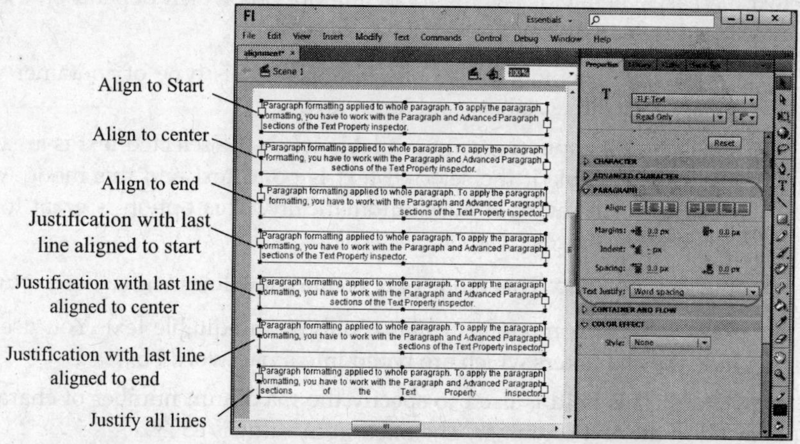

Figure 6.7 Different types of paragraph alignment

Margins: It sets the value for left and right text margins. The default value is 0.

Indent: It sets the indentation of the first word of the selected paragraph, in pixels.

Spacing: It specifies the space before and after a paragraph.

Text Justify: It controls the appearance of justified text. Text Justify can take following options:

- Letter Spacing: It adds spaces between letters to justify the text.
- Word Spacing: This is the default setting. It adds spaces between words.

Working with Container and Flow Properties

Container and flow properties are applied to the entire text container. To apply or set the container properties, you have to work with the Container and Flow section of the Text Properties Inspector.

There are two types of TLF text containers: point text *and* area text. *A point text container's size depends solely on the text it contains. An area text container's size is independent of the amount of text it contains. Point text is the default. To change a point text container to area text, resize it with the selection tool or double-click the small circle at the bottom-right corner of the container bounding box.*

To set container and flow properties, do this:

1. Select the container using the Selection tool.
2. The Container and Flow section of the Properties Inspector includes the following properties:

   Behavior: This option controls how the container expands as the amount of text increases. Behavior has the following options which depend on the text type (See Figure 6.8):

   - Single line: This mode uses one line only. This type of container work well for headlines, labels, and input text.

     Multiline: This option is only available when the selected text is area text. It is not available if the selected text is point text and this mode wraps word to form multiple lines automatically. This option is great for big paragraphs of text.

   - Multiline no wrap: This mode only creates new lines with a hard return.
   - Password: This mode is available only with editable text. You use it to hide the characters which are typed into a password box.

   Max chars: This field is used to specify the maximum number of characters allowed in the text container. The maximum value is 65535.

Alignment: To specify the alignment of text within the container. Options of Alignment include (See Figure 6.9):

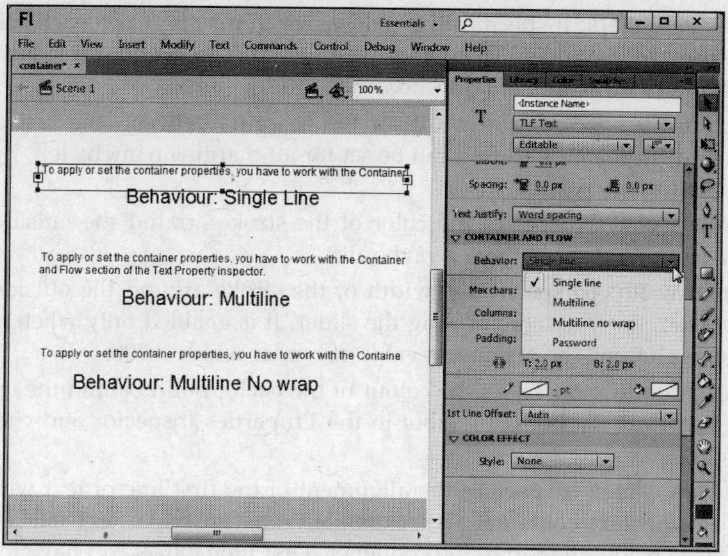

Figure 6.8 Different behavior of container

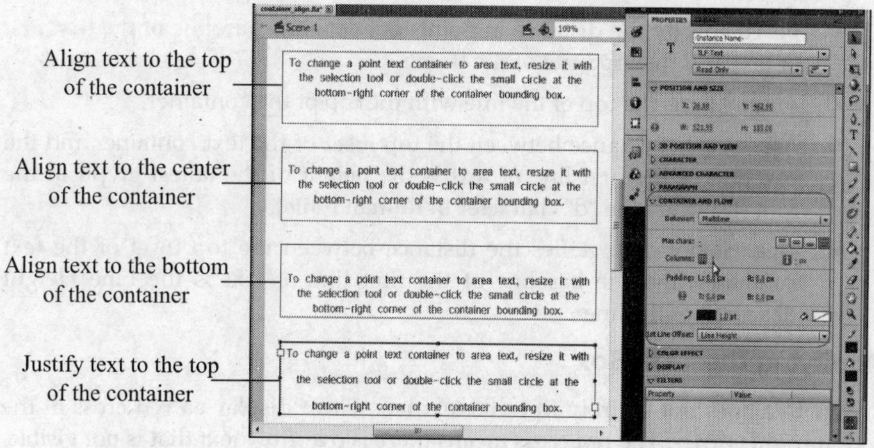

Figure 6.9 Different types of alignment of text within the container

- Top: It vertically aligns text down from the top of the container.
- Center: It centers lines of text in the container
- Bottom: It vertically aligns lines of text up from the bottom of the container.
- Justify: It evenly distributes lines of text vertically between the top and bottom of the container.

Columns: To specify the number of columns within the container. The default value is 1. The maximum value is 50.

Column Gutters: It specifies the spacing (or gutter) between each column in the selected container. The default value is 20. The maximum value is 1000. The unit of measurement depends on the Ruler Units.

Padding: It specifies the width of the margins between the text and the selected container. Padding can be set for all margins namely, left, right, top and bottom.

Border Color: To specify the color of the stroke around the outside of the container. By default, there is no border.

Border width: To specify the width of the stroke around the outside of the container, enter a value or drag the slider. It is enabled only when a border color is chosen. The maximum value of border width is 200.

Background Color: To set the colour of the background behind the text, click the box near the bucket symbol in the Properties Inspector and choose the colour.

1st Line Offset: It specifies the alignment of the first line of text with at the top of the text container. For example, you can make text fall a specific distance below the top of the container. First Line Offset can have following values:

- **pt:** To specify the distance in points between the baseline of the first line of text and the top inset of the frame.
- **Auto:** Aligns the top of the line with the top of the container.
- **Ascent:** The distance between the top inset of the text container and the baseline of the first line of text is the height of the tallest glyph in the font (typically the "d" character in Roman fonts).
- **Line Height:** It specifies the distance between the top inset of the text container and the baseline of the first line of text is the Line Height (leading) of the line.

Modifying the Text Box

If your text does not entirely fit in its text box, Flash displays a red cross at the bottom-right corner. The red cross means there is overflow text that is not visible. If you want to see more of the text, you have to enlarge the text box.

To modify (enlarge) the text box, do this:

1. Select the Text tool or the Selection tool.
2. Move your mouse cursor over one of the solid blue squares surrounding the text box.
3. Your mouse cursor changes to a double-headed arrow, indicating the direction in which you can modify the size of the text box.

4. Click and drag to make the text box wider or taller to fit the text. The text box gets resized, and the text reflows to accommodate the new dimensions. Figure 6.10 shows the text box before and after enlargement.

You can also resize a text box by entering new Width *and* Height *values in the* Properties Inspector.

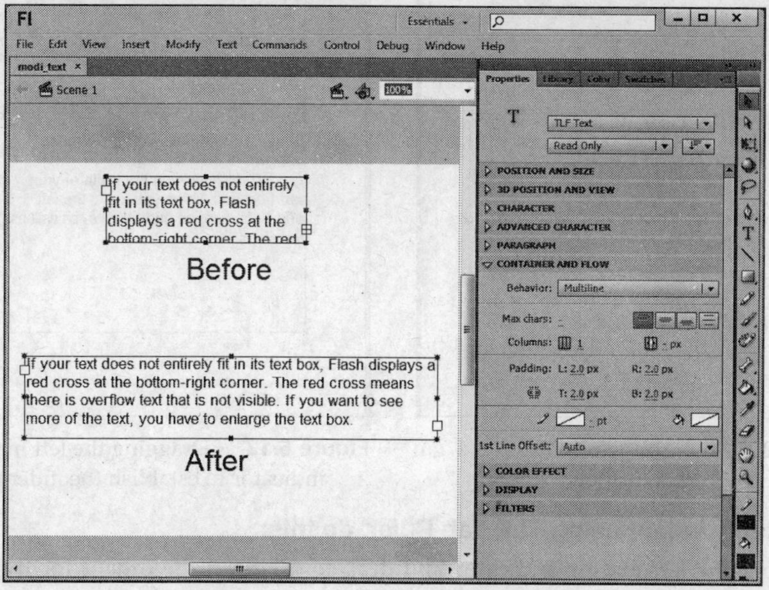

Figure 6.10 Modifying the Text box

Using the Tab Ruler

When you create TLF text boxes on the Stage, you will notice a handy ruler appears at their top edges. This shows you the width of your text field and allows you to set the left and right margins and indents, as well as tab stops.

To view the ruler, do this:

1. Double-click a TLF text box or select the Text tool and click in a TLF text box. You can also toggle to view or to hide the ruler by clicking the option TLF Tab Ruler from Text menu.

To set the margin using TLF Tab Ruler, do this:

1. Double-click the text box if it has not already selected. The TLF Tab Ruler is displayed at the top edge of the text box.
2. Drag the left margin indicator (solid black triangle) along the TLF Tab Ruler (See Figure 6.11).
3. The margin for the text increases.

If there were paragraph breaks in your text box, you would see the margin for only the selected paragraph change. But, if you want to change the margins for the entire contents of the text box, then click Edit *and then choose* Select All *before moving the margin indicator.*

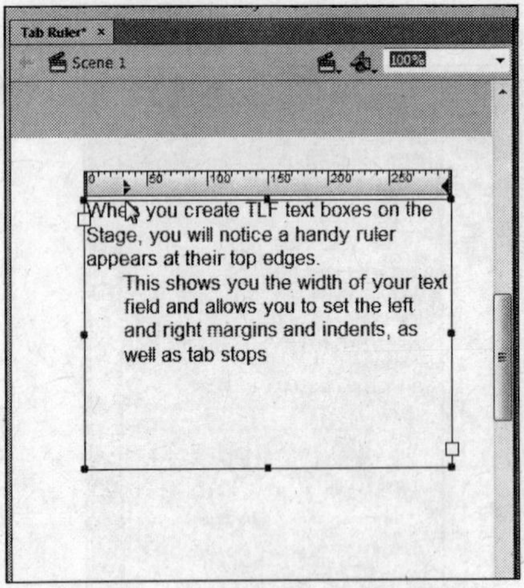

Figure 6.11 Dragging the left margin indicator

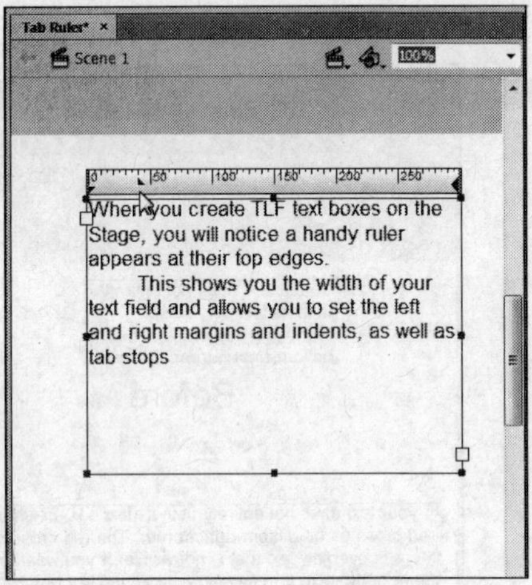

Figure 6.12 Dragging the left margin indicator to establish the indent

To modify indent using TLF Tab Ruler, do this:

1. Split the left margin indicator and drag to establish the indent for the first line of new paragraphs (See Figure 6.12).

To set or modify the tab stops using TLF Tab Ruler, do this:

1. Click inside the TLF Tab Ruler. Flash creates a tab stop (See Figure 6.13).

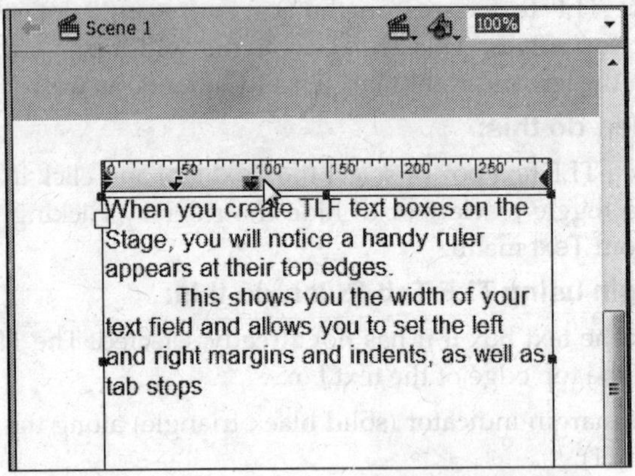

Figure 6.13 Setting or modifying the Tab stop

2. Drag the tab stop along the ruler to move the position of the tab.
3. To see the effects of the tab stop, press the Tab key.
4. Flash indents the text to the next tab stop on the TLF Tab Ruler.

Drag the tab stop off the ruler to delete it.

Flowing Text across Multiple Containers

Long passages of text are visually boring. Instead, you can wrap text around photographs or graphic elements to create more visual interest and a more pleasing design. You can create wrapping text by linking separate text boxes. Text will flow from one text box to another as if in a single container.

Threading, or linking between text containers is only available for TLF (Text Layout Framework) text and does not apply to Classic text blocks. Text containers can be threaded or linked from frame to frame, and inside symbols, as long as the linked containers are all within the same timeline.

Linked text boxes are also referred to as "threaded text containers."

Linking Text Boxes

To link text boxes, do this:

1. Drag any image on the Stage from Library Panel or paste from where you want to paste.
2. Then select the Text tool.
3. Click and drag out the first text box as shown in Figure 6.14.
4. Now add text in a text box by double-clicking the text box on the Stage and paste the text from where you want to paste.
5. Notice that the text box shows red cross inside the square (⊞) at its bottom-right corner, indicating overflow text that cannot be displayed (See Figure 6.15).

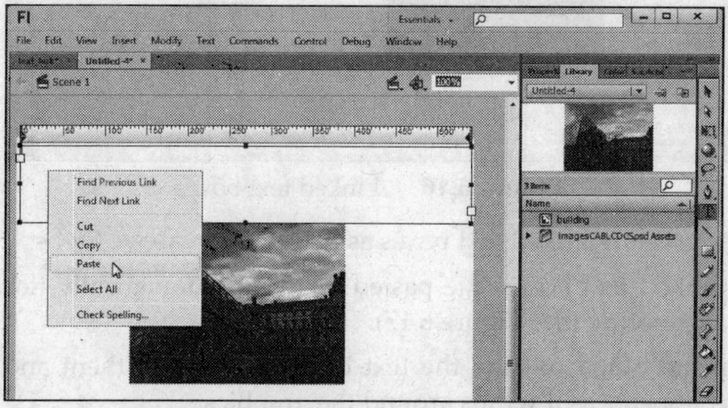

Figure 6.14 Creating Text box

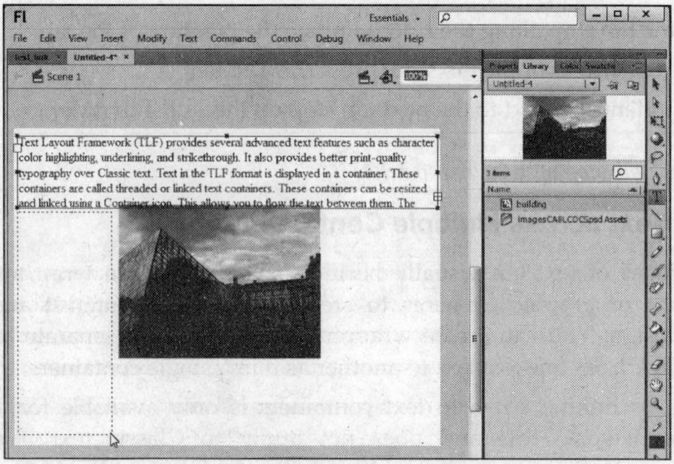

Figure 6.15 Creating another Text box

6. Click ⊕ icon on the lower-right corner of the text box (See Figure 6.15). Your pointer changes to the loaded text icon (▤).
7. Click and drag out second text box.
8. When you release your mouse cursor, your second text box becomes linked to the first text box. Blue lines that connect the first to the second represent the linkage (See Figure 6.16).

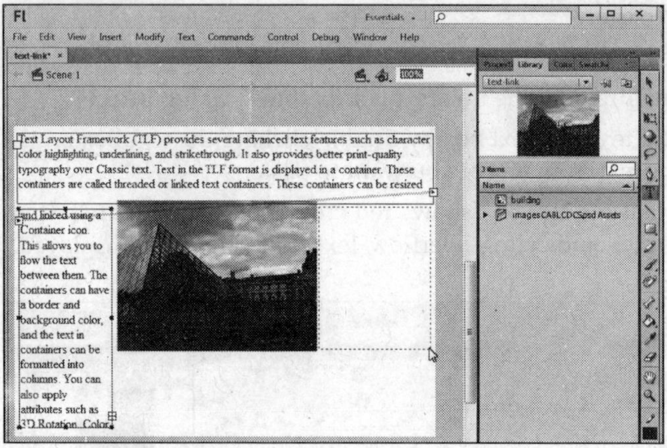

Figure 6.16 Linked text boxes

9. Continue creating linked text boxes as described in above Steps.
10. As you linked text boxes, the pasted text will automatically flow from one text box to another (See Figure 6.17).
11. Click on the Stage outside the text boxes to deselect them and view how your text appears as it wraps around the graphics.

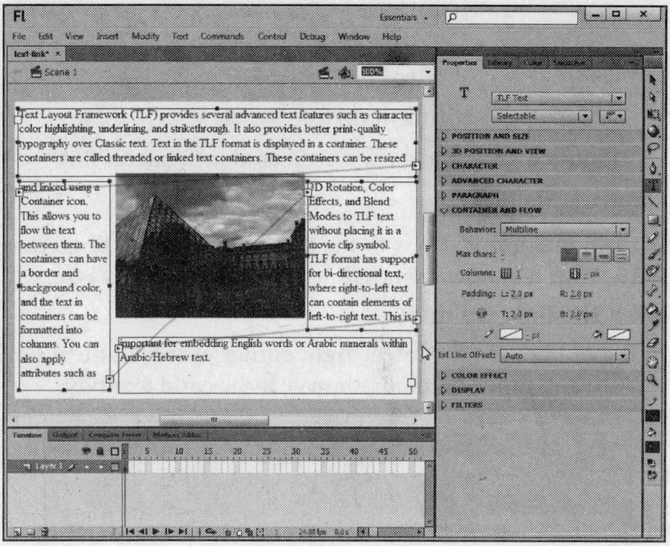

Figure 6.17 Flowing text across multiple text boxes or containers

If you simply click on the Stage to define your next linked text box, Flash creates a text box that is identical in size to the previous text box.

Deleting Text Boxes

If you need to edit the way the text flows, you can always delete linked text boxes and the linkages between the existing ones will be maintained.

To delete text box, do this:

1. With the Selection tool, select the linked text box which you want to delete.
2. Now, press the Del key from the keyboard.
3. The selected linked text box is deleted from the Stage, but the remaining text boxes maintain their linkages.

Breaking and Relinking Text Boxes

You can always break the links anytime between text boxes and create new linkages.

To break link between text boxes, do this:

1. Click on the box containing the small arrowhead on the lower-right corner of the first text box.
2. Now move your mouse cursor over the second text box.
3. Your cursor now changes to a broken link icon as shown in Figure 6.18, indicating that you can break the link to the text box that is currently below your cursor.

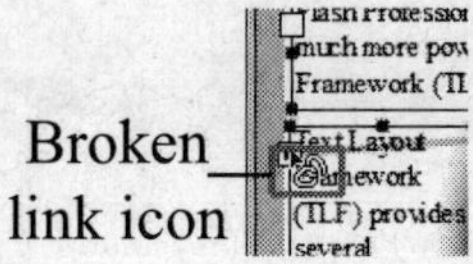

Figure 6.18 Broken link icon used to break the link

4. Click on the second text box.
5. The link from the first text box to the second text box is broken as shown in Figure 6.19. Your text now cannot flow out of the first text box.

To reestablish the link, do this:

1. Click on the red box on the lower-right corner of the first text box as shown in Figure 6.19 and move your cursor over the second text box.

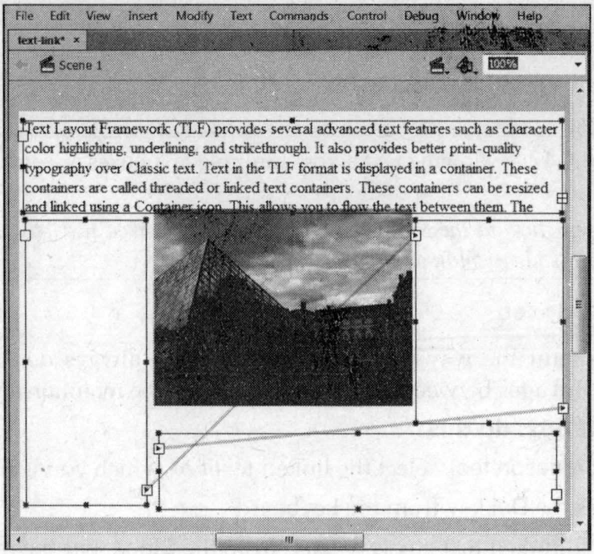

Figure 6.19 Broken link from first text box to other text boxes

2. Your cursor changes to a linked icon (), indicating that you can establish a link to the text box that is currently below your cursor.
3. Now click on the second text box.
4. The first text box is again linked to the second text box. Your text now flows throughout the text boxes as shown in Figure 6.17.

Finding the Next or Previous Link

Sometimes, if you have multiple linked text boxes, it may be confusing to see the linkages or difficult to select the boxes in succession.

To find next or previous link, do this:

1. Right-click over any text box that is linked as shown in Figure 6.20.

2. Then choose Find Previous Link or Find Next Link from the context menu. Here, we selected Find Previous Link.
3. The previous linked text box will become selected as shown in Figure 6.21.

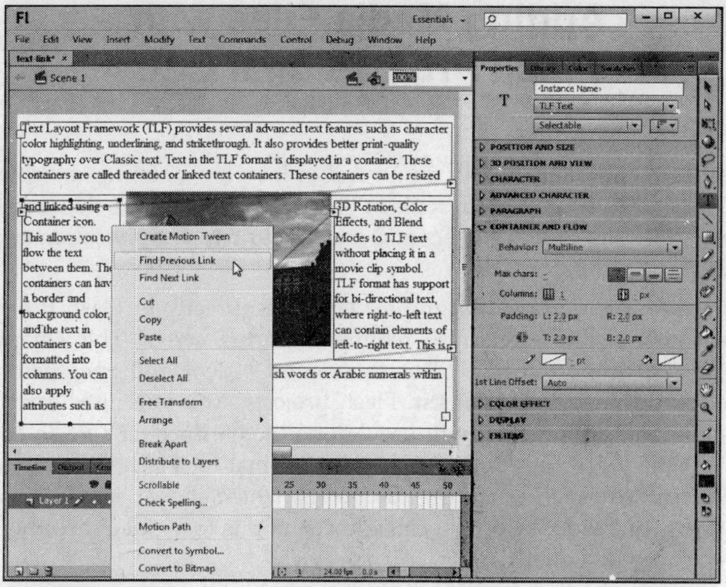

Figure 6.20 Context menu to select previous or next link

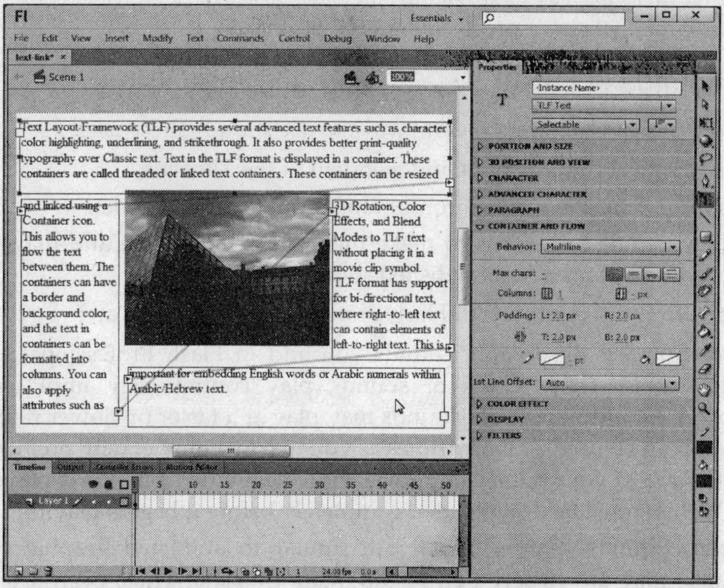

Figure 6.21 Selected Previous link

CHAPTER 7

Adding Media Files with Flash Professional CS6

Introduction

Like animation and interactivity, sound and video play an important role in any project. These are also important tools in Flash Professional CS6 that you can use to express a message, engage users and make your site or application appealing to visitors.

You can create a wide range of graphic elements directly in Flash Professional CS6. But sometimes, projects also require imported assets. This Chapter will explain how to import media files (sound and video) and put them on the Timeline to add new dimensions in Flash projects. You will also learn how to embed sounds in button. You will use Adobe Media Encoder CS6 to compress and convert the video files to the appropriate format for Flash. You can also use new video features, such as adding cue points, which allow users to navigate to different parts of a video clip. You can add cue points to a video directly in Flash using the Properties panel.

✍ *Effective and judicious use of sound and video files are key ingredients in making a Flash site or application a truly multimedia experience.*

Using Sounds in Flash

Flash Professional CS6 offers several ways to use sound. These are:

(a) It plays sound continuously, independent of the Timeline.

(b) It uses the Timeline to synchronize animation to a sound track.

(c) It adds sounds to buttons to make them more interactive and make sound fade in and out for a more polished sound track.

There are two types of sounds in Flash Professional CS6. These are:

(a) Event Sounds: By default, sounds you add in Flash Professional CS6 are *event sounds*. These types of sounds play continuously until explicitly stopped. In addition, event sounds may play at a faster or slower rate. Event sounds can be used as many times as you like in a movie, with no increase in the file size of your published movie. However, when a movie is played over the Web, it must be downloaded completely before it begins playing.

(b) Stream Sounds: *Stream sounds* are similar to animated graphic symbols because they are closely tied to the main Timeline. Thus, even if a stream sound is longer than a movie, a stream sound stops at the end of the movie. *Stream sounds* begin playing as soon as enough data for the first few frames have been downloaded, which prevent users from waiting for the entire sound file to download before the movie starts. Stream sounds are synchronized to the Timeline for playing on a Website.

Although you can add sounds to layers that contain other objects and actions, keeping sounds on their own layers helps organize your movie and make it easier to edit the sounds.

Importing Sound Files

One way to add sound to an object (such as a button) or the Timeline in Flash Professional CS6 is to import sound files to the Library panel. You can import several types of sound files into Flash Professional CS5, such as Adobe Sound Document (.ASND), Waveform Audio File (.WAV), Audio Interchange File (.aiff), (.aif), MPEG-1 Audio level 3 (.mp3), Sound only QuickTime movies (.mov), (.qtif), System 7 sounds (.snd), Sound Designer II (.sd2) and Sun AU (.au) files. But, MP3, WAV and AIFF files are common sound formats.

When you import sound files into Flash Professional CS6, they are stored in your Library panel. You can then drag the sound files from the Library panel onto the Stage at different points along the Timeline to synchronize those sounds to whatever may be happening on the Stage. In addition to imported sound files, it provides dozens of sound effects, such as sirens wailing, dogs barking, and lightening cracking. These sounds can be accessed by choosing Window menu, Common Libraries option and then Sounds sub-option. An External Library appears. Apart from this, you can also use ActionScript to add a sound during runtime.

To import sound file, do this:

1. Click the File menu, choose Import and then select Import to Library. An Import to Library dialog box appears as shown in Figure 7.1.
2. In Import to Library dialog box, navigate sound file (.wav file) from your local computer, and click Open. Here, we have selected **chimes.wav** file (See Figure 7.1).
3. Flash Professional CS6 stores a copy of sound file (**chimes.wav**) in the Library panel (See Figure 7.2). It is indicated by a unique icon, and the preview window shows a waveform—a series of peaks and valleys that represent the sound. When you click to select any of the frames in your Timeline, the Sound section appears in the Properties Inspector.
4. Click the Play button on the far upper-right corner of the Library Panel preview window to play the sound (See Figure 7.2).
5. Double-click the sound icon in front of your **chimes.wav** file as shown in Figure 7.2. It will display the Sound Properties dialog box as shown in Figure 7.3.

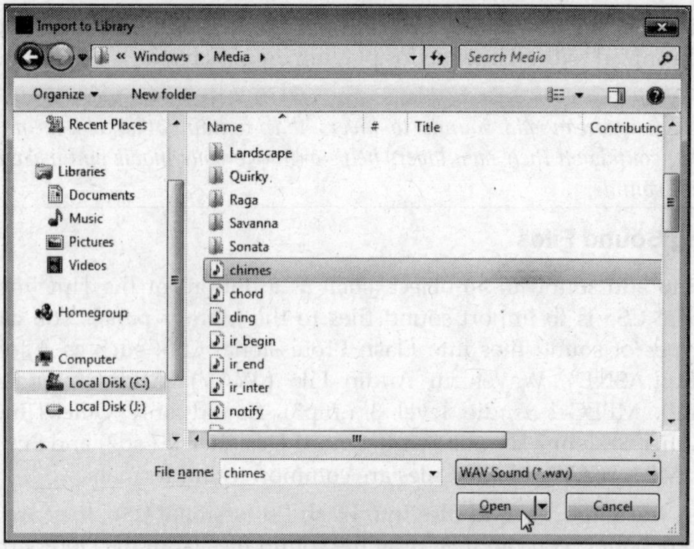

Figure 7.1 Import to Library dialog box

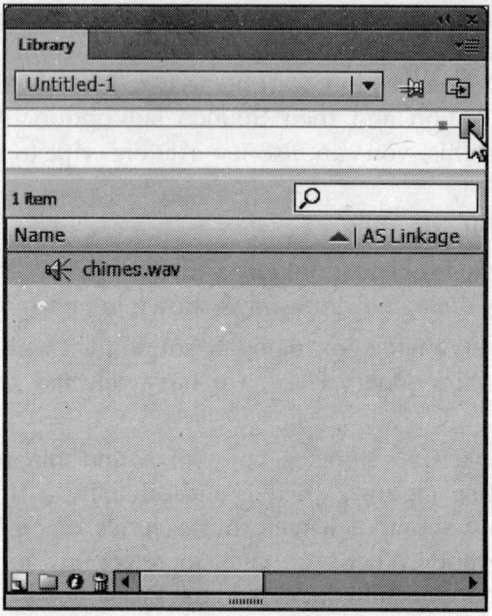

Figure 7.2 Library Panel showing sound file

6. This dialog box provides information about sound file, including its original location, size, and other technical properties.

Hold down the Shift key to select multiple sound files to import them all at once.

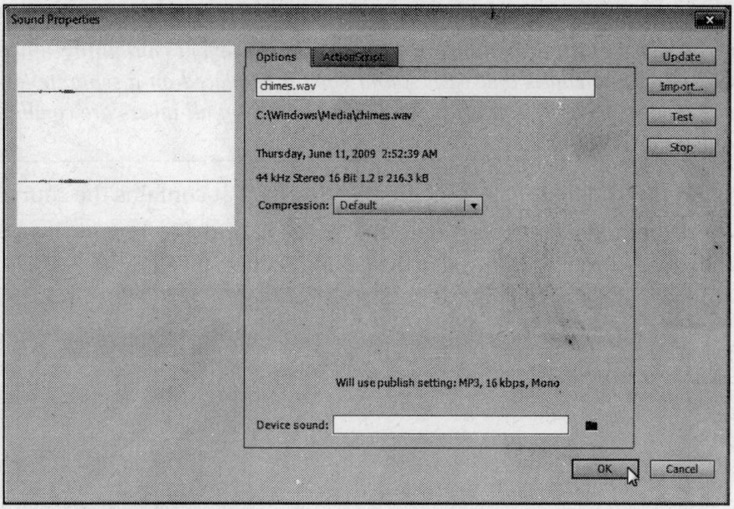

Figure 7.3 Sound Properties dialog box

Placing Sound on the Timeline

You can add a sound at any point along the Timeline using the library, or you can load a sound into a SWF (a file extension for Adobe Flash) file during runtime, using the loadSound method of the Sound object. Flash Professional CS6 will play that sound when the playhead reaches the keyframe.

To place sound on the Timeline, do this:

1. Click Insert menu, select Timeline and then choose Layer or click the New Layer button at the bottom of the Timeline. Rename it as **Sound**.
2. With new Sound layer selected, drag the sound file (i.e., **APPLAUSE.WAV**) from the Library panel onto the Stage (See Figure 7.4). The sound is added to the current layer and the waveform of sound appears on the Timeline.

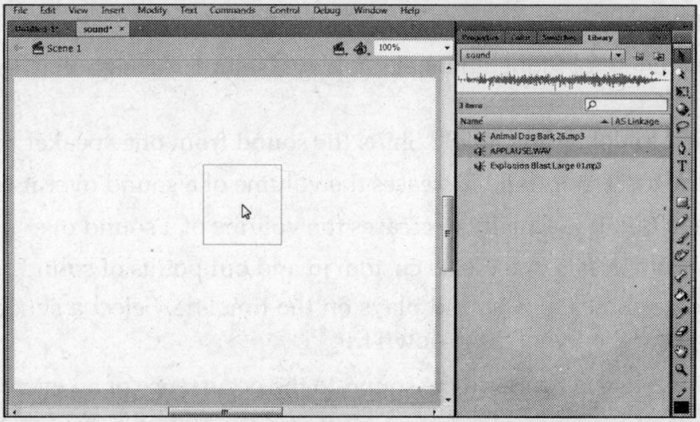

Figure 7.4 Dragging sound file from the Library panel to the Stage

You can place multiple sounds on one layer or on layers containing other objects. But, it is recommended that each sound should be placed on a separate layer. Each layer acts as a separate sound channel. The sounds on all layers are combined when you play the ***SWF*** *file.*

3. Now, in the Timeline, select the first keyframe that contains the sound file.
4. In the Properties Inspector, note that your sound file is now listed on the Name: drop-down menu under the Sound section (See Figure 7.5).

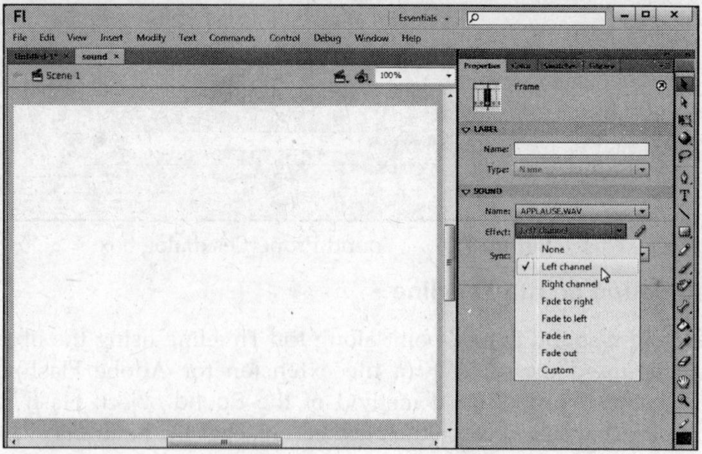

Figure 7.5 Sound section in the Properties Inspector

5. Then under the Sound section as shown in Figure 7.5, select one of the following options:
6. Click the Effects: drop-down list and select one of the effect options (See Figure 7.5).
   - None: It will not apply any effects to the sound file. Selecting this option will remove any previously applied effects.
   - Left channel/Right channel: It plays sound through the left or right speaker.
   - Fade to right/Fade to left: Shifts the sound from one speaker to the other.
   - Fade in: It gradually increases the volume of a sound over its duration.
   - Fade out: It gradually decreases the volume of a sound over its duration.
   - Custom: It lets you create custom in and out points of sound.

   Sync: determines how sound plays on the timeline. Select a synchronization option from the Sync: drop-down list.

   - Event: It synchronizes the sound to the occurrence of an event.
   - Start: It is same as Event, except that if the sound is already playing, no new instance of the sound plays.

- **Stop:** It silences the specified sound.
- **Stream:** It synchronizes the sound for playing on a Website. It is basically used for long passage of music. Stream sounds stop if the SWF file stops playing. Also, a stream sound can never play longer than the length of the frames it occupies. Voice of a character in an animation that plays in multiple frames is an example of stream sound. This option is best suited for *lip-synching*, when you are trying to match a voice over to an animated sequence featuring a talking head.

Enter a value for **Repeat** to specify the number of times the sound should loop.

Select **Loop** to repeat the sound continuously until the Timeline ends.

7. Move the playhead back and forth on the Timeline. The sound plays as you scrub the Timeline.
8. Click **Control** menu, select **Test Movie** and then choose **in Flash Professional** or press **Ctrl + Enter** keys together to test sound in Flash player.

You add a sound to a button in the same way as you add sound on the Timeline, but with two exceptions: (i) You have to add a sound file for a button to the button's third or (ii) ***Down*** *frame so that the sound plays when your audience clicks down on the button and you leave the synchronization option set to* ***Event****.*

Adding Frames to the Timeline

Adding frames to the Timeline means extending the Timeline so that the entire sound (or at least the portions that you desire) plays before the stop action halts the playhead.

To extend the Timeline, do this:

1. Deselect the Timeline by clicking on the Stage.
2. Then place the playhead between frames 1 and 9 by clicking on the top frame numbers.
3. Press **F5** key or click **Insert** menu, select **Timeline** and then choose **Frame** to insert frames between frames 1 and 9.
4. Insert enough frames so that there are about 50 frames to play the sound before the stop action in the second keyframe of the actions layer.
5. Click **Control** menu, select Test Movie and then choose **in Flash Professional** or press **Ctrl + Enter** keys together to test sound in Flash player.
6. The sound lasts longer because it has more frames to play before the playhead stops.

Editing Sound Clips in Flash

If you find you need to adjust imported sounds, Flash Professional CS6 offers some very useful tools for basic editing, effects, and sound manipulation. Using this, you can define the starting point of sound or control the volume of the sound as it plays. You can also change the point at which the sound starts and stops playing. This is useful for making sound files smaller by removing unused sections.

To edit the sound clips, do this:

1. Add a sound to a frame, or select a frame that already contains a sound.
2. In the Properties Inspector, click the Edit Sound Envelope button (pencil icon) on the right side of the Effect: drop-down list of the Sound section as shown in Figure 7.6.
3. The Edit Envelope dialog box appears as shown in Figure 7.7.
4. In this dialog box, choose and apply some of the Preset effects from the pull-down menu.
5. To change the start and end points of a sound, drag the Time In and Time Out controls in the Edit Envelope.
6. To change the sound envelope, drag the envelope handles to change levels at different points in the sound. Envelope lines show the volume of the sound as it plays.

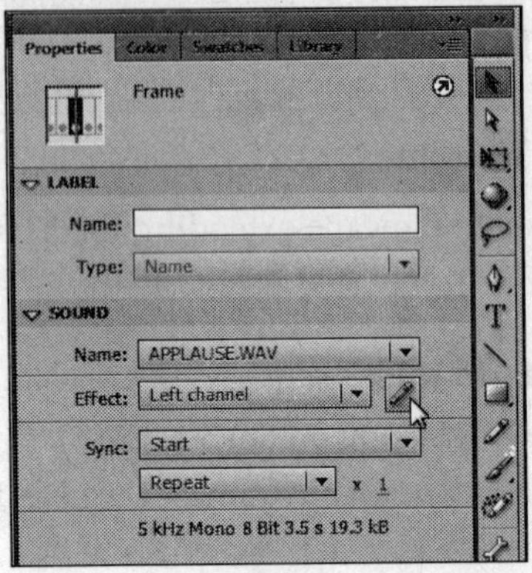

Figure 7.6 Edit Sound Envelope button in Properties Inspector

7. To create additional envelope handles (up to eight in total), click the envelope lines.
8. To remove an envelope handle, drag it out of the window.
9. To display more or less of the sound in the window, click the Zoom In or Out buttons from the **View options**.
10. To switch the time units between seconds and frames, click the Seconds and Frames buttons from the **View options**.
11. To hear the edited sound, click the Play button.
12. Finally, click OK button.

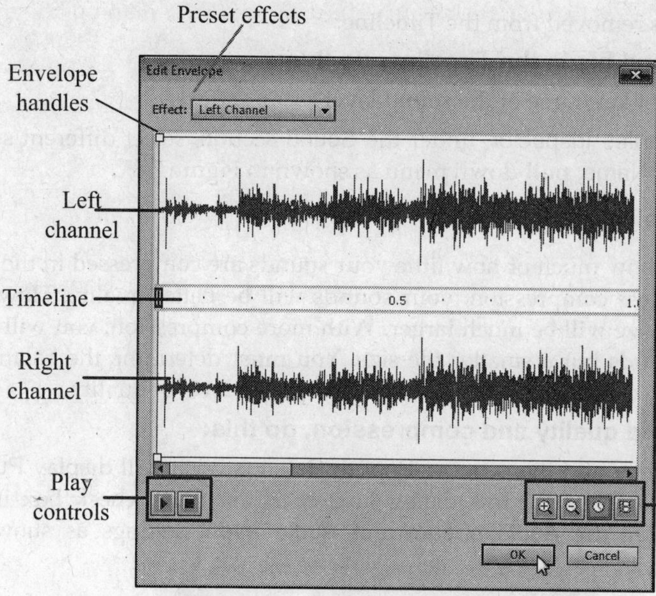

Figure 7.7 Edit Envelope dialog box

Removing or Changing the Sound File

If you do not want the sound on Timeline, or you want to change to a different sound tune, you can make those changes in the Properties Inspector.

To remove sound file from the Timeline, do this:

1. Select the first keyframe of the sound layer.
2. In the Properties Inspector, under the Sound section, select None in the Name: pull-down menu as shown in Figure 7.8.

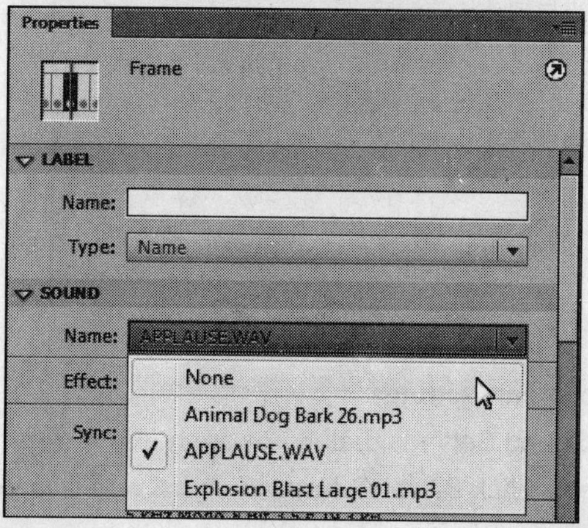

Figure 7.8 Properties Inspector with Sound section

3. The sound is removed from the Timeline.

To change sound file in the Timeline, do this:

1. Select the first keyframe of the sound layer.
2. In the Properties Inspector, under the Sound section, select different sound file from the Name: pull-down menu as shown in Figure 7.8

Setting the Quality of the Sound

You can control how much or how little your sounds are compressed in the final SWF file. With less compression, your sounds will be better quality. However, your final SWF size will be much larger. With more compression, you will have poor quality sounds but a smaller file size. You must determine the balance of quality and file size based on the minimum acceptable level of quality.

To set the sound quality and compression, do this:

1. Click File menu and then choose Publish Settings… . It will display Publish Settings dialog box. In this dialog box, click the Flash check box in the Publish to see the Audio stream and Audio event settings as shown in Figure 7.9.

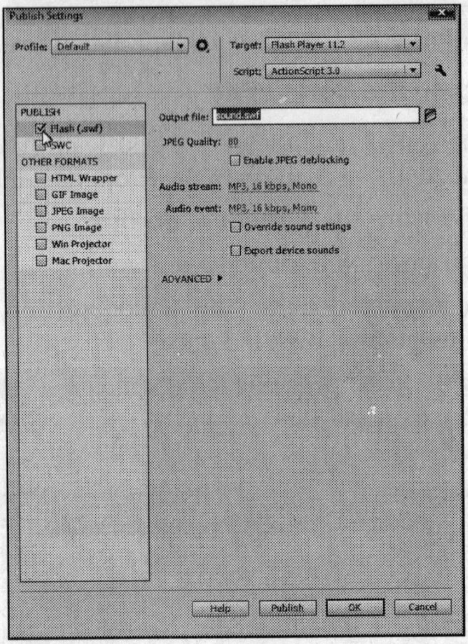

Figure 7.9 Publish Setting dialog box

2. Click the Audio stream settings.
3. It will display Sound Settings dialog box as shown in Figure 7.10.
4. In this dialog box, click Bit rate: drop-down list and change the bit rate to 64 kbps.

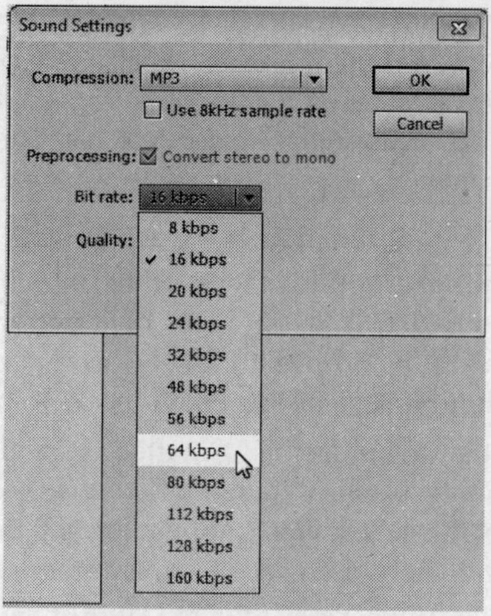

Figure 7.10 Sound Settings dialog box

5. Deselect the option Convert stereo to mono in Preprocessing: setting.
6. Click OK to accept the settings.
7. Then do the same for the Audio event: options.
8. Now both the Audio stream: and Audio event: settings should be at 64 kbps with stereo sounds preserved.
9. Then click OK button.

The Bit rate is measured in kilobits per second (kbps), and it determines the quality of sound in final exported Flash movie. The higher the bit rate the better the quality. However, the higher the bit rate the larger the size of the sound file.

---

10. Select Override sound settings check box in Audio event: setting. This option is useful if you want to create a larger high-fidelity audio file for local use and a smaller low-fidelity version for the Web.
11. Then click OK to save the settings.

The sound settings in the Publish Settings dialog box will determine how all your sounds are exported.

Using Video in Flash Professional CS6

Adobe Flash Professional CS6 is the most common method of delivering video over the Web. Today, most Internet users can view video with Flash than with any other technology including *QuickTime*, *Windows Media Player*, or *RealPlayer*. Content-sharing sites, such as *YouTube* rely on Flash to present video.

Flash Professional CS6 allows you to import FLV (Flash Video) files that can be used in a Flash document. There are several ways to add video into Flash Professional CS6. It will depend on the application, especially, on the file size.

The FLV *and* F4V (H.264) *video formats offer technological and creative benefits that let you fuse video together with data, graphics, sound, and interactive control.* FLV *and* F4V *video let you easily put video on a Web page in a format that almost anyone can view.*

Adding video to Flash is easy, whether you want to present straight video alone, or whether you want to incorporate it with other animated elements. There are two options to display video in Flash. The first option is to keep the video separate from your Flash file and use a playback component from Flash to play the video. The second option is to embed the video in your Flash file.

Both methods require that the video be formatted correctly first. The appropriate video format for Flash is Flash Video, which uses the extension .flv or the extension .f4v. F4V is the latest Flash Video format that supports the H.264 standard, a state-of-the-art video codec (compression-decompression) that delivers high quality with remarkably efficient compression.

A codec (compression-decompression) is a method in which computers use to compress a video file to save space, and then decompress it to play it back.

Using the Adobe® Media® Encoder CS6

Adobe® Media® Encoder CS6 is a stand-alone encoding application that comes with Flash Professional CS6 to convert various video file formats, such as .mov, .avi, and .mpeg, to the FLV (Flash Video) format so the videos can be used with Flash. Adobe Media Encoder can convert single files or multiple files (batch processing) to make your workflow easier.

The Adobe Media Encoder provides a specialized Export Settings dialog box that accommodates the numerous settings associated with certain export formats, such as Adobe Flash Video and H.264. For each format, the Export Settings dialog box includes a number of presets that are tailored for particular delivery media. You can also save custom presets, which you can share with others or reload as needed.

The Adobe® Media® Encoder CS6 can be accessed through the Import Video Wizard *of Adobe Flash Professional CS6.*

Adding a Video File to Adobe Media Encoder CS6

To add a video file to Adobe Media Encoder, do this:

1. First of all, launch Adobe Media Encoder CS6 by clicking Start menu, highlight All Programs, again highlight Adobe Master Collection CS6 and then select Adobe Media Encoder CS6 (See Figure 7.11).

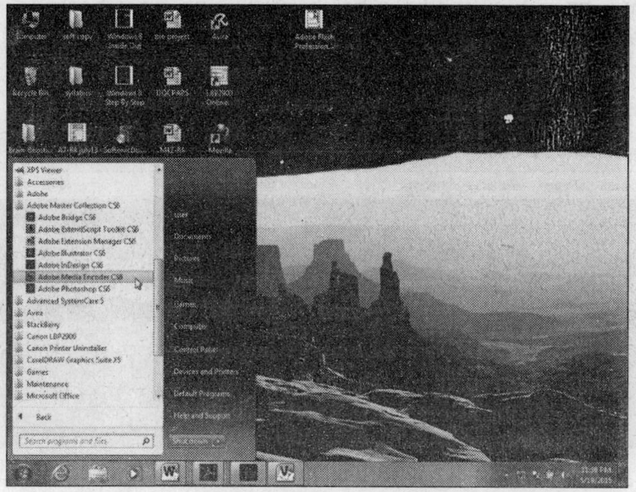

Figure 7.11 Starting Adobe Media Encoder CS6

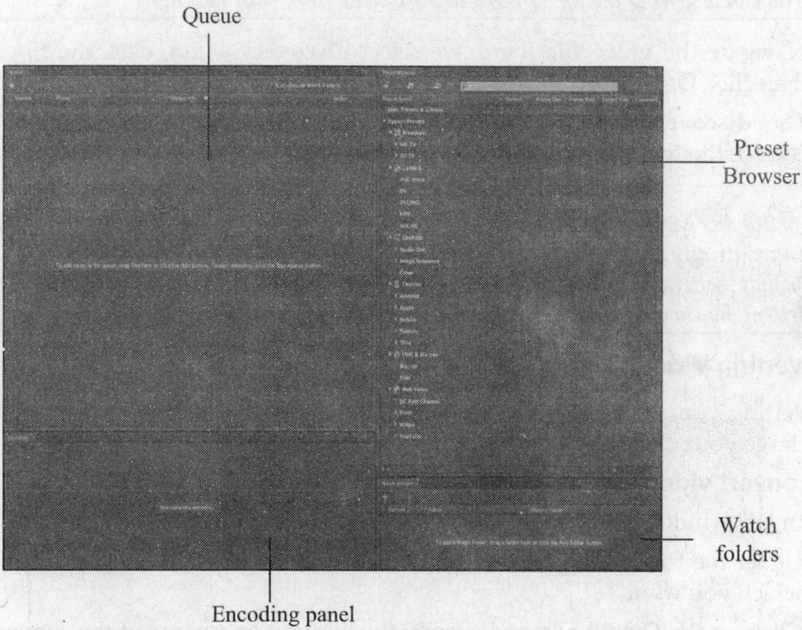

Figure 7.12 Opening screen of Adobe Media Encoder CS6

2. The opening screen of the Adobe Media Encoder CS6 looks like as shown in Figure 7.12. It displays the Queue in the upper left which lists any current video files that have been added for processing. The Queue panel should be empty. Another one is Encoding panel, which shows any video currently being processed. Next in a line is the Watch Folders, which shows folders

that have been identified for batch processing and the last one is Preset Browser, which provides common predefined settings.

3. Click File menu and then choose Add Source or click Plus (+) button from the Queue Panel (See Figure 7.13).

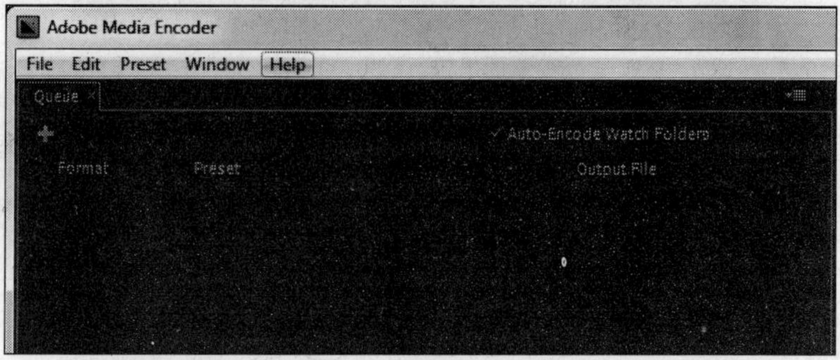

Figure 7.13 Queue panel of Adobe Media Encoder CS6

You can also drag the file directly to the Queue from your desktop.

4. Navigate the video file (here, we select **discovery.wmv)**, click the file and then click Open.
5. The **discovery.wmv** file is added to the display list and is ready for conversion to either an FLV or F4V format.

In Adobe Media Encoder CS6, the default setting is not to start the Queue automatically when the program is idle. But, in Adobe Media Encoder CS5, the default setting was to start the Queue automatically. You can still change the setting by choosing Adobe Media Encoder CS6 > Preferences.

Converting Video Files to Flash Video

Converting your video files is easy, and the length of time it takes depends on how large your original video file is.

To convert video files to Flash Video, do this:

1. In this window, under the Format drop-down list, select the **F4V** option.
2. Under the Preset drop-down list, choose one of the standard preset options which you want.
3. Click on the Output File and specify the location and name of the converted file.
4. Then click Start Queue button to begin the encoding process. Flash displays the settings for the encoded video, and shows the progress and a preview of the video in in the Encoding panel.

5. When the encoding process finishes, a "Done" label and green check appear in the Status column of the Queue panel indicates that the file has been converted successfully. Now you get **discovery.f4v** file to be used in Flash.

Setting Encoding Options

You can customize many settings when converting original video to the Flash Video format. You can crop and resize video to specific dimensions, convert a snippet of the video, adjust the type of compression and also the compression levels, and even apply filters to the video.

To display the encoding options, do this:

1. Click Edit menu and then choose Export Settings.
2. The Export Settings dialog box appears as shown in Figure 7.14.

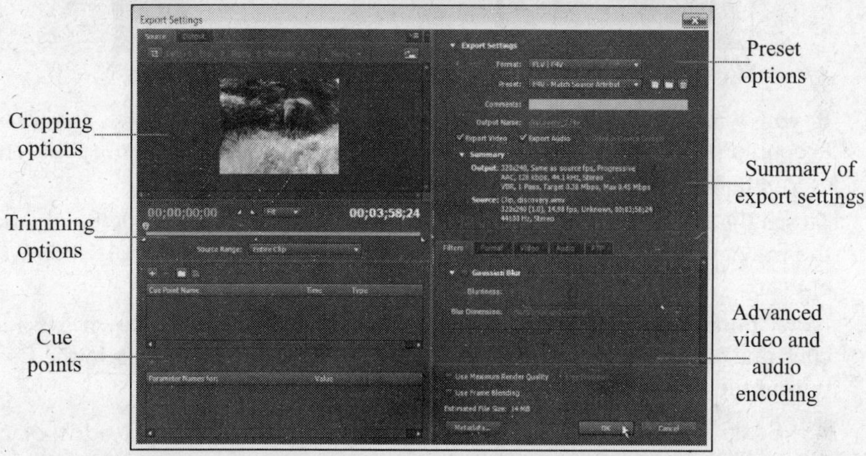

Figure 7.14 Export Settings dialog box

Cropping Video

Cropping is the process of removing some portions of an image or a video. If you only want to show a portion of the video, you can crop it.

To crop video, do this:

1. In the Export Settings dialog box, under the Source tab, click the Crop button at the upper-left corner. The cropping box appears over the video preview window.
2. Drag the sides inward to crop from the *top, bottom, left,* or *right*. The grayed-out portions outside the box will be discarded as shown in Figure 7.15. Flash displays the new dimensions next to the cursor. You can also use the Left, Top, Right, and Bottom settings above the preview window to enter exacted pixel values.

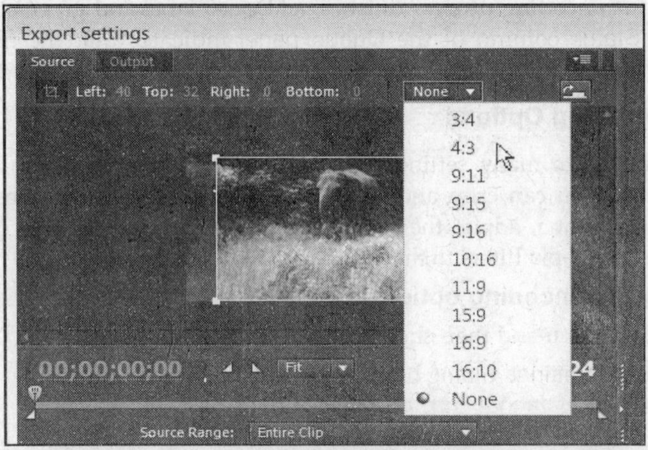

Figure 7.15 Cropping options in Export Settings dialog box

3. If you want to keep the crop in a standard proportion, click the Crop Proportions menu and choose the desired ratio as shown in Figure 7.15. The cropping box will be constrained to the selected proportions.
4. To see the effects of the crop, click the Output Tab in the upper-left corner of the preview window. The preview window shows how the final video will appear.
5. Now, under the Output tab, click the Source Scaling: drop-down list and click one of the following options to set how the crop will appear in the final output file (See Figure 7.16).

   - Scale To Fit: It adjusts the dimensions of the crop and adds black borders to fit the output file.

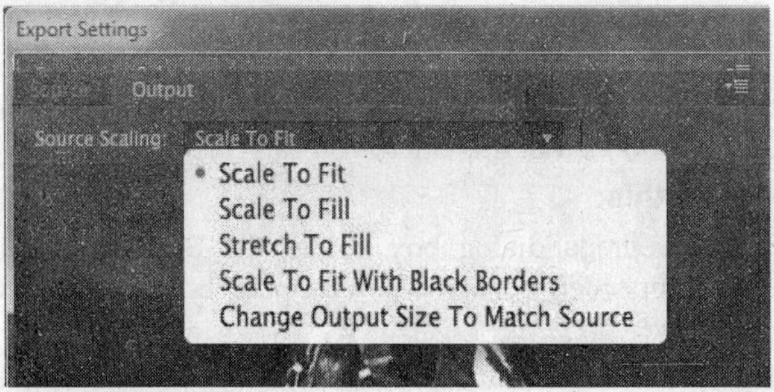

Figure 7.16 Source Scaling: drop-down list

   - Scale To Fill: It adjusts the dimensions of the crop to fill the size of the output file.
   - Stretch To Fill: It adjusts the dimensions of the crop by distorting the image, if necessary, to fill the size of the output file.

- Scale To Fit With Black Borders: It adds black bands at either the top or at the sides to fit the crop in the dimensions of the output file.
- Change Output Size To Match Source: It changes the dimensions of the output file to match the crop dimensions.

6. To exit from the cropping mode without making the crop, click the Source tab and then click Crop button again to deselect it.

Adjusting Video Length

If your videos have unwanted segments at the beginning or at the end, you can cut off footage from either end to adjust the overall length of the video.

To adjust the video length, do this:

1. In the Export Settings dialog box, under the *Trimming options*, click and drag the playhead (top yellow marker) to scrub through the video to preview the footage. Place the playhead at the desired beginning point of the video.
2. Click the Set In Point icon.
3. The In point moves to the current position of the playhead (See Figure 7.17).
4. Drag the playhead to the desired ending point of your video.
5. Click the Set Out Point icon as shown in Figure 7.17.

Figure 7.17 Adjusting video length using Trimming options

6. The Out point moves to the current position of the playhead.
7. You can also simply drag the In and Out point markers to set the desired video segment.
8. The highlighted portion of your video between the In and Out point markers will be the only segment of your original video that will be encoded.

Playback of External Video Using the Import Video Wizard

Now you have successfully converted your video to the correct Flash-compatible format, you can use it in Flash. You will keep your videos external to the Flash project. By keeping videos external, your Flash project remains small, the videos can be edited separately, and the videos can maintain different frame rates from your Flash project.

The Import Video Wizard guides you step-by-step process through a series of windows to add video into Flash. The Video Import Wizard provides a basic level of configuration for the import and playback method you choose, which you can later modify for your specific requirements.

To import video into Flash, do this:

1. Click File menu, select Import and then choose the Import Video. The Import Video Wizard appears as shown in Figure 7.18.

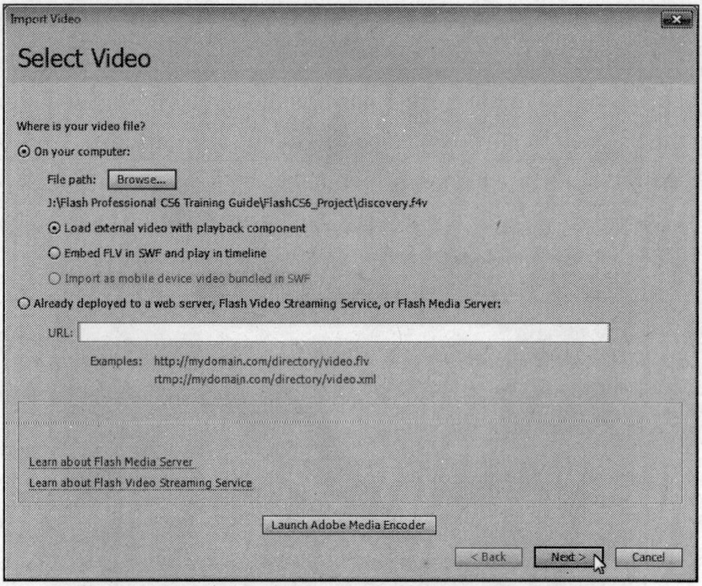

Figure 7.18 Import Video Wizard–Select Video

2. In the Import Video wizard, select On your computer radio button and then click Browse.
3. Navigate to the drive and folder where your .flv or .f4v files are stored. Click the file and then click Open.
4. The path to the video file appears below the Browse button as shown in Figure 7.18.
5. Then click one of the following video import options:

- **Load external video with playback component**: It imports the video and creates an instance of the FLV Playback component to control video playback. When you want to publish the Flash document as a SWF file and upload it to your Web server. You must also upload the video file to either a Web server or Flash Media Server, and configure the FLV Playback component with the location of the uploaded video file.
- **Embed FLV or F4V in SWF and play in timeline**: It embeds the FLV or F4V into the Flash document. When you import video in this way, the video is placed in the **Library panel** and the video layer on the **Timeline** where you can see the individual video frames represented in the **Timeline** frames. The embedded video plays when the **Play** button is clicked.
- **Import as mobile device video bundled in SWF**: It is similar to embedding a video in a Flash Professional document. You can bundle a video into a Flash Lite document for deployment to a mobile device.

✍ *An embedded FLV or F4V video file becomes part of the Flash Professional CS6 document.*

---

6. Click **Launch Adobe Media Encoder** button if you want to convert any video file formats, such as .mov, .avi, and .mpeg, to the FLV (Flash Video) format so that the videos can be used with Flash Professional CS6.
7. Then click **Next>** button.
8. In the next screen of the Import Video wizard, you have to select the skin, or the interface controls for the video from the **Skin**: drop-down list (See Figure 7.19). The skinning feature is useful to determine the appearance and position of the play controls.

✍ *The skin is a small SWF file that determines the functionality and appearance of the video's controls. You can use one of the skins provided with Flash Professional CS6, or you can choose* **None** *from the top of the menu.*

---

9. Select the colour of controls from the **Color**: box.
10. A preview of the skin and its controls appear in the preview window.
11. Then click **Next>** button.
12. On the next screen of the Import Video wizard, review the information for the video file, and then click **Finish** button to place the video.
13. Video with the selected skin appears on the **Stage** and an FLV Playback component also appears in the **Library panel** (See Figure 7.20).

✍ *Component is a special widget that is used on the* **Stage** *to play external video.*

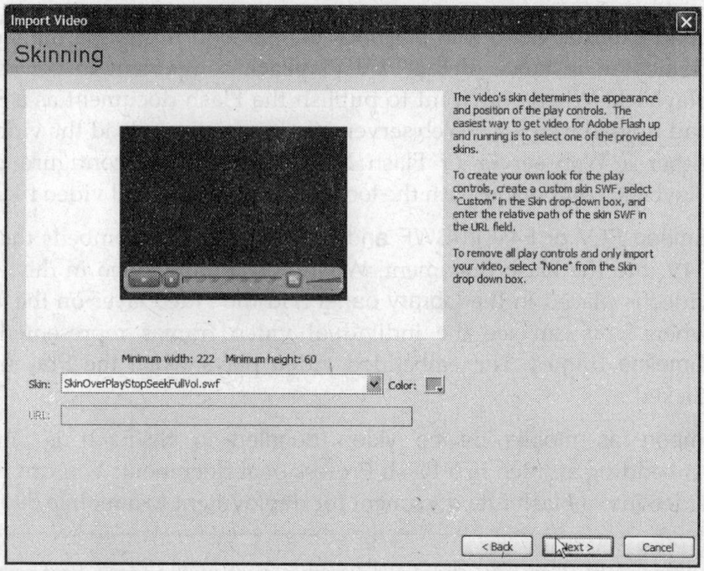

Figure 7.19 Import Video Wizard–Skinning

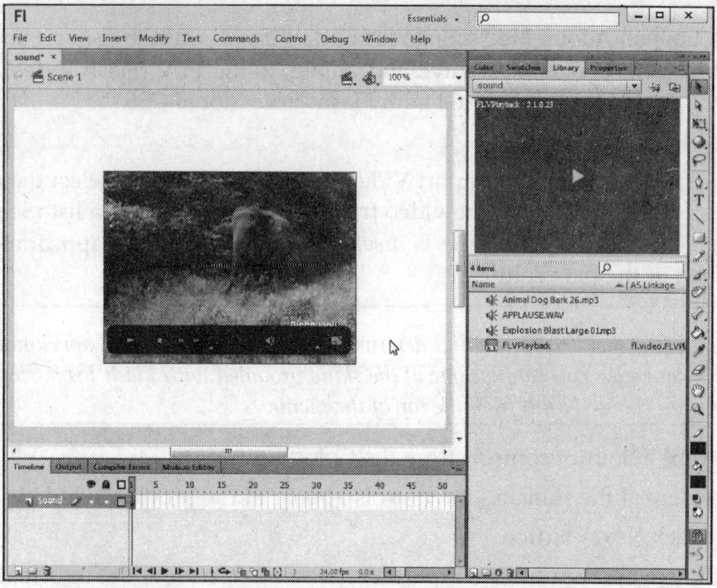

Figure 7.20 Video on the Stage and on the Library panel

14. Click the Play button on the skin of your video to preview the video. The video plays on the Stage. Use the controls to *play, stop, scrub,* and *change the volume* of the movie.

15. Click Control menu, select Test Movie and then choose in Flash Professional or press Ctrl + Enter keys together to test video in Flash player (See Figure 7.21).

Figure 7.21 Video played on Flash Player

Controlling the Video Playback

The FLVPlayback component lets you control which video is to be played, whether the video plays automatically, and other aspects of playback. The options for playback can be accessed in the Properties Inspector.

To control the video playback using Properties Inspector, do this:

1. Select the videos on the Stage.
2. In the Properties Inspector, under the Component Parameters, choose out of the following options (See Figure 7.22):
   - Click autoPlay check box, if you want that the video plays automatically. When the check box is deselected, the video is paused on the first frame.
   - Click skinAutoHide check box to hide the controller and only display it when users roll their mouse cursor over the video.
   - To choose a new skin, click the name of your skin file and select a new skin in the dialog box that appears.
   - To change the transparency of the skin, enter a decimal value from 0 (totally transparent) to 1 (totally opaque) in the skinBackgroundAlpha text box.

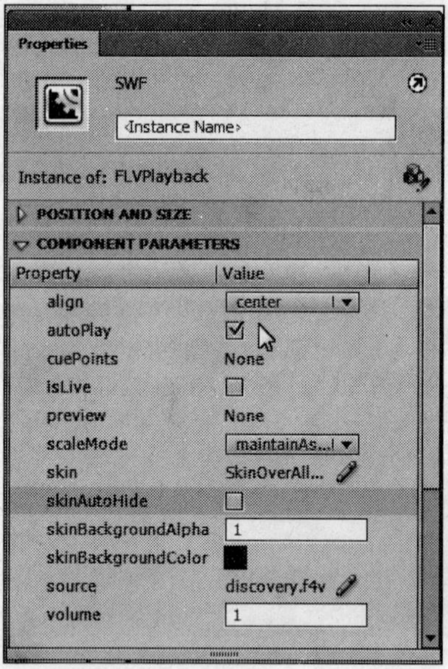

Figure 7.22 Controlling video playback using Properties Inspector

- To change the color of the skin, click on the skinBackgroundColor box.
- To change the video file or the location of the video file that Flash plays, click the source option.
- To change the volume, enter values from 0 to 100 in the volume text box.

Working with Cue Points

Cue points are special markers that are placed in the video to allow events to be triggered at specific times in the video. It can transform an ordinary, linear video into a true interactive, immersive video experience. There are two types of cue points that you can work with in Flash Professional CS6. These are:

(a) Encoded cue points: You can add these cue points to a video when encoding video with Adobe Media Encoder takes place. Encoded cue points can be accessed by other applications in addition to Flash.

(b) ActionScript cue points: You can add these cue points to a video with the Properties Inspector in Flash Professional CS6. ActionScript cue points are accessible only to Flash and Flash Player.

When an FLVPlayback component instance is selected on the Stage, the video cue points list appears in the Properties Inspector. *You can also preview the entire video on the* Stage *and add* ActionScript *cue points using the* Properties Inspector *while previewing the video, including videos served by* Flash Media Server.

To insert cue points in the Properties Inspector, do this:

1. Import video as a progressive download, or place the FLVPlayback component on the stage and specify the source video. You can specify the source video in the Properties Inspector.

✍ *If the FLVPlayback component on the Stage does not show a preview of the video, right-click on the video and make sure that the Preview option is selected.*

---

2. In the Properties Inspector, under the Cue Points section make the changes or add the cue points as you want (See Figure 7.23).
   - Click the + (Add ActionScript Cue Point) button to add an ActionScript cue point.

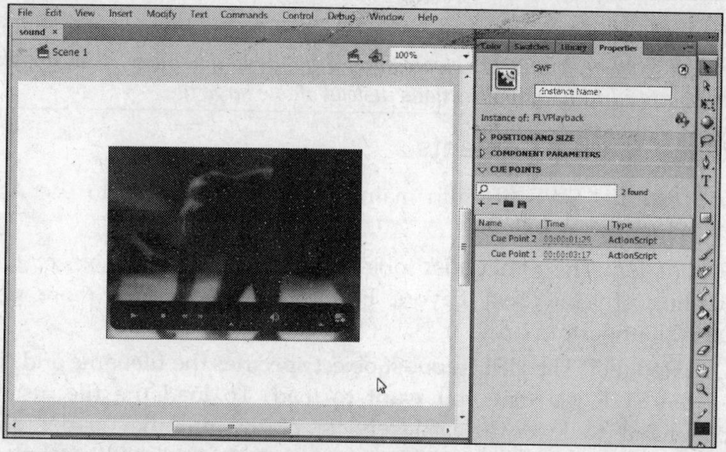

Figure 7.23 Cue Points section of the Properties Inspector

   - Click the – (Delete ActionScript Cue Point) button to delete an existing cue point.
   - To specify the time, under the Time column, drag the mouse right or left to increase or decrease the time code value, or type in a value.
   - To add a parameter to a cue point, select the ActionScript cue point and click the + (Add Cue Point Parameter) button at the bottom of Parameters section.
   - To rename the ActionScript cue points and any parameters, click in the Name field and change the name.

✍ *In the Properties Inspector, double-click any cue point in the Type column, and video on the Stage will immediately jump to that particular cue point.*

CHAPTER 8

Loading and Controlling Flash Contents

Introduction

In this Chapter, you will learn how to load an external Small Web Forma or SWF (a file extension for Adobe Flash) file, remove a loaded SWF file and control a movie clip's Timeline. We use ActionScript to load external Flash contents. By keeping Flash content modular, Flash projects remain more manageable and easier to edit.

Loading external content keeps overall project in separate modules and prevents the project from becoming too bloated and difficult to download. It also makes it easier for you to edit individual sections instead of one large file.

Loading External Contents

To load external SWF file into main Flash file, you have to use ActionScript objects, which are as follows:

(a) ProLoader: The ProLoader object is an ActionScript object handles the loading of TLF (Text Layout Format) text better for more reliable and consistent performance.

(b) URLRequest: The URLRequest object specifies the filename and file location of the SWF file that you want to load. To load the file, use the load() command to load the URLRequest object into the Loader object. Then display the Loader object on the Stage with the addChild() command.

To load the external files using Actions panel, do this:

1. Open a Flash file containing movie clip symbol.
2. Now insert a new layer and rename it as **ActionScript**.
3. Now drag a movie clip symbol (**building**, in our case) from the Library and select it as shown in Figure 8.1.
4. Then in Properties Inspector, under the Instance name box name it as **building_plane** as shown in Figure 8.2.
5. Click the Window menu and choose Actions. Or *alternatively*, press F9 key. The Actions Panel window appears as shown in Figure 8.3.
6. Then type the following two line (See Figure 8.3):

   ```
   import fl.display.ProLoader;
   var myProLoader:ProLoader=new ProLoader();
   ```

   This code first imports the necessary code for the ProLoader class, and then creates a ProLoader object and names it myProLoader.

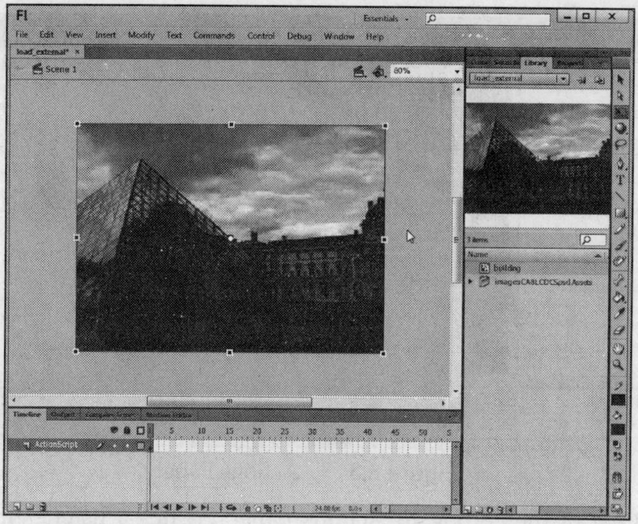

Figure 8.1 Dragging movie clip symbol from Library panel

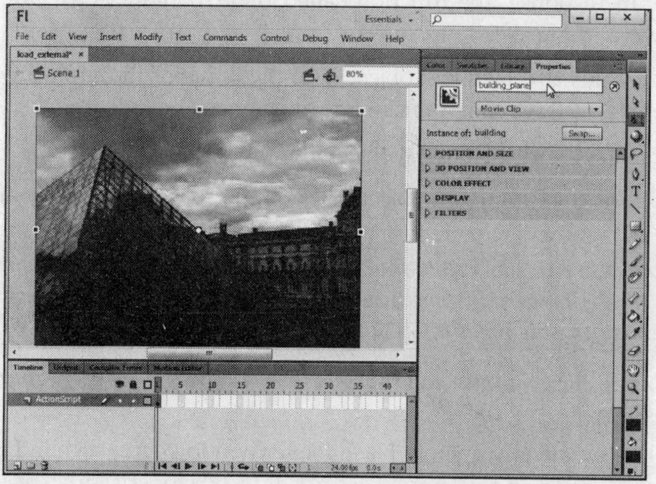

Figure 8.2 Giving name to movie clip instance in the Properties Inspector

7. On the next line, type the following lines (See Figure 8.3):

```
building_plane.addEventListener(MouseEvent.CLICK, page1content);
function page1content(myevent:MouseEvent):void {
var myURL:URLRequest=new URLRequest("plane.swf");
myProLoader.load(myURL);
addChild(myProLoader);
}
```

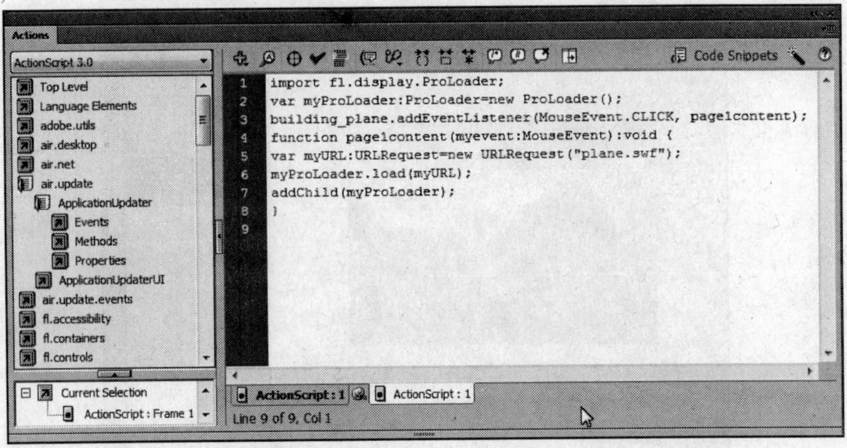

Figure 8.3 Actions Panel

8. Line three of the coding in Actions panel, creates a listener that detects a mouse click on the object called building_plane. This is a movie clip on the Stage. In response, the function called page1content is executed and does the several things:
   - It creates URLRequest object with the name of the file we want to load. (Here, we give the **plane.swf** as file name).
   - It loads the URLRequest object into the ProLoader object.
   - It adds the ProLoader object to the Stage so that we can see it.

You can also use the ProLoader and URLRequest objects to dynamically load image files. The syntax is identical. Simply replace the SWF filename with a JPEG (Joint Photographic Experts Group) filename, and Flash loads the specified image.

---

9. After that click Control menu, select Test Movie and then choose in Flash Professional.
10. It will automatically open in Flash Player window as shown in Figure 8.4.
11. When you click the building movie clip symbol, the file called **plane.swf** loads and is displayed as shown in Figure 8.5.

Adding event listeners to movie clips can make them respond to mouse clicks, but the cursor does not automatically change to a hand icon to indicate that it is clickable. In the Actions panel, set the property buttonMode to true for each movie clip instance to enable the hand cursor. For example, building_plane.buttonMode = true makes the hand cursor appear when you move your mouse over that movie clip on the Stage.

Figure 8.4 Flash Player window

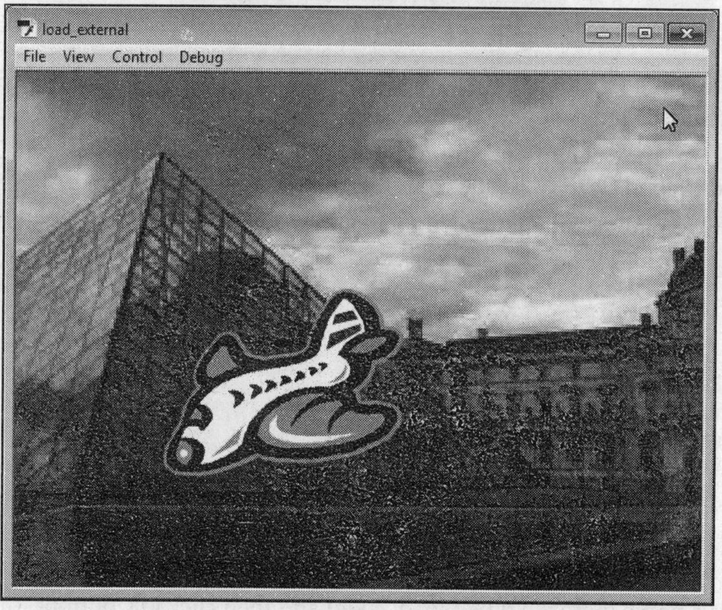

Figure 8.5 Flash Player window after loading external plane.swf file

You can also use the Code Snippets panel to visually point and add code to load external SWF or image files.

To load external contents using Code Snippets panel, do this:

1. Click the Window menu and then choose Code Snippets. It will display Code Snippets panel as shown in Figure 8.6.

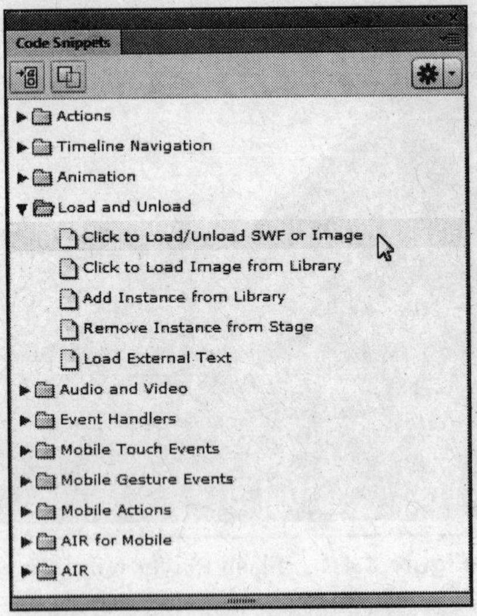

Figure 8.6 Code Snippets panel

2. In the Code Snippets panel, click the Load and Unload folder to expand its contents.
3. Select a movie clip on the Stage and double-click the option Click to Load/Unload SWF or Image from the Code Snippets panel.
4. Flash displays Set Instance Name dialog box as shown in Figure 8.7.

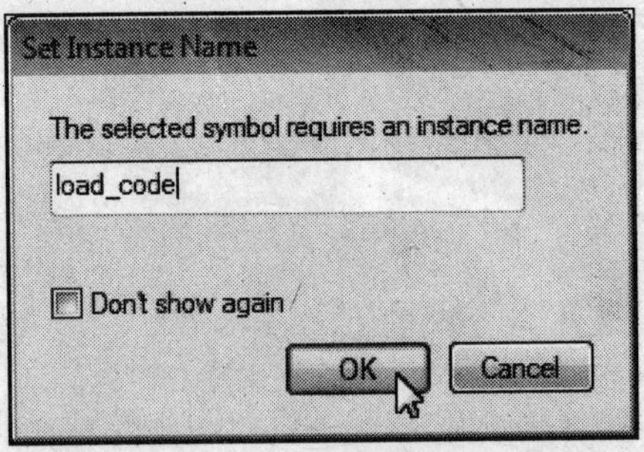

Figure 8.7 Set Instance Name dialog box

5. Give a name (here we typed load_code) and then click OK button.
6. After that it will display the necessary ActionScript code to load a SWF or an image.
7. In the code, replace the path and filename in the sample code with your own (See Figure 8.8).

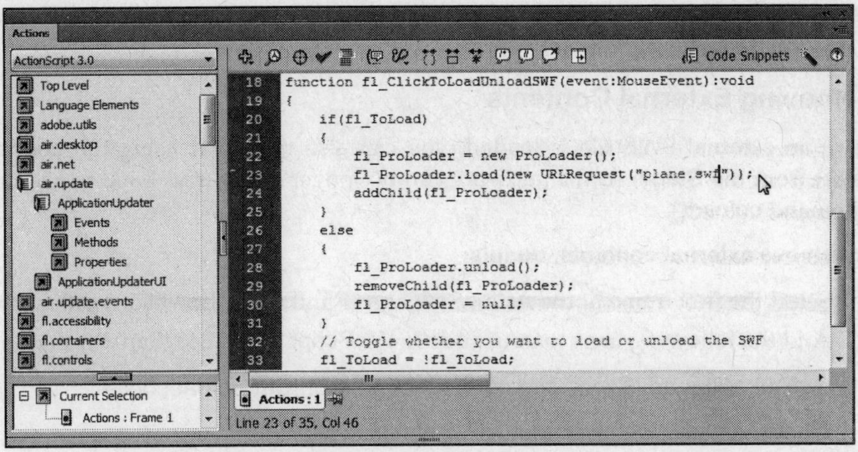

Figure 8.8 ActionScript code to load a SWF or an image

8. After that click Control menu, select Test Movie and then choose in Flash Professional.
9. It will automatically open in Flash Player window. When you click the movie clip symbol, the SWF file or an image loads and is displayed.

Using the Code Snippets panel can save your time and effort, but understanding how the code works and writing code is the only way to begin building more sophisticated, customized projects.

Positioning the Loaded Content

Loaded content is aligned with the Stage or the registration point of the ProLoader object that it is loaded into. By default, the ProLoader object is positioned at the registration point of the Stage (the top-left corner). However, you can position the ProLoader object wherever you want.

If you want to place the ProLroader object in a different horizontal position, you can set a new x value for the Loader object with ActionScript.

If you want to place the ProLoader in a different vertical position, you can set a new y value for the Loader.

In the Actions panel, enter the name of the ProLoader object, followed by a period (.), the property x or y, and then an equals symbol and a new value. In the following example, the ProLoader object called myProLoader is repositioned 200 pixels from the left edge and 100 pixels from the top edge (See Figure 8.9).

```

myProLoader.x = 200;
myProLoader.y = 100;
```

Figure 8.9 Positioning (horizontal and vertical) the loaded content

When the external content loads, it shows up exactly 200 pixels to the right and 100 pixels down.

Removing External Contents

Once an external SWF file is loaded, you can also unload it using the Loader object from the Stage, so the audience can no longer see it. You have to use the command unload().

To remove external contents, do this:

1. Select the first frame of the ActionScript layer and open the Actions panel.
2. Add the following lines to your code in the Script pane (See Figure 8.10):

```
myProLoader.addEventListener(MouseEvent.CLICK, unloadcontent);
function unloadcontent(e:MouseEvent):void {
myProloader.unload();
}
```

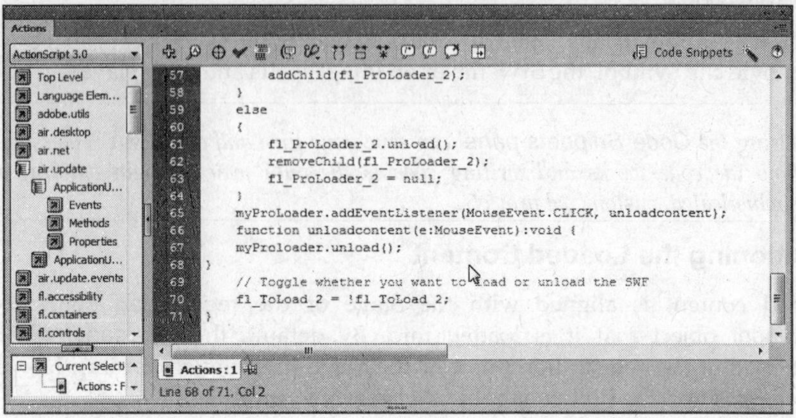

Figure 8.10 Code entered in Actions panel to remove external contents

3. Above written code adds an event listener to the ProLoader object called myProLoader. When you click on the ProLoader object, the function called unloadcontent is executed. The function performs just one action. It removes any loaded content from the ProLoader object.
4. After that click Control menu, select Test Movie and then choose in Flash Professional to preview the movie.

---

*If you want to remove the **ProLoader** object from the Stage entirely, you can use the **removeChild()** command. The code **removeChild (myProLoader)** removes the **ProLoader** object called **myProLoader** so that it is no longer displayed on the Stage.*

CHAPTER 9

Publishing Flash Professional CS6 Documents

Introduction

The most common use of Flash Professional CS6 is to develop movies that provide Web content and applications. Flash Professional CS6 provides several features that help you generate the files that are necessary for delivering movies successfully to the target audience over the Internet. When you deliver a movie over the Internet, you have to keep the file size small so that the movies play smoothly even when user's Internet connection speed is low. It will also allow you to test movies to determine where problems might arise during download and to make changes to optimize the play of movies.

Adobe provides a program called Device Central, which allows you to preview and test contents on mobile devices. This is especially useful when designing Flash movies because of the reduced viewing size for mobile devices, such as cell phones, and the limited download speeds available for mobile devices.

✍ *Using Device Central, you can specify the model of a cell phone and simulate the display of Flash movies for that phone. Then you can make adjustments in your movie to optimize the design and lighting.*

Adobe also provides a version of its Flash Player, called Flash Lite, which is specifically developed to optimize the playing of Flash movies using mobile devices.

In the earlier Chapters, you saw that a Flash movie played only on your computer system. But in this Chapter, you will come to know how you can upload Flash movie to a Web Server. For this, you must publish the Flash file (having .FLA extension) in another file format. You will also learn how to customize publish settings for a variety of output formats across Web, mobile and desktop (AIR or Adobe Integrated Runtime).

✍ *Flash is commonly thought of as a Web design and development program, it is also a full-featured multimedia authoring tool. With Flash Professional CS6, you can publish content for distribution to the Web, mobile devices and even as full-featured desktop applications.*

Testing a Flash Document

As you create a final movie, you should play it back to preview animation and test interactive controls. If you test a scene or movie after each step, you know which changes you made and therefore what might have gone wrong. You can also test a scene or an entire movie using the Test Scene or Test Movie command to test downloading performance (where a movie may pause during downloading). You can test movies or scenes in Flash Professional CS6 with two different ways. These ways are:

(a) In a Flash Professional

(b) In a Web browser

✍ *It is a good habit and necessary for user to test the movie using the Test Movie command to see how the SWF (Small Web Format) file works before publishing the movie on the Web. The SWF is an Adobe Flash file format which is used for multimedia, vector graphics and ActionScript.*

To test a movie or a scene in separate window, do this:

1. Click Control menu, select Test Movie or Test Scene according to your need to test movie in Flash player.
2. This command creates a SWF file in the same location as your FLA file so you can play and preview the movie directly within the Flash application (See Figure 9.1).

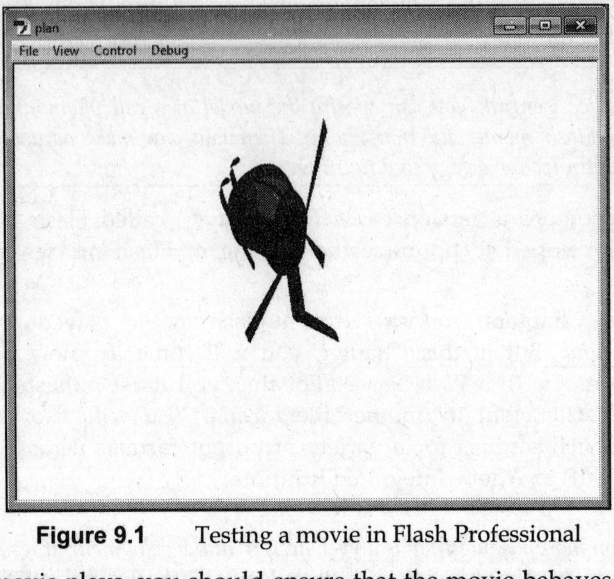

Figure 9.1 Testing a movie in Flash Professional

3. As the movie plays, you should ensure that the movie behaves as expected. You should check every possibility that a user may encounter.

✍ *Test Movie or Test Scene command does not create the HTML (HyperText Markup Language) file or any other files necessary to play the movie using a Web browser.*

To test movie or scene in Web browser, do this:

1. Click File menu and then choose Publish Preview and then select Default-(HTML). *Alternatively*, press F12 key to export a SWF file and an HTML file required to play in a Web browser and to preview the movie.
2. A browser opens, if one is not already open, and plays the final movie. Figure 9.2 shows testing of a scene or movie as if it is in a Web browser.

Figure 9.2 Testing a movie or scene in a Web browser

The default behavior for your movie in the **Test Movie** *mode is to loop. You can make your* **SWF** *file to play differently in a browser by selecting different publish settings or by adding* **ActionScript** *to stop the* **Timeline**. *ActionScript is an object-oriented programming language used on Web pages in the form of embedded SWF files.*

Using the Bandwidth Profiler

When you publish a movie over the Web, the contents of each frame are sent to the user's computer. When the frame's contents are downloaded in user's computer, the movie may pause because of the amount of data in the frame and the slow Internet connection speed. To overcome this problem, you have to improve a movie by testing it and determining which frames may create a pause during playback. The test should be done using a simulated Internet connection speed that is representative of the speed of your target audience. You can set a simulated speed using the Bandwidth Profiler.

You can preview how your final project might behave under different download environments by using the Bandwidth Profiler, a useful panel that is available when you are in Test Movie mode.

The Bandwidth Profiler provides following information (See Figure 9.3):

(a) **Movie information**: dimensions of the Stage, frame rate, file size, duration, and preload.

(b) **Settings**: simulated bandwidth (specified in the **View** menu option).

(c) **State**: number of the selected frame and size of the contents in that frame.

(d) Each bar of a Bandwidth profiler represents one frame of the movie, and the height of the bar corresponds to the frame size. If a bar extends above the red baseline, the movie may need to pause to allow the frame's contents to be downloaded.

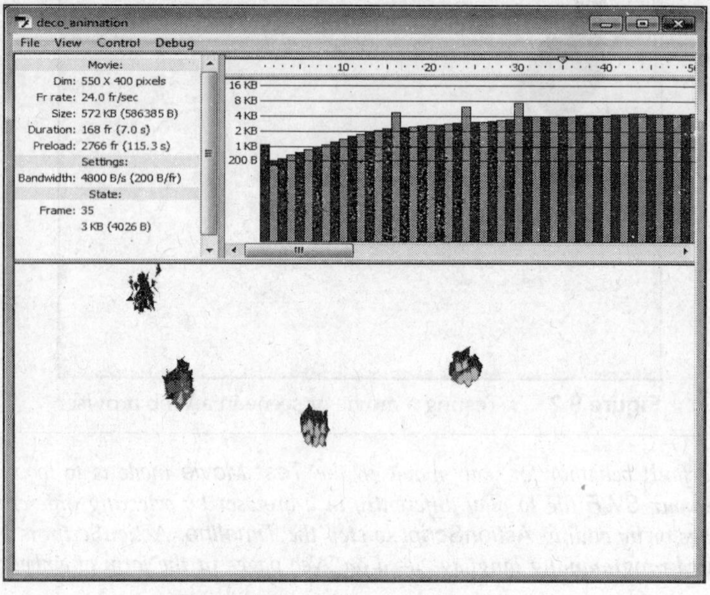

Figure 9.3 Bandwidth Profiler

To view the Bandwidth Profiler, do this:

1. Click **Control** menu, select **Test Movie** and then choose in **Flash Professional**.
2. Flash exports a SWF and displays your movie in a new window.
3. In this window, click **View** menu and then select **Bandwidth Profiler**.
4. A new window appears above your movie as shown in Figure 9.3. Basic information about movie is listed on the left side of the profiler. A timeline appears on the right side of the profiler with gray bars representing the amount of data in each frame. The higher the bars the more data it includes.

Test Document Download Performance

You can set different download speed and test the playback performance of the movie while testing a movie. The most common connections are as follows:

(a) **Dial-up**: Dial-up is a phone connection that provides a relatively slow download speed.

(b) **Broadband (both DSL or Digital Subscriber Line and Cable)**: Broadband is a type of data transmission in which a wide band of frequencies are available to transmit more information at the same time. DSL provides a broadband Internet connection speed that is available through phone lines. It is widely used by business organizations.

(c) **T1**: T1 provides an extremely fast connection speed and is widely used in businesses, especially for intranet applications.

✍ *Testing the movie means that you are developing the different speed to evaluate the download experience for potential users.*

To test download performance, do this:

1. While in **Test Movie mode**, choose **View** menu, select **Download Settings** and then select a download speed to determine the streaming rate that Flash Professional CS6 simulates (here, we choose, DSL). To enter a custom user setting, select **Customize** (See Figure 9.4).

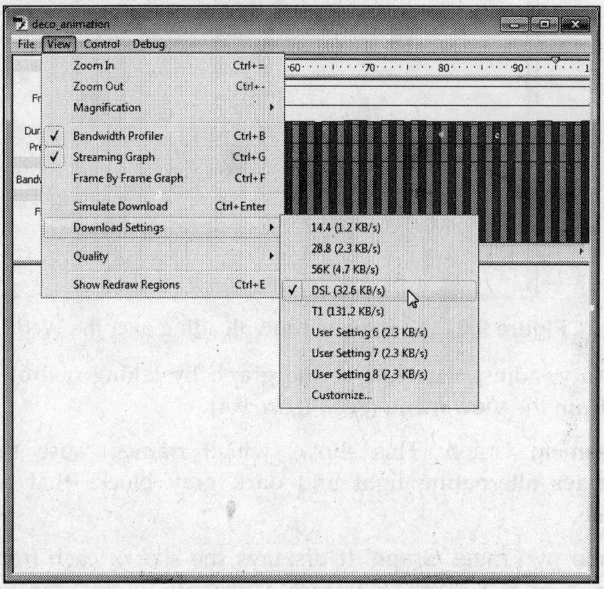

Figure 9.4 Flash Player with View menu selected

DSL setting is a type of Internet connection and it is a measure of the download speed that you want to test. It corresponds to 32.6 kilobytes per second (32.6 KB/s). Choose higher or lower speeds depending on your target audience.

2. Click View menu and then select Simulate Download as shown in Figure 9.4 to turn streaming off or on. If you turn streaming off, the document starts over without simulating a Web connection.
3. Flash Professional CS6 simulates playback over the Web for different bandwidth settings. A green horizontal bar at the top of the window indicates which frames have been downloaded. The triangular playhead marks the current frame that plays currently (See Figure 9.5).
4. Once sufficient data is downloaded, the movie plays and you may still see some pauses when the playhead catches up to the downloaded portions.

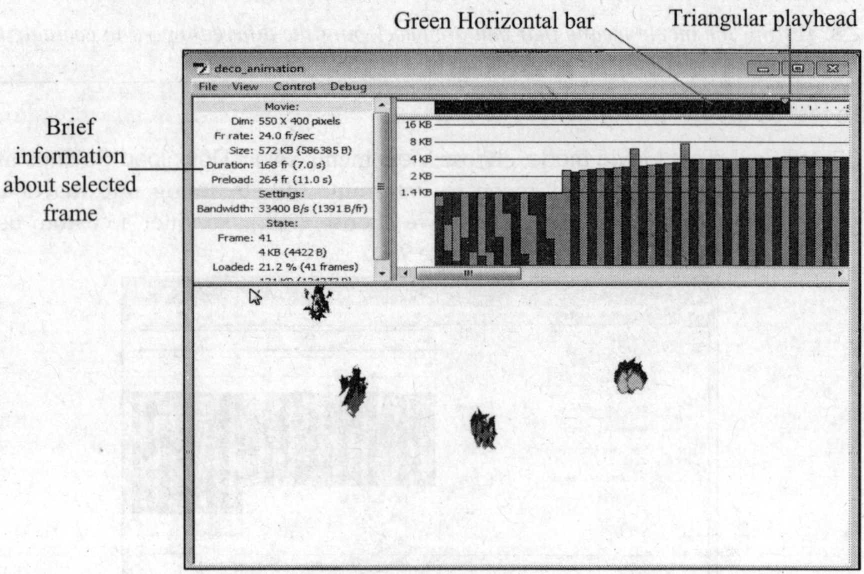

Figure 9.5 Simulates downloading over the Web

5. If necessary, adjust the view of the graph by taking one of the following actions from the View menu (See Figure 9.4):
   - Streaming Graph: This shows which frames cause the pause and displays alternating light and dark gray blocks that represent each frame.
   - Frame by Frame Graph: It displays the size of each frame. This view helps you to see which frames contribute to streaming delays. If any frame block extends above the red line in the graph, Flash Player stops playback until the entire frame is downloaded.

6. Finally, close the test window.

Adding Metadata

Metadata is information about data. It describes your Flash file so other developers with whom you share your FLA can see details that you want them to know, or a search engine on the Web can find and share your movie.

> *Metadata includes a document's title, a description, keywords, the date the file was created, and other information about the document.*

You can add metadata to a Flash document, and that metadata is embedded in the file. Metadata makes it easier for other applications and Web search engines to catalog your movie.

To add metadata, do this:

1. Click File menu and choose Publish Settings... or *alternatively,* press Ctrl + Shift + F12 keys together. A Publish Setting dialog box will appear.
2. Select Flash (.swf) check box in Publish section. A Publish Setting dialog box with Flash setting appears as shown in Figure 9.6.

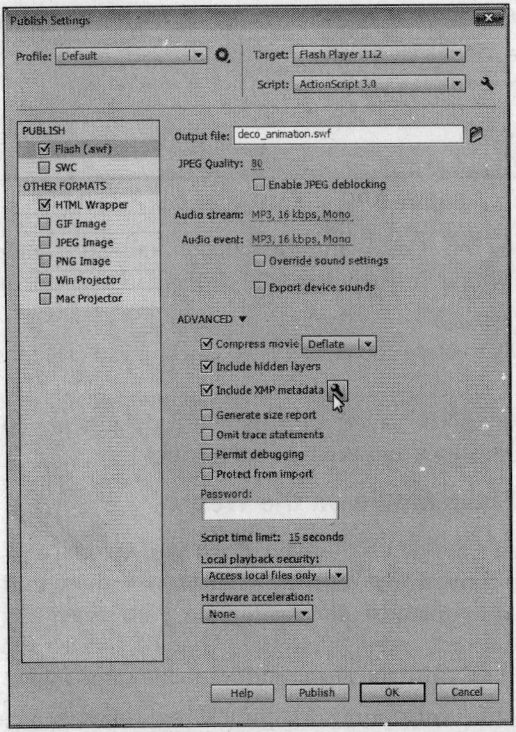

Figure 9.6 Publish Settings dialog box with Flash settings

3. In the Advanced section, click the Include XMP metadata check box and then click the wrench icon as shown in Figure 9.6. XMP stands for eXtensible Metadata Platform.
4. The XMP Metadata dialog box appears as shown in Figure 9.7.

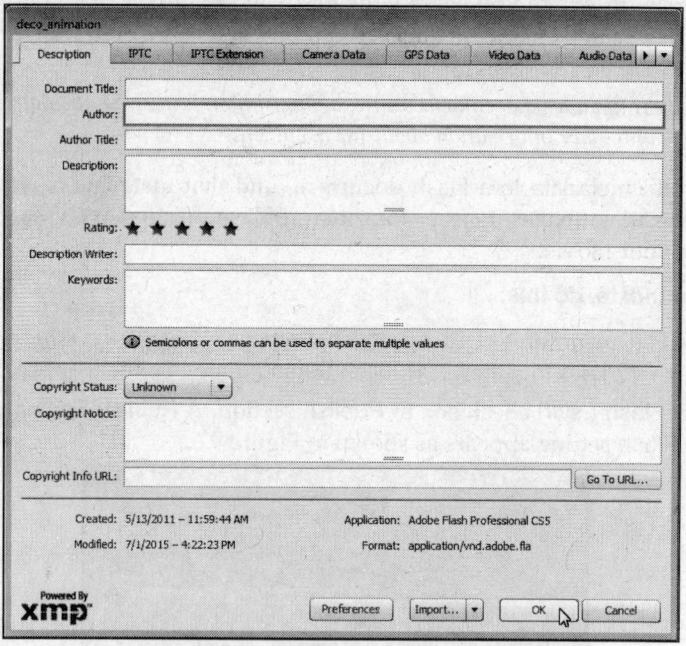

Figure 9.7 XMP Metadata dialog box

5. In this dialog box, click the Description tab and enter any descriptive information which you want to add with the Flash document in the space provided.
6. Then click OK to close the dialog box. Click OK to close the Publish Settings dialog box.
7. The metadata will be saved with the Flash document and will be available for other applications and Web search engines.

Publishing a Flash Movie on the Web

When you publish a movie for the Web, Flash Professional CS5 creates a SWF file and an HTML document that tells the Web browser how to display your Flash content. You need to upload both files to your Web server along with any other files your SWF file references (such as FLV or F4V video files and skins). The Publish command saves all the required files to the same folder.

You can specify different options for publishing a movie, including whether to detect the version of Flash Player installed on the viewer's computer. When you change the settings in the **Publish Settings** dialog box, they are saved with the document. You can publish a Flash movie on the Web in the following two steps:

(a) First of all, prepare all required files for the complete Flash application with the **Publish Settings** command and then set its setting according to requirement.

(b) Finally, publish the movie and all its files with the **Publish** command.

Using Publish Settings

To prepare Flash contents for use in other applications or to export the contents of the Flash Movie in a particular file format, you need to use the Export command. The Export command (Export image, selection and movie) do not store export settings with each file, as does the **Publish** command.

Flash Publish feature generates the necessary files to deliver the movies on the Web. When you publish a movie using the default settings, a Flash (.swf) file is created that can be viewed using the Flash Player. In addition, an HTML file is created with the necessary code to instruct the browser how to show or play the SWF file using the Flash Player.

With the Publish command, you can choose the particular file format in which you want the file to be delivered. You can also adjust its settings. Flash automatically publishes the file in the selected formats, creates additional files based on the selected settings, and stores the settings with the movie file for reuse. But, Export Movie option does not save the settings for reuse.

After, creating file formats, such as GIF (Graphics Interchange Format), JPEG (Joint Photographic Experts Group), PNG (Portable Network Graphics), QuickTime, HTML displays them in the browser window. But, another format, such as Windows Projector (.exe) and Macintosh Projector (.app) enables a browser to display movie's animation interactivity for users who do not have the Flash Player installed on their device.

✍ *If you are not distributing the movie over the Internet or if you know the Flash Player will not be available, you can use the Publish Settings feature to create alternate images and stand-alone projector files.*

Changing Publish Settings and Publishing a Flash Movie

To change Publish Settings, do this:

1. Create a file (having object with animation) and save it.
2. Click on **File** menu and choose **Publish Settings...** . Or *alternatively,* press **Ctrl + Shift + F12** keys together. A **Publish Settings** dialog box will appear as shown in Figure 9.6.
3. In this dialog box, select the profile from **Profile**: drop-down list.

Publish profiles let you save a publish settings configuration, export it, and import the publish profile to other documents or for others to use.

4. In this dialog box, from the left pane, select the option for file format you want to create. When you select any file format, corresponding settings will appear in the right pane of this dialog box.
5. HTML format is selected automatically, because an HTML file is required to display the Flash movie in a browser. Choosing an image format such as *GIF, JPEG,* or *PNG* automatically adds the required HTML code to display the image if the Flash Player is not available.
6. Now, if you want to generate all the specified files, then click the Publish button and then click OK. Otherwise click the OK button to save the settings with your file.

To publish a Flash movie, do this:

1. If you set the publish setting, set it as described above.
2. Then, click File menu and choose Publish. Or *alternatively*, press Alt + Shift + F12 keys together.

Publishing a Desktop Application

Most desktop computers have the Flash Player installed with their browsers. If you want to distribute movie to someone who does not have the Flash Player or who has an older version, or you want movie to run without a browser, then there are two ways available in Flash Professional CS6. These are as follows:

(a) You can output your movie as a projector, which is a stand-alone file that includes the Flash Player with your movie. Because a projector contains the Flash Player, projector files are larger than SWF files.

(b) You can also output your movie as an AIR file, which installs an application on the user's desktop. Adobe AIR is a more robust runtime environment that supports a broader range of technologies.

Publishing as a Standalone Projector

A projector is the equivalent of a .swf file and a copy of Flash Player all rolled up into a single executable file. When you create a projector, your audience does not need to have either a Web browser or Flash Player installed on their computers: All they need to do to play your animation is to run the projector file. Tutorials, product demonstrations, and program mock-ups (as well as the programs themselves) are all examples of the kinds of animations you might want to publish as projectors.

You must create a projector that is specific for Windows or for the Macintosh. However, you can create both kinds of projectors from either platform.

To create a projector, do this:

1. Click on File menu and choose Publish Settings... . Or *alternatively*, press Ctrl + Shift + F12 keys together. A Publish Settings dialog box will appear as shown in Figure 9.6.
2. In this dialog box, from the left pane, deselect the formats, such as Flash and HTML Wrapper in Other Formats section. Select Win Projector and Mac Projector check boxes in Other Formats section (See Figure 9.8).
3. Then click Publish button.
4. When the files have been published, click OK to close the dialog box.

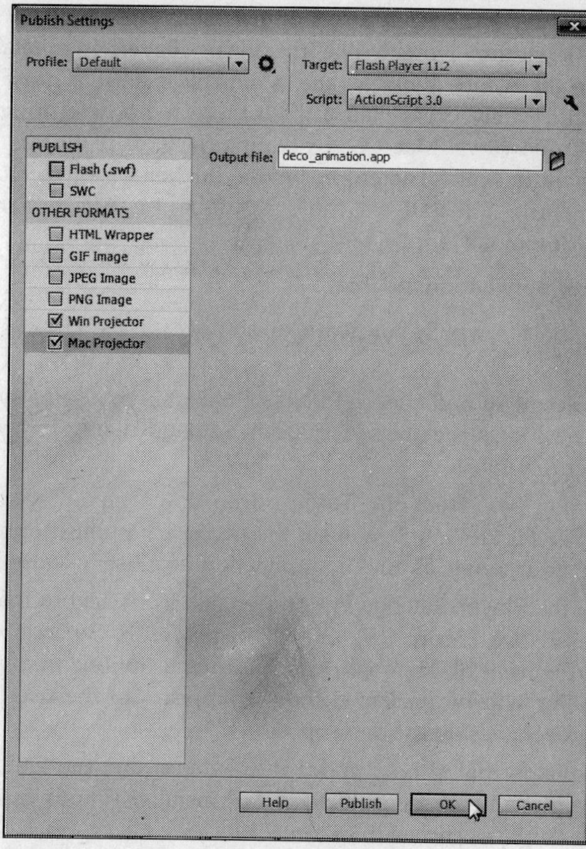

Figure 9.8 Publish Settings dialog box with Projector settings

5. The Windows Projector file has an .exe extension and the Mac Projector file has an .app extension, though operating system may hide the extension in the filename.

6. Open the projector file for your platform (Windows or Mac). Both the Windows and the Mac projectors can be double-clicked to play without a browser.

Creating an AIR Application

The Adobe AIR (Adobe Integrated Runtime) makes it possible to use your Flash movies as full-blown desktop applications in a few clicks from your Publish Settings dialog box. Your movies will behave exactly as they do in a browser, and with a bit of ActionScript you can extend their capabilities to interact with the user's operating system, work with local files, and connect to outside services to get data.

The Adobe AIR runtime, much like the Flash Player, is available as a free download from the Adobe Website, and is a quick install for most users. Best of all, AIR applications are cross-platform, so there is no need to create separate installers for Windows vs. Mac OS (Operating System) platforms. One installer package can handle both. Therefore, before further proceed, make sure you download and install the Adobe AIR runtime at filehippo.com/download_adobe_air/.

To create an AIR application, do this:

1. Open any .fla file which you want to publish for the **Desktop with Adobe** AIR.
2. Click on File menu and choose Publish Settings... or alternatively, press Ctrl + Shift + F12 keys together. A Publish Settings dialog box will appear as seen in Figure 9.6.
3. In this dialog box, from the Target: drop-down menu, select AIR 3.2 for Desktop (See Figure 9.9). It will set the necessary publish options to deploy and install your movie as an AIR application on a user's computer.
4. Then click the Player Settings button (wrench icon) next to the Target: drop-down menu (See Figure 9.9). It will display AIR Settings dialog box as shown in Figure 9.10. Here you can set several options that will affect how your installer will be packaged, how it appears to the user, and how the application behaves on the desktop.
5. In AIR Settings dialog box, under the General tab, the Output file: option shows the filename of the published AIR installer (in our case, it will show classic tween.air) as shown in Figure 9.10.
6. The Output as: option provides three ways to create an AIR application. Choose the way as per you choice or requirement:
   - AIR package: It creates a platform-independent AIR installer.
   - Windows installer: It creates a platform-specific AIR installer.

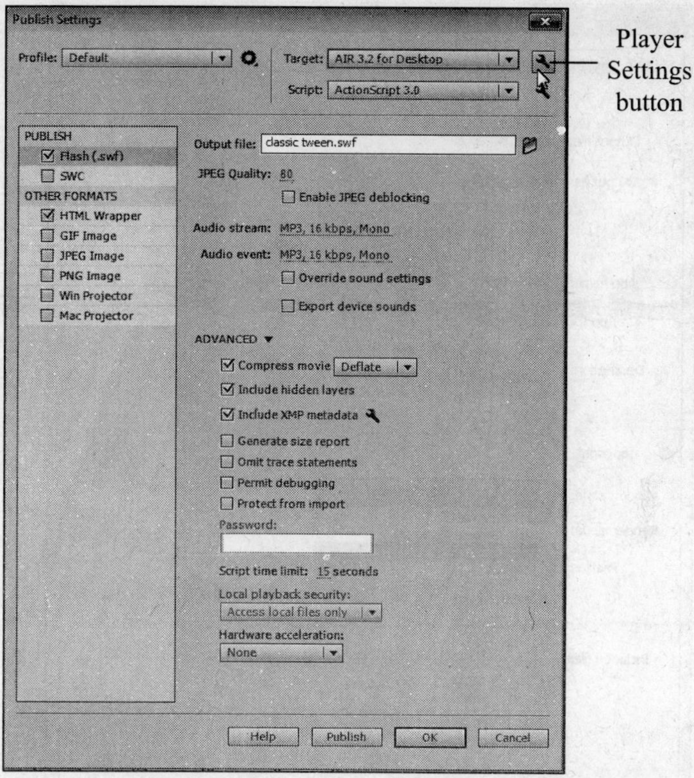

Figure 9.9 Publish Settings dialog box

- Application with runtime embedded: It creates an application without an installer or the need for the AIR runtime already on the desktop.

7. In the App Name: enter the name of your application (See Figure 9.10).
8. In the Version: enter a version number to correspond with the specific release you are offering. If you are not creating an official release, you can enter temporary information and set a default Version number. It will help your users identify your application.
9. In App ID: enter a unique ID for your application to distinguish it from other applications the user may have installed on their system. The suggested convention is known as "reverse DNS"—which includes your company domain and application name.
10. Next, enter some descriptive text in the Description:, and relevant copyright info in the Copyright. These are optional, so you can leave them blank if nothing comes to mind at the moment (See Figure 9.10).

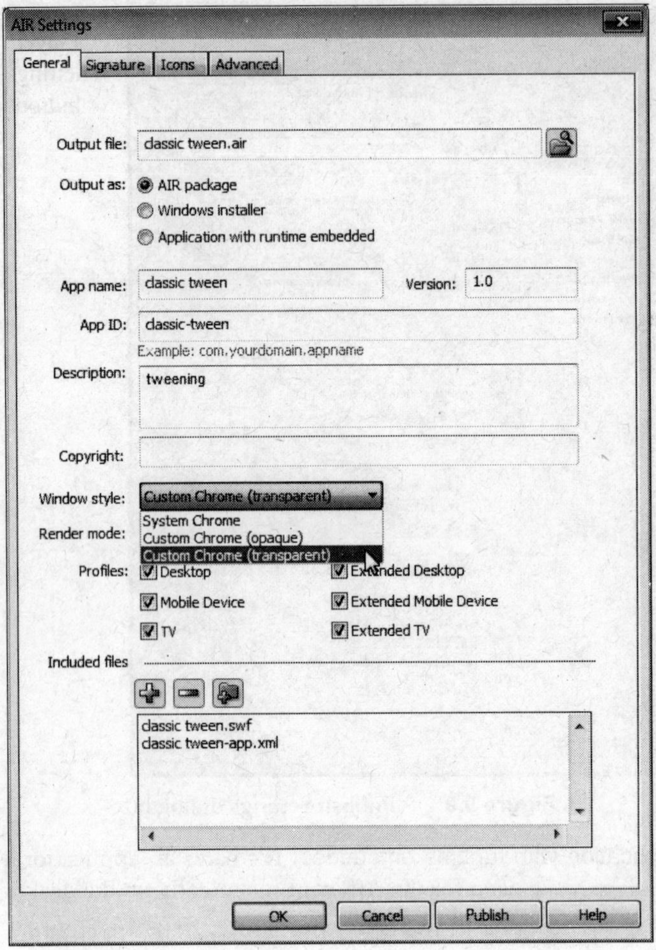

Figure 9.10 AIR Settings dialog box with General Tab

11. Window Style determines how your application is framed, and how it appears on the desktop. The default option is System Chrome, which places a system window around your application. However, you can choose Custom Chrome (transparent) to create an application without any interface or frame elements (known as chrome), and with a transparent background.
12. Then click the Signature tab of the AIR Settings dialog box. It will display AIR Settings dialog with Signature Tab as shown in Figure 9.11.

Creating an AIR application requires a certificate so that users can trust and identify the developer of the Flash content.

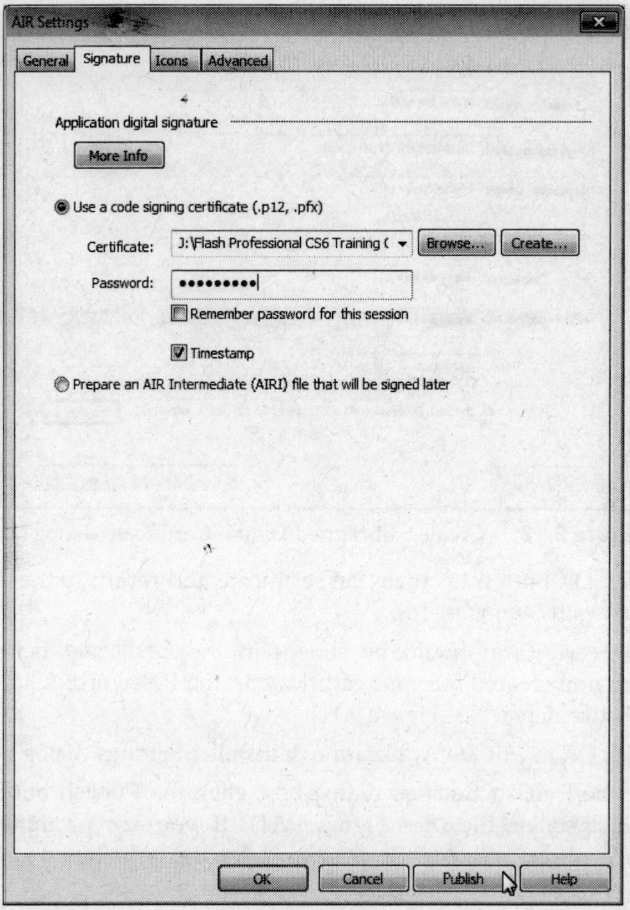

Figure 9.11 AIR Settings dialog box with Signature Tab

13. In this dialog box, click the Create... button next to Certificate drop-down list. It will display another dialog box named Create Self-Signed Digital Certificate (See Figure 9.12).
14. Fill the information, such as Publisher Name, Organization Unit, Organization Name, and Country (See Figure 9.12).
15. Then create a password by entering it in the Password and Confirm Password fields.

Creating a self-signed certificate allows you to install and run your application for testing or limited distribution.

---

16. Then click the Folder icon next to Save As and select a location on your computer to save the certificate in.

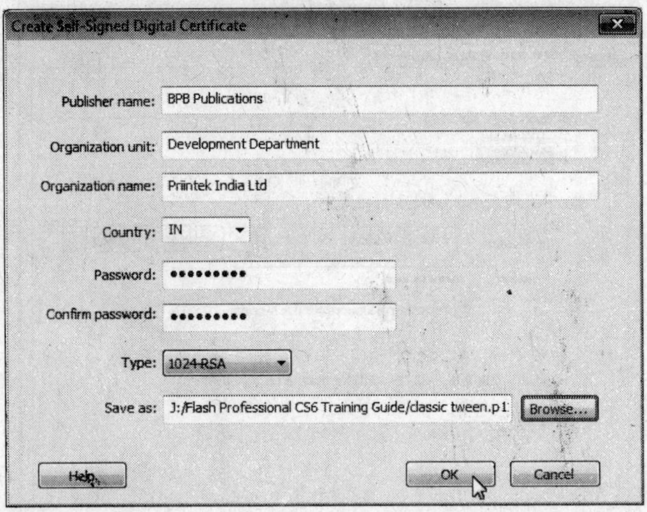

Figure 9.12 Create Self-Signed Digital Certificate dialog box

17. Then click OK button to create the certificate and return to the AIR Settings dialog box with Signature Tab.
18. The new certificate should be shown in the Certificate field. Enter the password you created for your certificate in the Password: field, and for the sake of convenience (See Figure 9.11).
19. Then click OK to exit the Application & Installer Settings dialog box.
20. Then in the Publish Settings dialog box, click the Publish button to create your .air installer file (See Figure 9.11). If you are prompted for your password, please re-enter the password for the Self-signed certificate you created.
21. Flash creates an AIR installer (.air).

Installing an AIR Application

Installing a new AIR application is an easy task, especially if you have already installed the Adobe AIR Runtime. Adobe AIR does the work for you, registering your new application on the system and making it available, just like any other application on your computer.

The AIR installer is platform-independent, but requires that the AIR runtime is installed on the user's system.

To install the new AIR application, do this:

1. Double-click the AIR installer that you just created (classic tween.air in our case) as shown in Figure 9.13.

Figure 9.13 classic tween AIR installer

2. The Adobe AIR Application Installer dialog box opens and asks to install the application (See Figure 9.14).

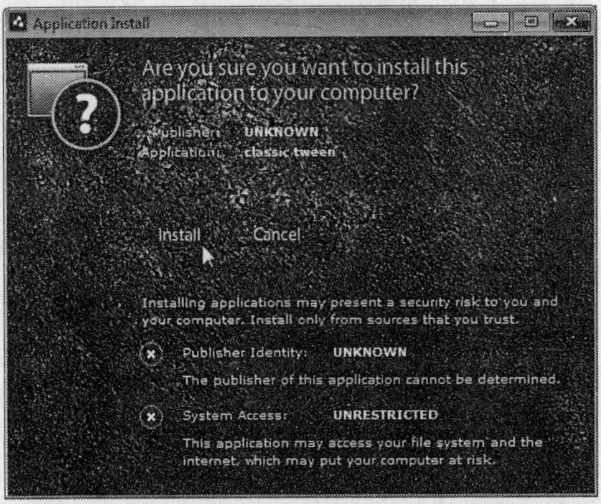

Figure 9.14 Application Installer dialog box

3. Click Install, and then click Continue to proceed with the installation at the default settings.
4. The application is installed on your computer and automatically opens.

Publishing for a Mobile Devices

You can also publish Flash content for mobile devices running on Android or on Apple's iOS, such as the iPhone or iPad. To publish Flash content for a mobile device, you target AIR for Android or AIR for iOS to create an application that viewers download and install on their devices.

Creating an app for mobile devices is a little more complicated than creating an application for the desktop because you have to obtain specific developer certificates for distribution. Moreover, you have to factor in the additional time and effort required for testing and debugging on a separate device. However, Flash Professional CS6 features a mobile device simulator that can help make that testing and debugging easier. The simulator can emulate specific mobile device interactions such as tilting the device (using the accelerometer), touch gestures such as swiping and pinching, or even using the geolocation functions.

Adobe SimController is used to simulate mobile device interactions within Flash Professional CS6.

To simulate a mobile app, do this:

1. Open any .fla file.
2. In the Properties inspector, under the Target: drop-down list select AIR 3.2 for Android (See Figure 9.15).

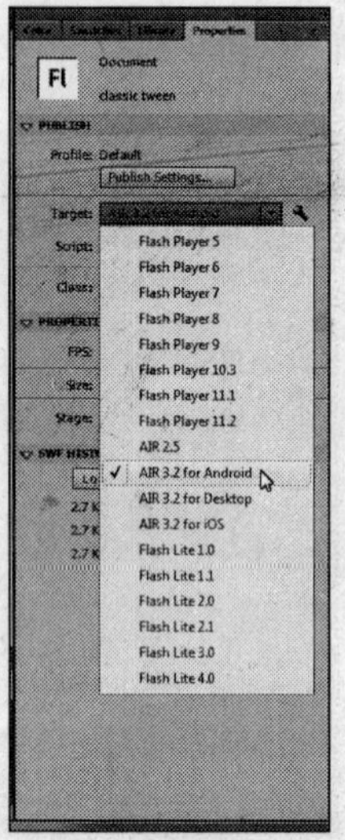

Figure 9.15 Properties Inspector with Publish Section

3. Click on the Control menu and choose Test Movie and then choose in AIR Debug Launcher (Mobile).
4. The project publishes to a new window and the SimController launches, which provide options to interact with the Flash content (See Figure 9.16).
5. In the Simulator panel, click Touch and Gesture section.
6. Click the Touch layer check box to enable it. The simulator overlays a transparent gray box over the Flash content to simulate the touch surface of the mobile device.

7. You can change the opacity of the touch layer by changing the Alpha value, if you wish.

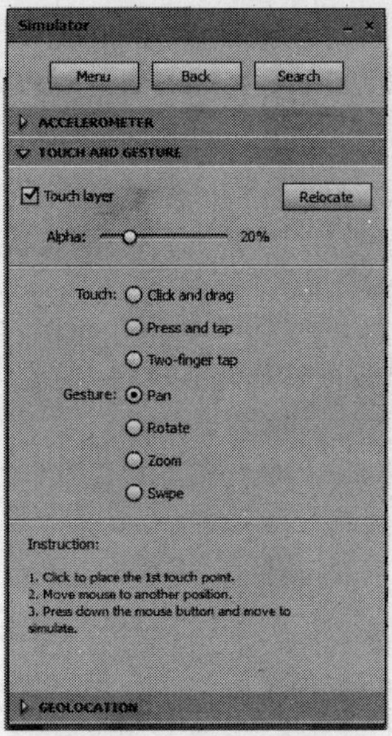

Figure 9.16 Simulator Panel

Publishing a Movie for HTML5

A free extension available for Flash Professional CS6 called Toolkit for CreateJS allows you to publish your Flash content as HTML5. HTML5 is the latest Web standard for browsers. One of the key features of HTML5 is the new <canvas> tag, which supports more sophisticated rendering and animation without the need for the Flash Player.

Once installed, the Toolkit for CreateJS extension appears as a new panel within FlashProfessional CS6. From the panel, you can export Flash content, including animation, sounds, and images, to HTML5. The Toolkit uses several JavaScript libraries (collectively known as CreateJS) to output a faithful representation of your Flash content.

At the time of this publication, the Toolkit supports only Classic Tween animations and a small subset of Flash Professional's capabilities. The Toolkit for CreateJS is in only its first iteration, and in time, Adobe will be adding additional support and features. Keep your eye on Adobe's Web site for any updates and news about this exciting new tool. It will undoubtedly become a valuable bridge between the Flash Professional platform and the emerging standard of HTML5.

CHAPTER 10

Introduction about Flash® Professional CC

Introduction

Adobe Flash Professional® CC provides an authoring environment for creating animation and multimedia content for the Web. It enables visual designers to build interactive experiences that present consistently across desktops and mobile devices. The minimum system requirements to install and run Adobe Flash Professional CC version are listed below:

- Windows 7 or higher Operating System
- Intel Pentium 4 or equivalent processor
- At least 4GB RAM Memory
- 2.5 GB of free space
- 1024x768 display
- QuickTime 10 is optional, even though it must be installed for multimedia purpose
- Broadband connection to activate, validate and access to the Cloud service
- Available through Adobe AIR application

New Features of Adobe Flash Professional CC

Till now, the new features of Adobe Flash Professional CC are as follows:

Updated Bone Tool

The Bone Tool gives you Inverse Kinematics (IK) capabilities within Flash. IK is a way of animating objects using bones chained into linear or branched armatures in parent-child relationships. When one bone moves, connected bones move in relation to it. Inverse kinematics lets you easily create natural motion. To animate using inverse kinematics, specify the start and end positions of bones on the Timeline. Flash automatically interpolates the positions of the bones in the armature between the starting and ending frames.

Bone Tool comes with on Stage controls to ensure greater precision in movements (See Figure 10.1). The on Stage control allows you to switch between Locked, Open, and Constrained states for Rotation and Translation properties of individual bones in the IK armature. You can now directly adjust these constraints on Stage with accuracy using clear visual feedback.

Figure 10.1 On-Stage controls for the bone tool

Import H.264 Videos with Audio

In addition to FLV videos, it also introduces an option to embed H.264 videos in Timeline. When an H.264 video is embedded, the frames of the video are rendered on the Stage when you scrub the Timeline. This feature enables you to use videos as a guide to synchronize your animation on the Stage. Since the Flash Player and other run-times do not support rendering embedded H.264 videos, they are not published. Importing H.264 videos is a design-time-only feature. Audio playback is enabled for H.264 videos. You can now select the 'Include audio' option while importing H.264 videos. Once imported to the Stage (with 'place instance on Stage' option selected), scrubbing the Timeline must play the audio for the relevant frames. Playing the Timeline must play back the animation at the fps (frame per second) of the imported video so that the audio is in sync with the video frames on Stage.

Click **File > Import > Import Video** and select the **Embed H.264 video** in the Timeline (design time only – the video cannot be exported) option as shown in the Figure 10.2.

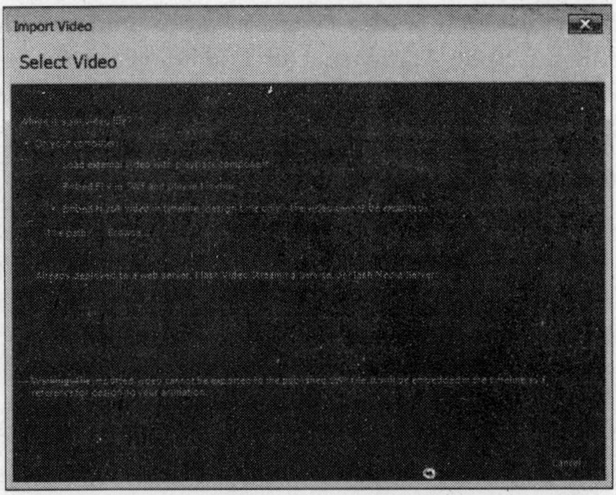

Figure 10.2 Import Video

Export bitmaps as sprite sheet for HTML5 Canvas

Export bitmap as sprite sheet allows you to pack all the bitmaps in canvas document in to a sprite sheet. A new Export the Bitmap as Sprite Sheet check box has been added and enabled by default. You can specify the maximum size of the sprite sheet by giving the height and width values in the publish settings.

Brush Scaling with Stage Zoom

Flash Professional CC scales the brush size proportionately to the changing zoom level of the Stage. Proportionate zooming allows you to draw seamlessly adjusting to any zoom level and preview your work as you draw. If you want to revert to the earlier default behavior of brushes maintaining a constant pixel size even when you change the zoom level of the Stage, you must disable the 'Stage zoom level' checkbox in the brush Properties Inspector.

Universal Document Type Converter

The universal document type converter enables conversion of your existing FLA projects (of any type) to any other document type such as HTML5 Canvas or WebGL.

Improved Audio Workflows

In earlier versions of Flash, you had to import the audio file in to the Library and then add it to a layer on the Timeline. In this release, you can directly import audio in to your Stage/Timeline by dragging and dropping the file to a layer or by using the File > Import > Import to Stage option.

Split Audio option in Context menu

The stream audio embedded on the Timeline can be split at ease using the Split Audio context menu. Split Audio enables you to pause the audio when it is necessary and then resume the audio playback from the point it was stopped at a later frame on the Timeline.

Remember audio sync options in Properties Inspector

Flash now remembers the sync options in Properties Inspector. If a sound is selected from the "Sound" section of the Properties Inspector, then on trying to set another sound on a new keyframe from the Properties Inspector, Flash remembers the sync options "Stream" or "Event" of the previous sound.

Panel Locking

A new option, Lock/Unlock, has been added to the fly-out menu of the panels to lock the dock. Once a dock is locked, all the panels in the dock can be resized, but cannot be moved. This feature helps you prevent accidental drag and resize of panels.

Paste and Overwrite Frames

The new 'Paste and Overwrite Frames' Timeline context menu option enables you to paste the copied frames by replacing the exact number of frames without pushing the frames forward. This replaces the existing way of selecting the exact number of frames which you want to replace with the same number of copied frames. For example, if you want to copy ten frames from a Timeline and replace the exact number of frames in another Timeline, copy the ten frames and use the Paste and Overwrite Frames frames to paste it at the starting frame-the next ten frames are overwritten with the copied frames.

Miscellaneous Features

- Publish fully interactive animations – with scripting and audio – to the WebGL format. They can run in modern browsers without Flash Player and take advantage of GPU-accelerated hardware.
- Create your own brushes to get the ideal shape, angle, and flatness save them for future use and access them across multiple computers.
- Animation guide now helps you enhance the animation you create by defining a path for the objects you animate.
- Custom platform support will help you extend the capabilities of the powerful Flash platform to custom formats that are not natively supported by Flash. It allows you to create plugins for new formats and distribute them through the Adobe Add-ons website.
- Export any frame in your Flash project as an SVG file that can be scaled up and used in posters and other promotional materials.
- An updated Motion Editor gives you precise control over motion tween properties like color effects and transformations.
- Object-level undo lets you undo an action on one object without having to undo actions on other objects you changed more recently.
- Publish videos as Flash projector (.exe) files so they are viewable even on systems that do not have Flash Player installed.
- Supports HTML5-based panels, so that developers can extend the app's capabilities with new features and content.
- Built-in 64-bit structure delivers unprecedented speed and stability. Easily manage multiple large files, publish more quickly, and experience a more responsive Timeline.
- Real-time drawing to see full previews instantly as you draw. So that your designs will take shape faster than ever before.
- Synchronize your workspace settings to Creative so they go where you go.
- Simplified user interface, dialog boxes and panels are more intuitive and easier to navigate.
- Manage properties across multiple selected layers in the Timeline panel. Easily swap symbols or bitmap images on the Stage. Select multiple objects on a layer and distribute them to keyframes with a single click.
- Easily manage large backgrounds or content that's positioned off Stage with an unlimited pasteboard/work area.
- Test and debug your content in fewer steps by connecting multiple iOS and Android mobile devices directly to your computer via USB.